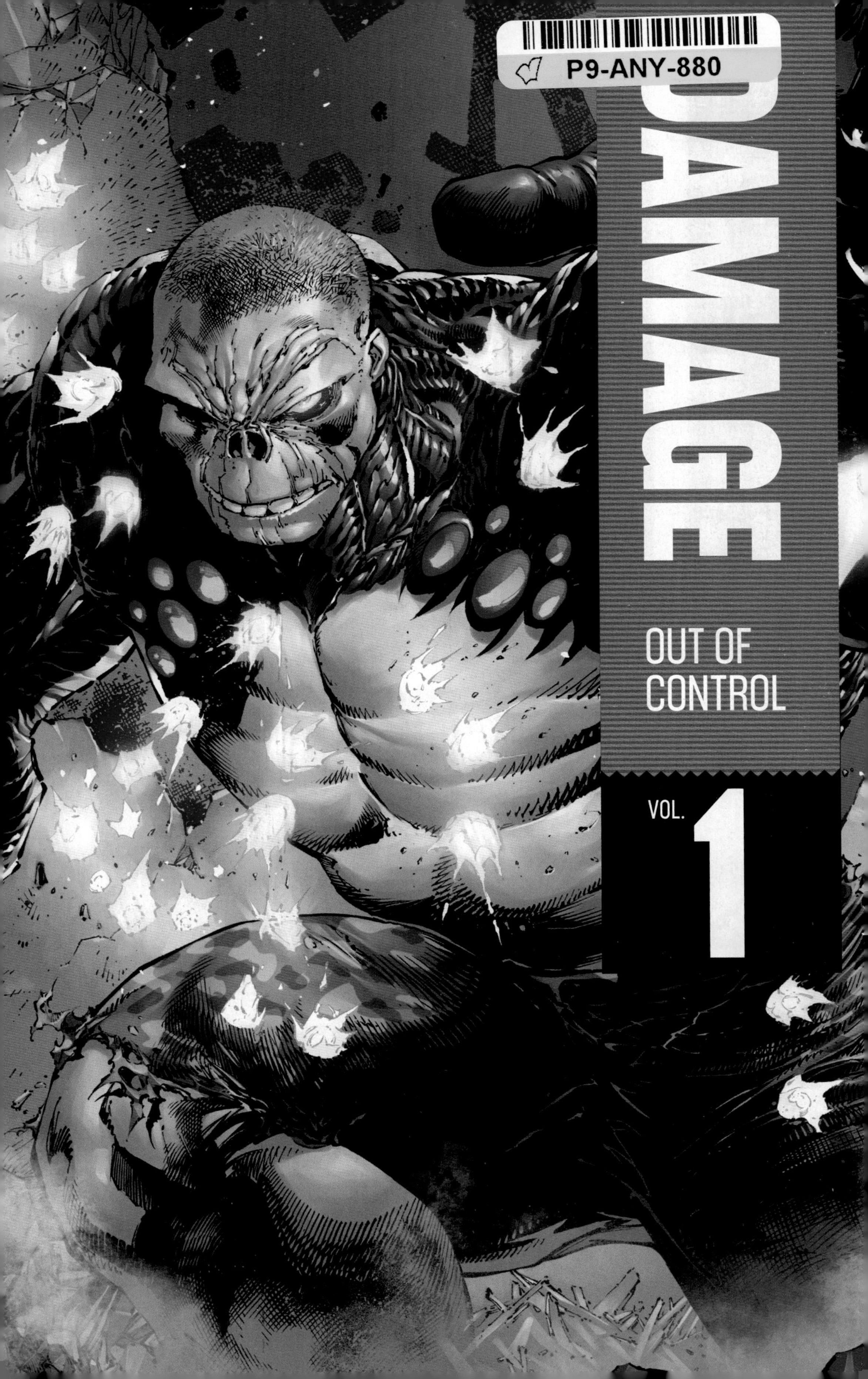
DAMAGE
OUT OF CONTROL
VOL. 1

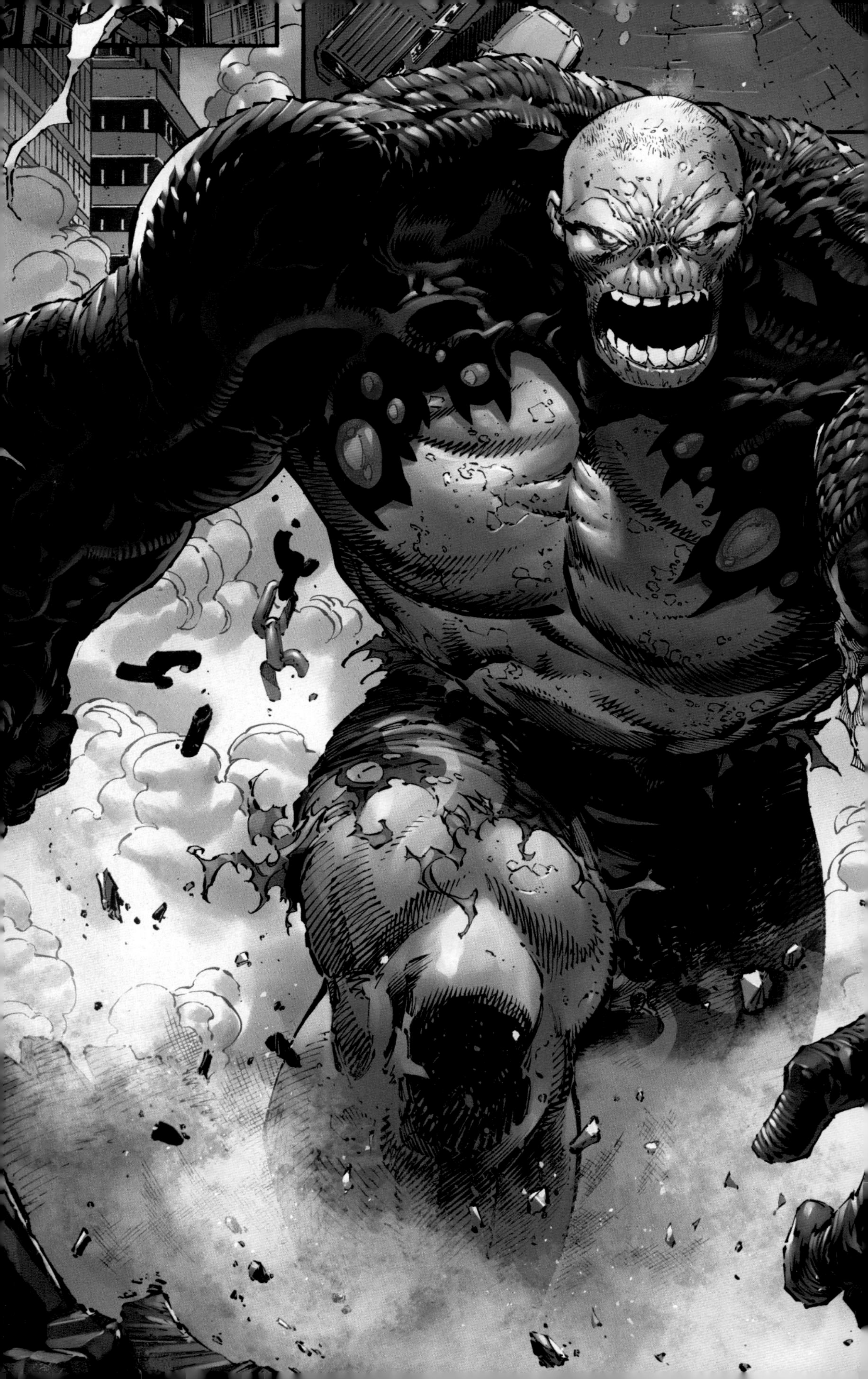

DAMAGE
OUT OF CONTROL

artists
TONY S. DANIEL \ DIOGENES NEVES
CARY NORD \ DANNY MIKI
TREVOR SCOTT \ LARRY HAMA

writer
ROBERT VENDITTI

colorists
TOMEU MOREY
ALLEN PASSALAQUA

letterer
TOM NAPOLITANO

collection cover artists
TONY S. DANIEL, DANNY MIKI
and **TOMEU MOREY**

DAMAGE created by **TONY S. DANIEL** and **ROBERT VENDITTI**
SWAMP THING created by **LEN WEIN** and **BERNIE WRIGHTSON**
SUPERMAN created by **JERRY SIEGEL** and **JOE SHUSTER**
By special arrangement with the Jerry Siegel family

VOL.
1

JESSICA CHEN \ JAMIE S. RICH \ MIKE COTTON \ EDDIE BERGANZA Editors – Original Series
BRITTANY HOLZHERR Associate Editor – Original Series
JEB WOODARD Group Editor – Collected Editions
ERIKA ROTHBERG Editor – Collected Edition
STEVE COOK Design Director – Books
DAMIAN RYLAND \ MONIQUE NARBONETA Publication Design

BOB HARRAS Senior VP – Editor-in-Chief, DC Comics
PAT McCALLUM Executive Editor, DC Comics

DAN DiDIO Publisher
JIM LEE Publisher & Chief Creative Officer
AMIT DESAI Executive VP – Business & Marketing Strategy, Direct to
 Consumer & Global Franchise Management
BOBBIE CHASE VP & Executive Editor, Young Reader & Talent Development
MARK CHIARELLO Senior VP – Art, Design & Collected Editions
JOHN CUNNINGHAM Senior VP – Sales & Trade Marketing
BRIAR DARDEN VP – Business Affairs
ANNE DePIES Senior VP – Business Strategy, Finance & Administration
DON FALLETTI VP – Manufacturing Operations
LAWRENCE GANEM VP – Editorial Administration & Talent Relations
ALISON GILL Senior VP – Manufacturing & Operations
JASON GREENBERG VP – Business Strategy & Finance
HANK KANALZ Senior VP – Editorial Strategy & Administration
JAY KOGAN Senior VP – Legal Affairs
NICK J. NAPOLITANO VP – Manufacturing Administration
LISETTE OSTERLOH VP – Digital Marketing & Events
EDDIE SCANNELL VP – Consumer Marketing
COURTNEY SIMMONS Senior VP – Publicity & Communications
JIM (SKI) SOKOLOWSKI VP – Comic Book Specialty Sales & Trade Marketing
NANCY SPEARS VP – Mass, Book, Digital Sales & Trade Marketing
MICHELE R. WELLS VP – Content Strategy

DAMAGE VOL. 1: OUT OF CONTROL

DC Comics, 2900 West Alameda Ave., Burbank, CA 91505
Printed by Times Printing, LLC, Random Lake, WI, USA. 8/17/18. First Printing.
ISBN: 978-1-4012-8333-9

Library of Congress Cataloging-in-Publication Data is available.

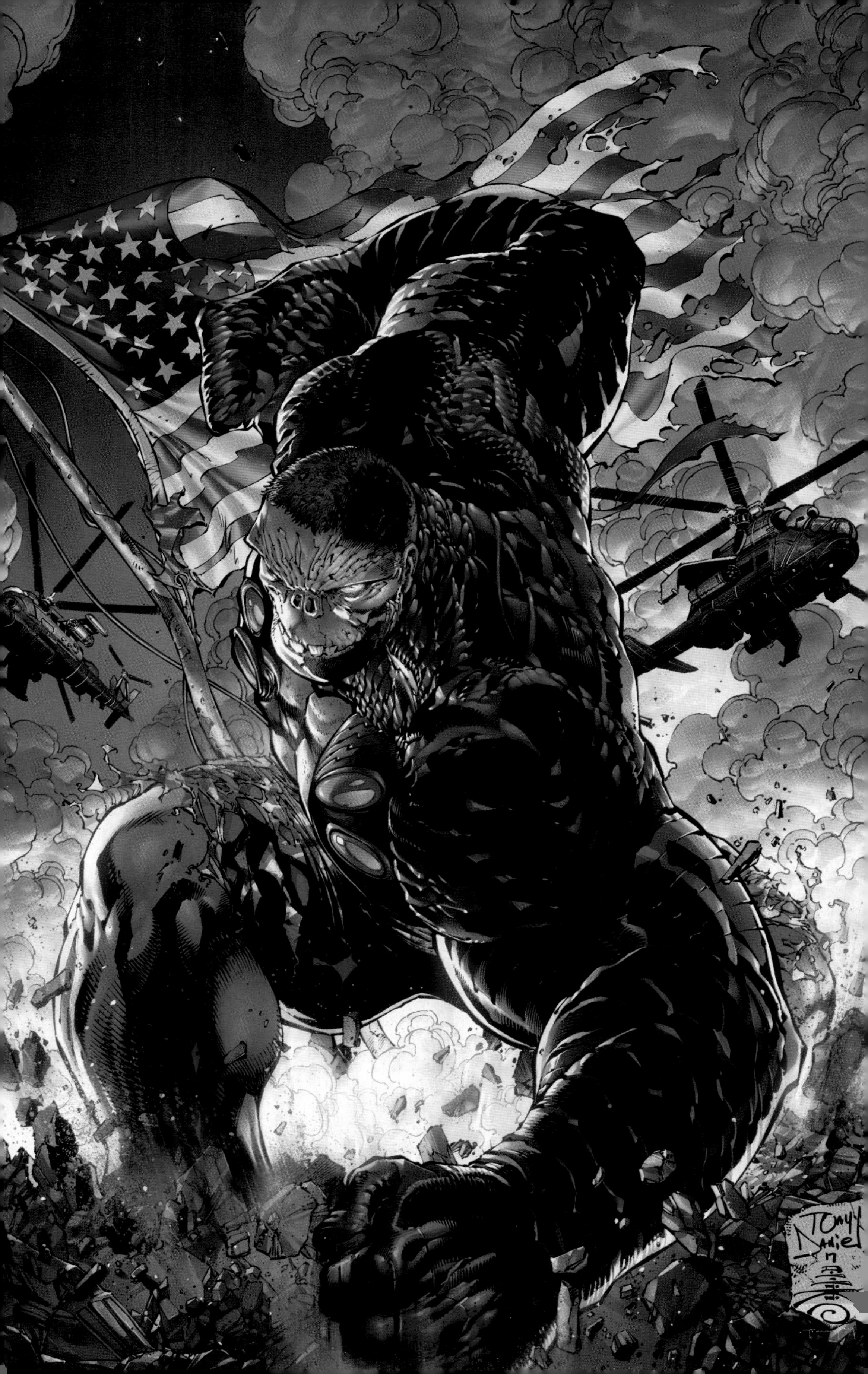

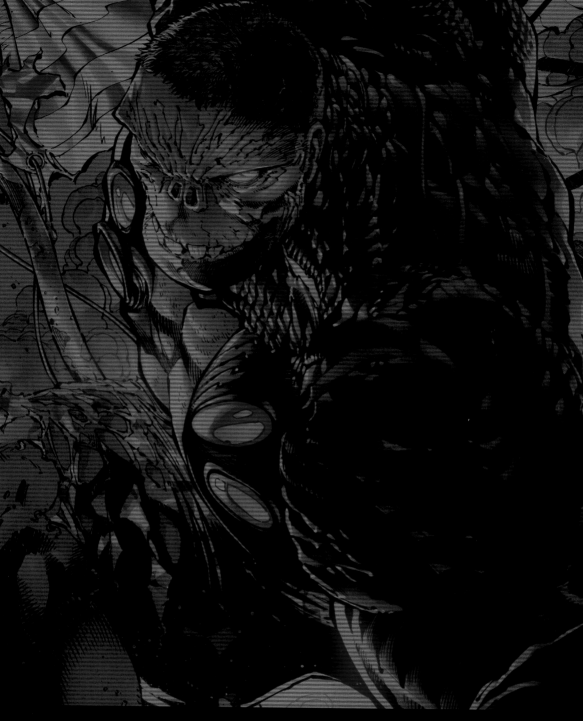

DAMAGE
#1

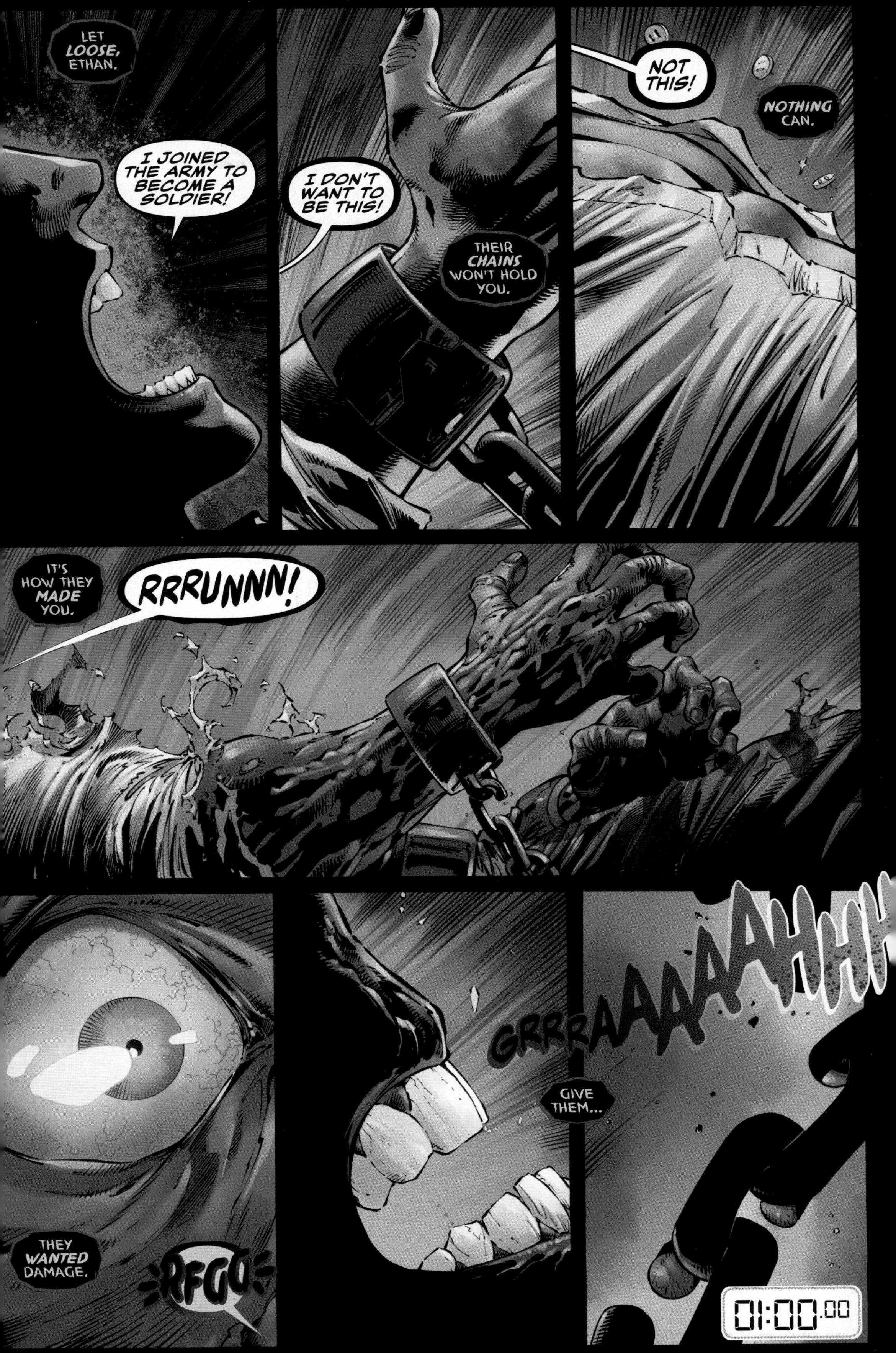
LET LOOSE, ETHAN.
I JOINED THE ARMY TO BECOME A SOLDIER!
I DON'T WANT TO BE THIS!
THEIR CHAINS WON'T HOLD YOU.
NOT THIS!
NOTHING CAN.
IT'S HOW THEY MADE YOU.
RRRUNNN!
THEY WANTED DAMAGE.
RFGG
GIVE THEM...
GRRRAAAAAAHHH
01:00.00

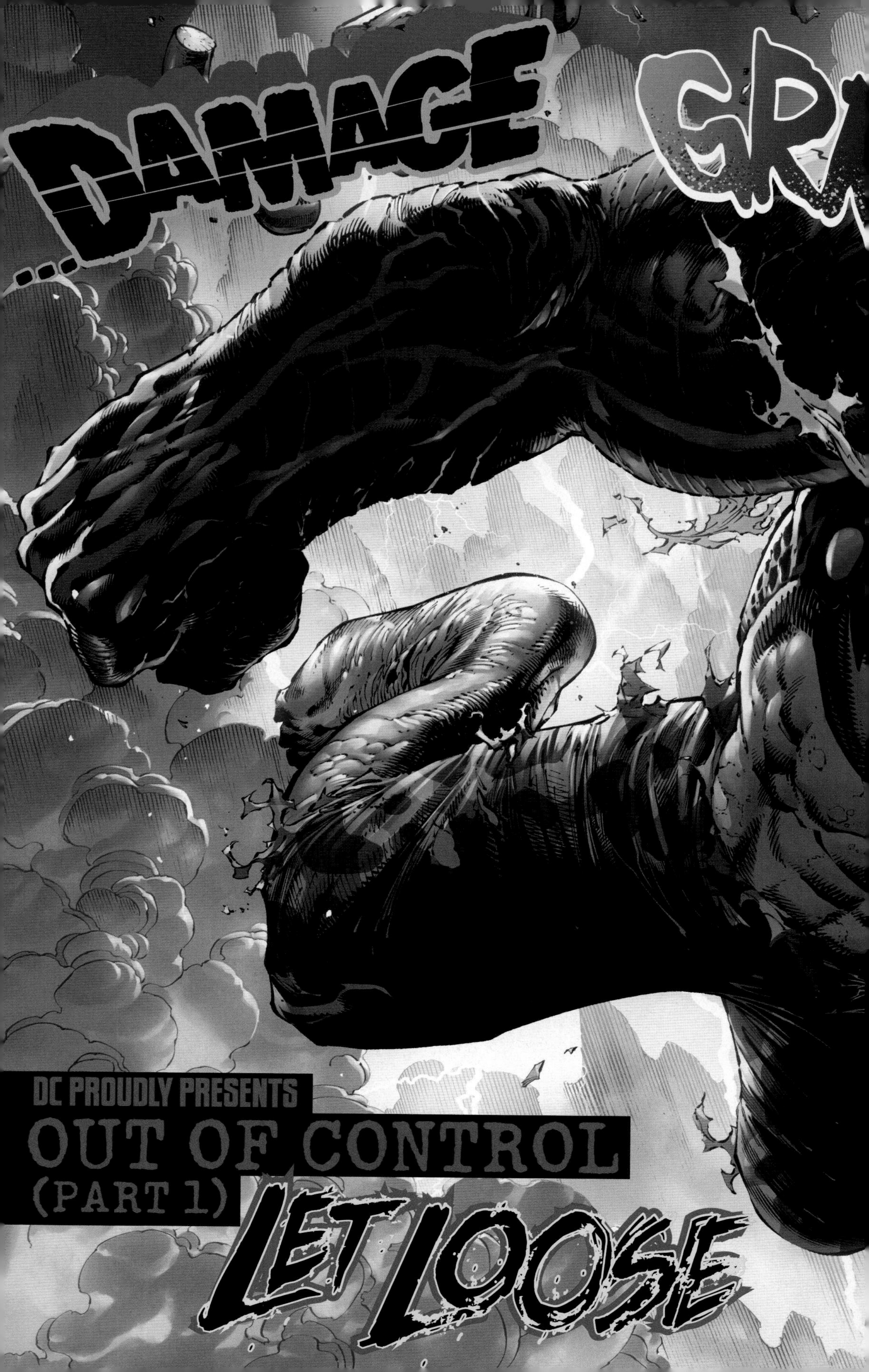
...DAMAGE
DC PROUDLY PRESENTS
OUT OF CONTROL
(PART 1)
LET LOOSE

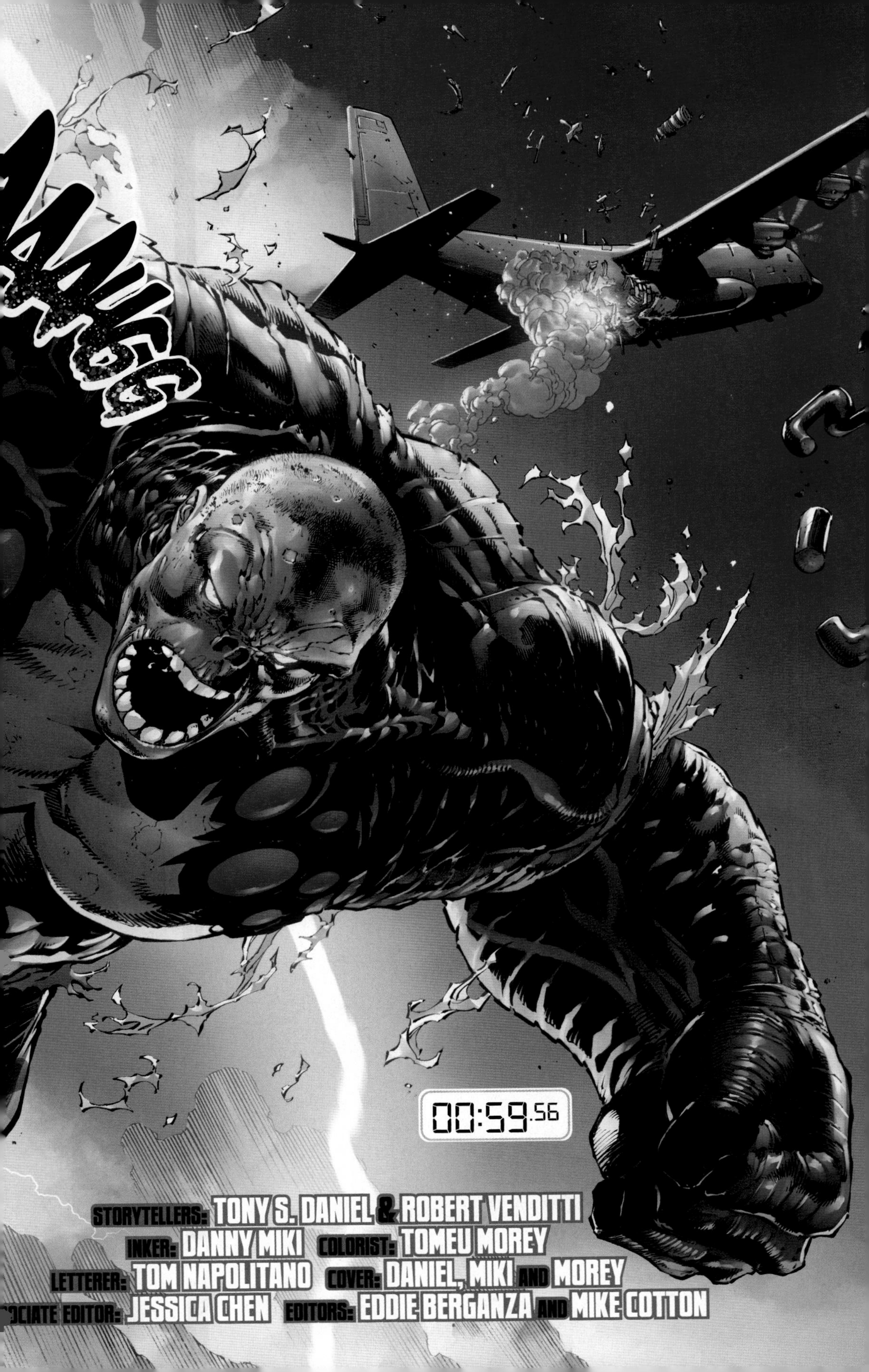
00:59.56
STORYTELLERS: TONY S. DANIEL & ROBERT VENDITTI
INKER: DANNY MIKI COLORIST: TOMEU MOREY
LETTERER: TOM NAPOLITANO COVER: DANIEL, MIKI AND MOREY
OCIATE EDITOR: JESSICA CHEN EDITORS: EDDIE BERGANZA AND MIKE COTTON

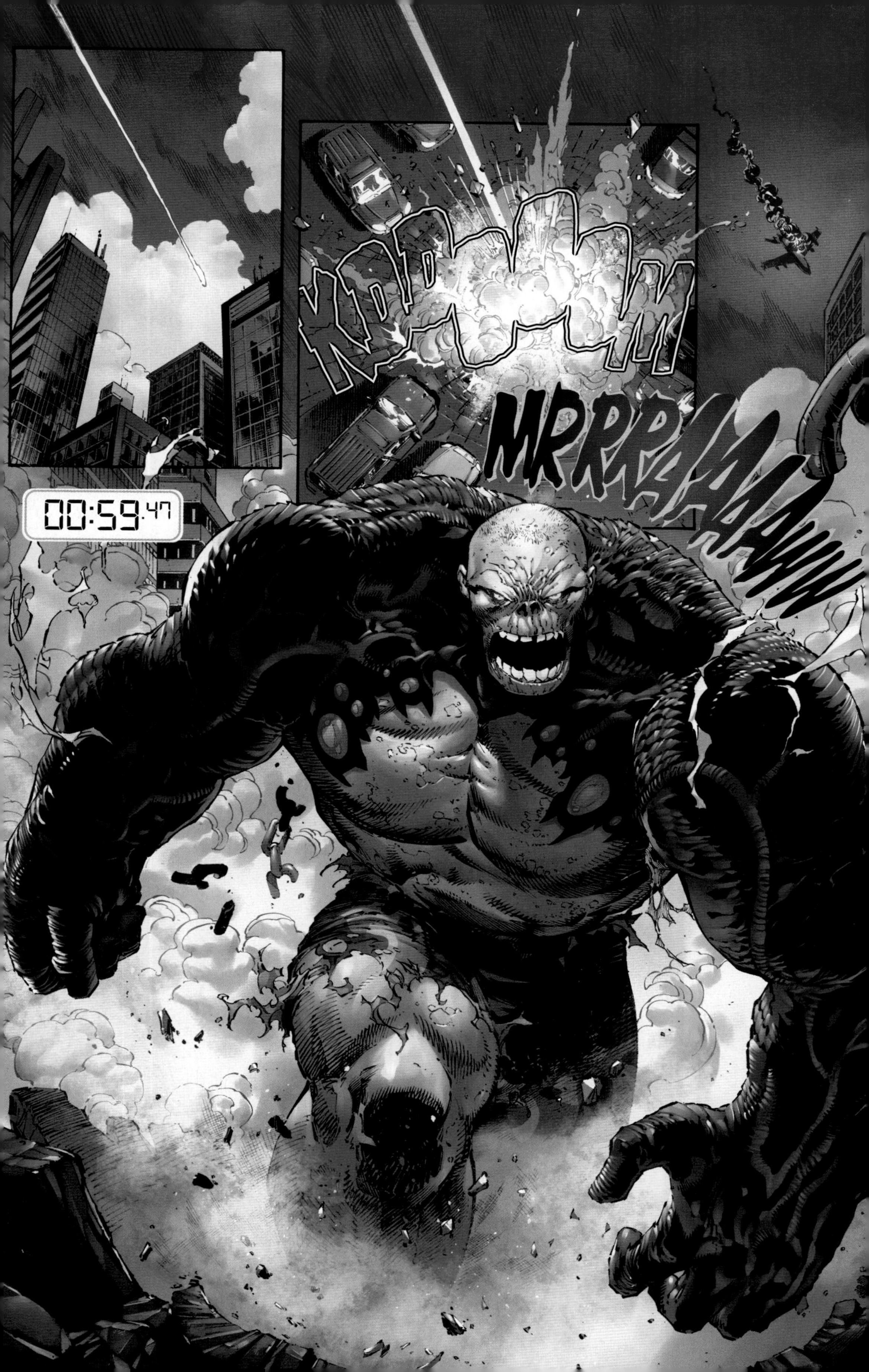
00:59.47

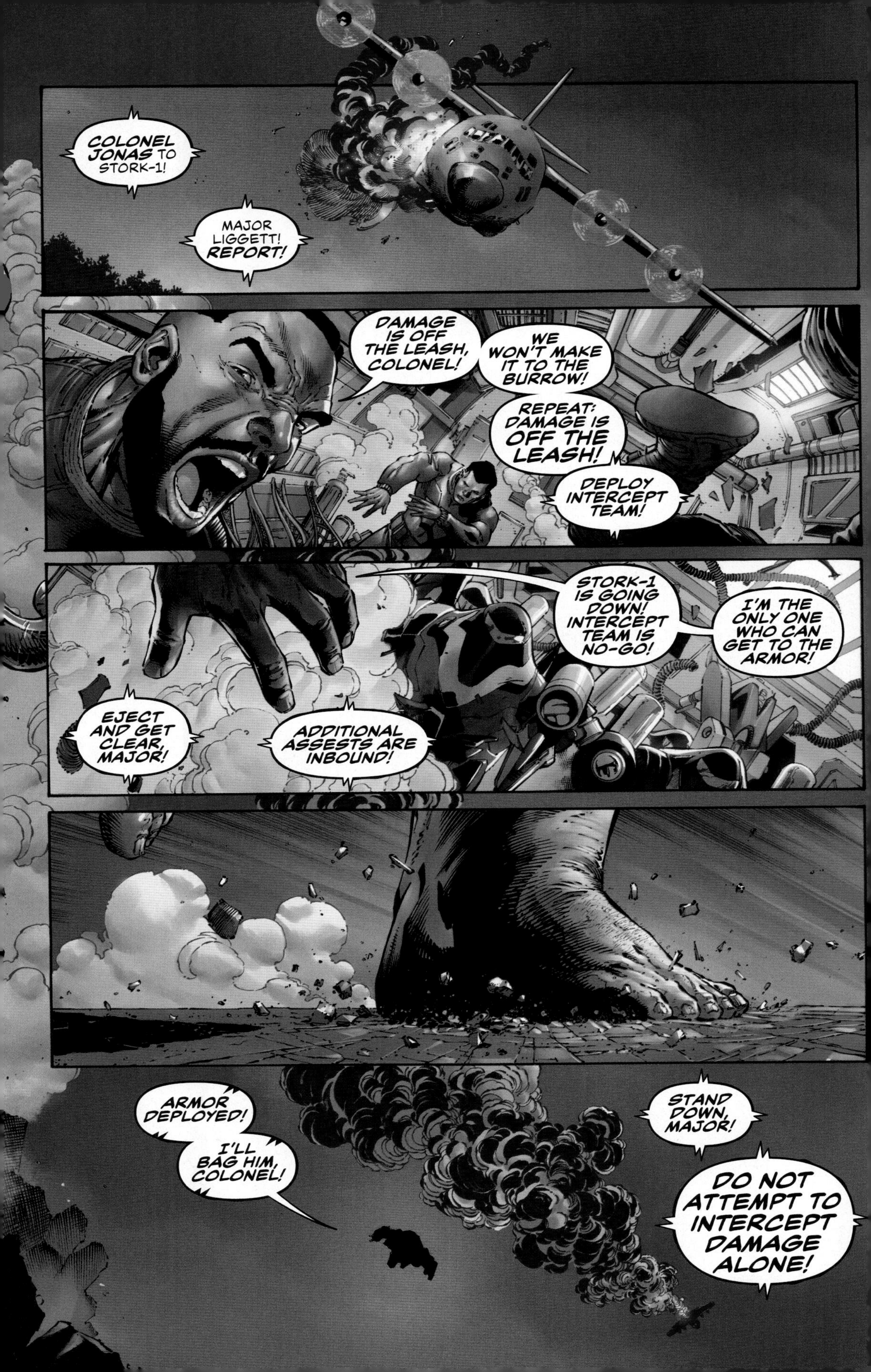
COLONEL JONAS TO STORK-1!
MAJOR LIGGETT! REPORT!
DAMAGE IS OFF THE LEASH, COLONEL!
WE WON'T MAKE IT TO THE BURROW!
REPEAT: DAMAGE IS OFF THE LEASH!
DEPLOY INTERCEPT TEAM!
STORK-1 IS GOING DOWN! INTERCEPT TEAM IS NO-GO!
I'M THE ONLY ONE WHO CAN GET TO THE ARMOR!
EJECT AND GET CLEAR, MAJOR!
ADDITIONAL ASSESTS ARE INBOUND!
ARMOR DEPLOYED!
I'LL BAG HIM, COLONEL!
STAND DOWN, MAJOR!
DO NOT ATTEMPT TO INTERCEPT DAMAGE ALONE!

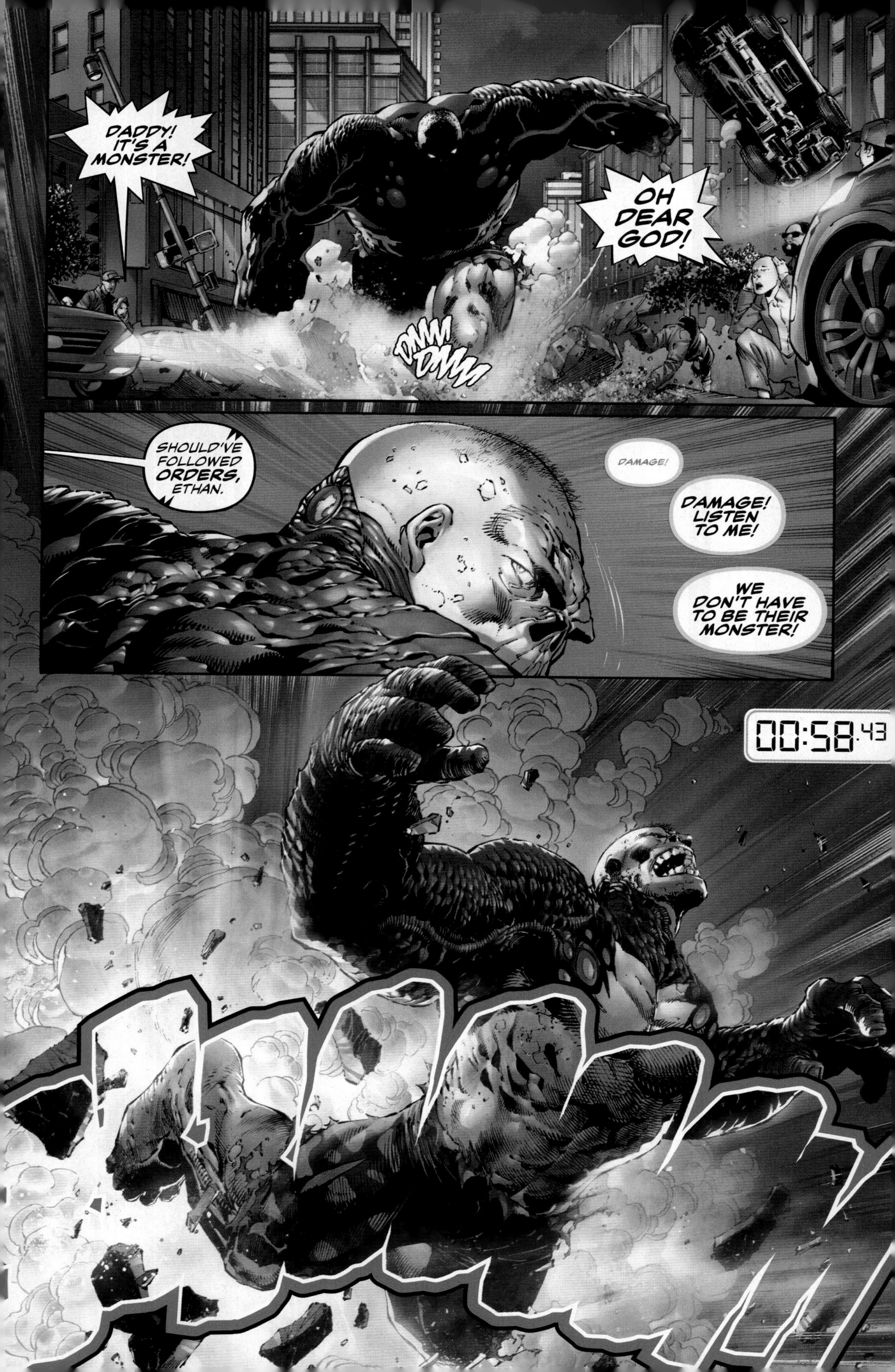
DADDY! IT'S A MONSTER!
OH DEAR GOD!
DMM DMM
SHOULD'VE FOLLOWED ORDERS, ETHAN.
DAMAGE!
DAMAGE! LISTEN TO ME!
WE DON'T HAVE TO BE THEIR MONSTER!
00:58.43

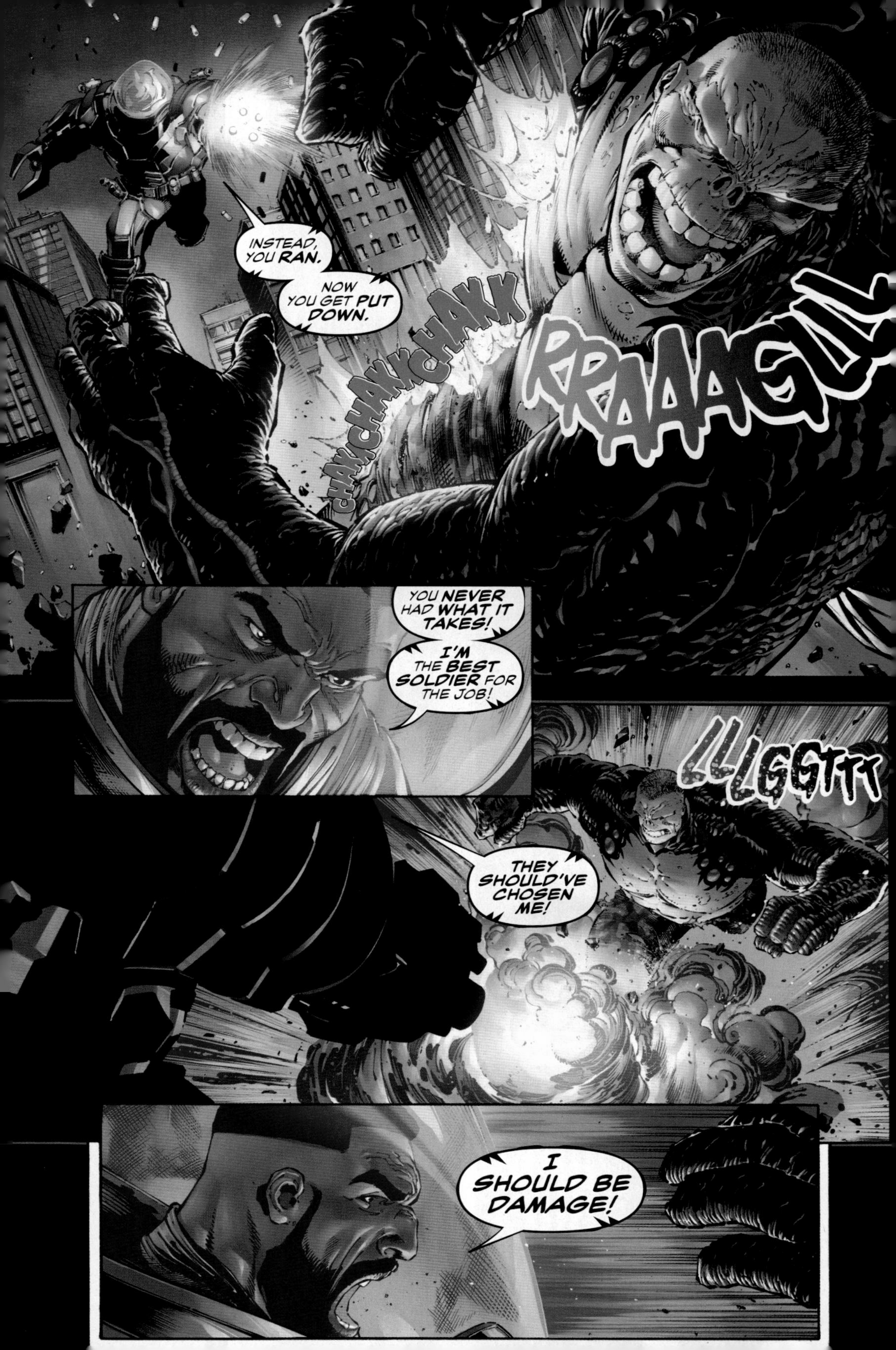
INSTEAD, YOU RAN.
NOW YOU GET PUT DOWN.
CHAKCHAKKCHAKKCHAKK
RRAAAAGH
YOU NEVER HAD WHAT IT TAKES!
I'M THE BEST SOLDIER FOR THE JOB!
LLLGGTTT
THEY SHOULD'VE CHOSEN ME!
I SHOULD BE DAMAGE!

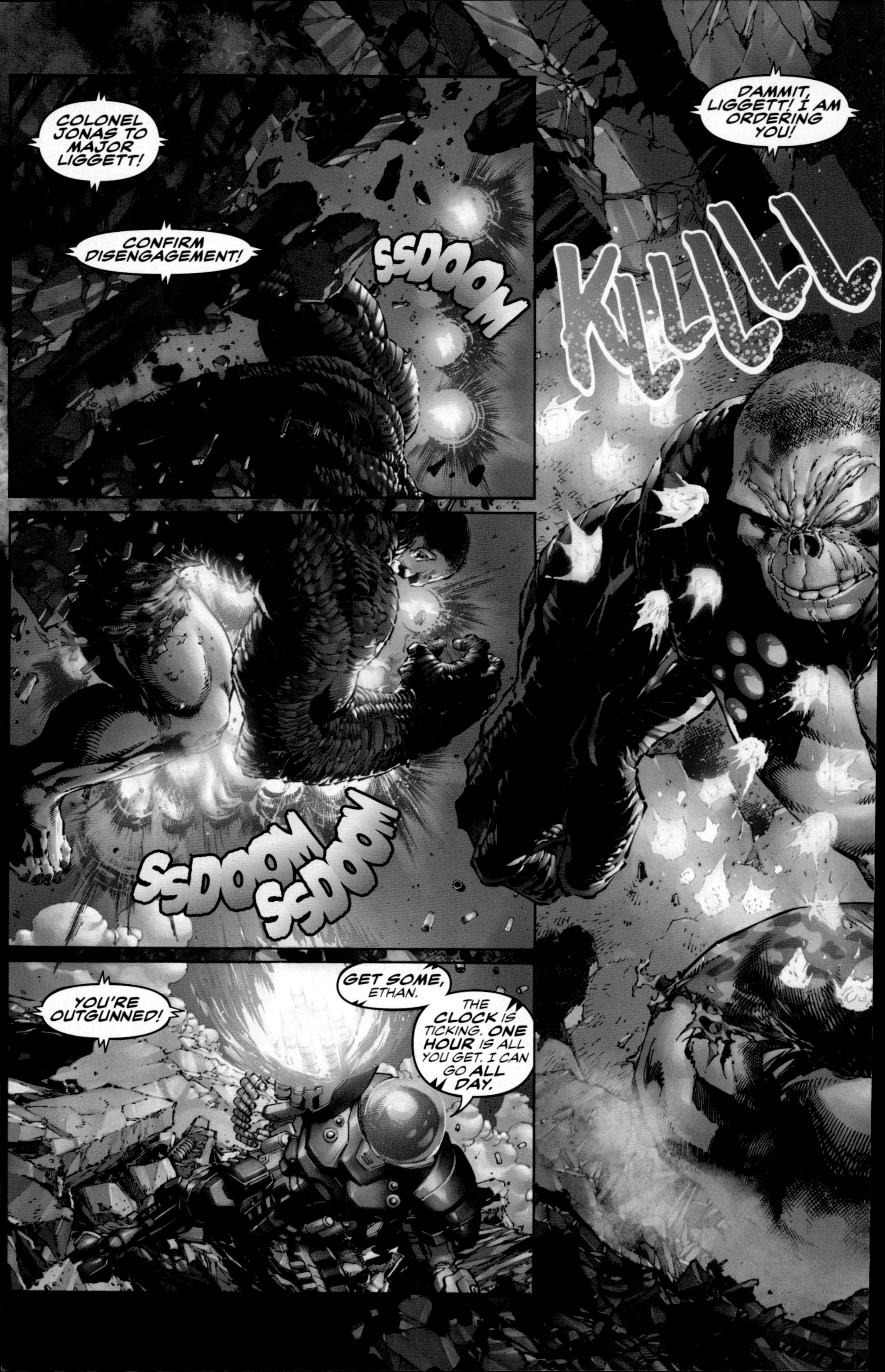
COLONEL JONAS TO MAJOR LIGGETT!
CONFIRM DISENGAGEMENT!
SSDOOM
SSDOOM SSDOOM
YOU'RE OUTGUNNED!
GET SOME, ETHAN.
THE CLOCK IS TICKING. ONE HOUR IS ALL YOU GET. I CAN GO ALL DAY.
DAMMIT, LIGGETT! I AM ORDERING YOU!
KILLLL

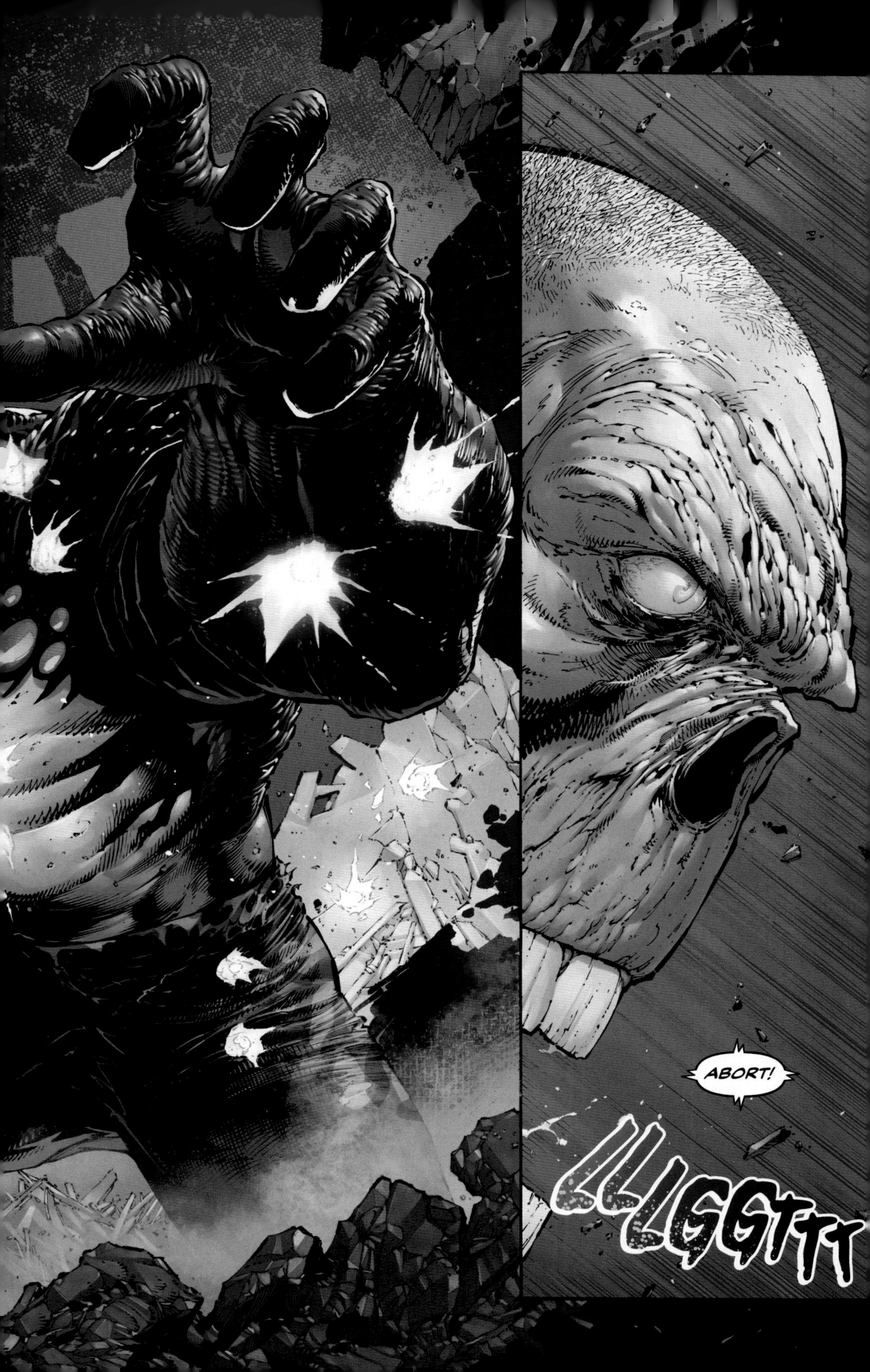
ABORT!
LLLGGTTT

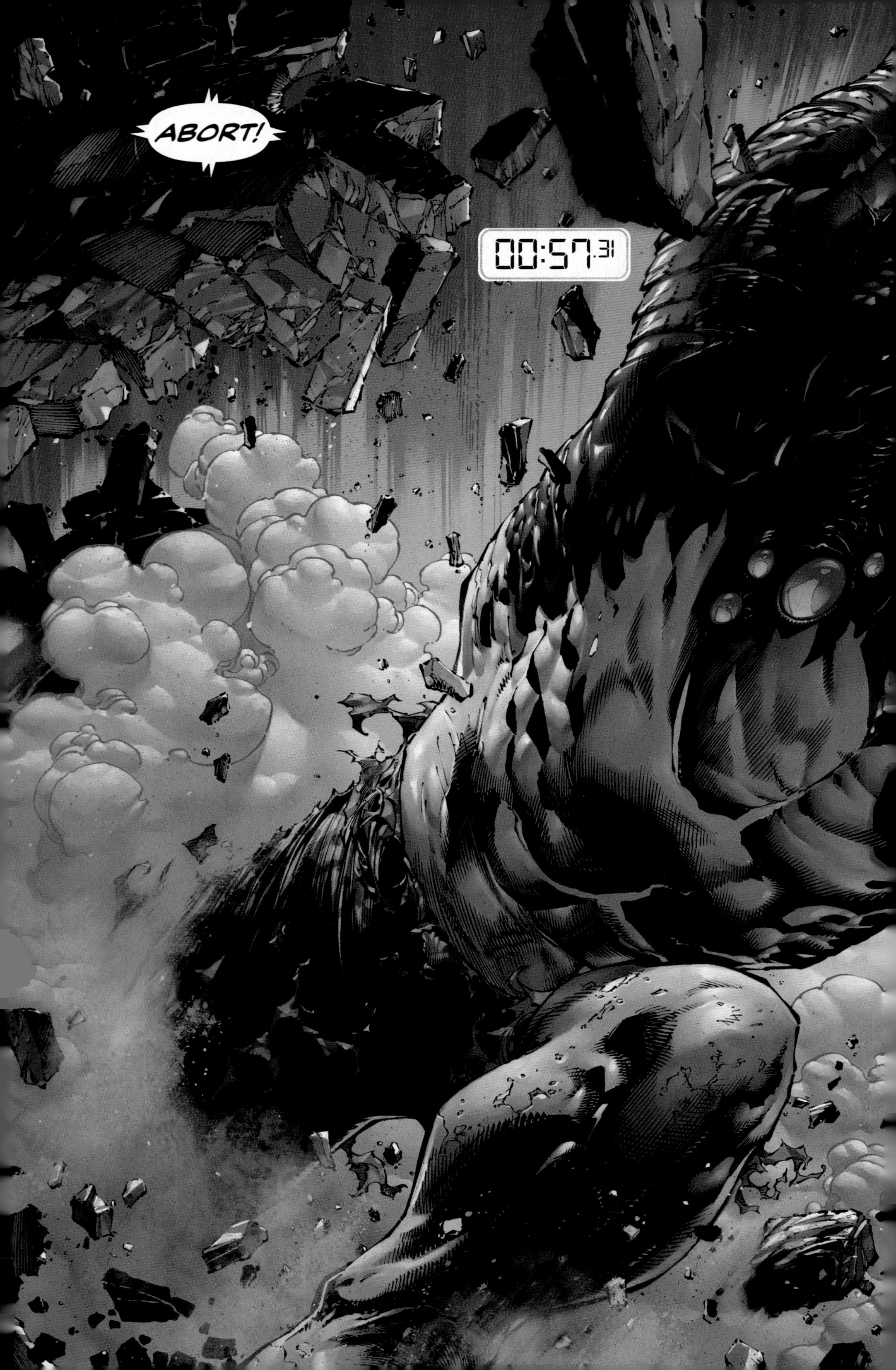
ABORT!
00:57.31

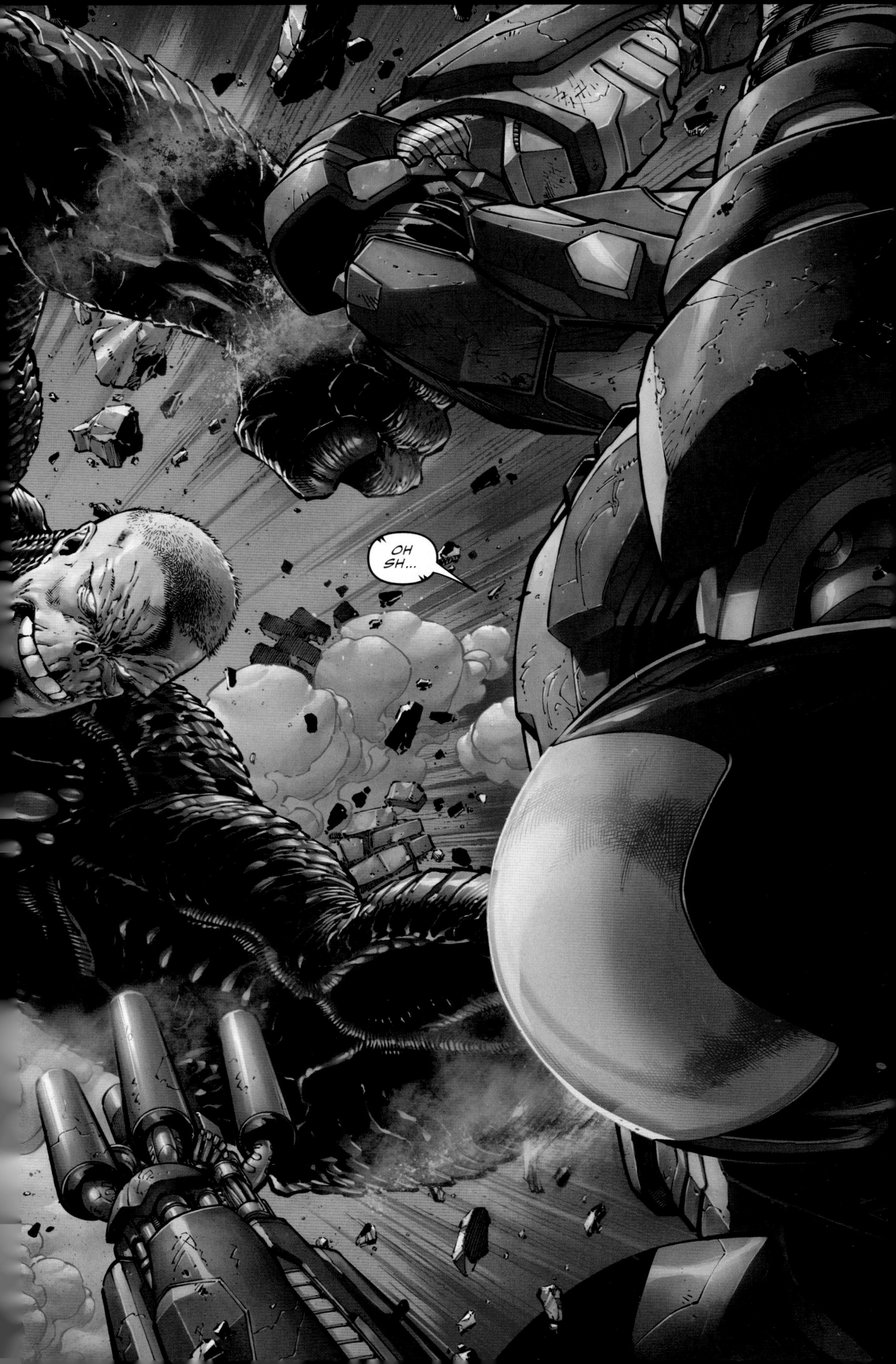
OH SH...

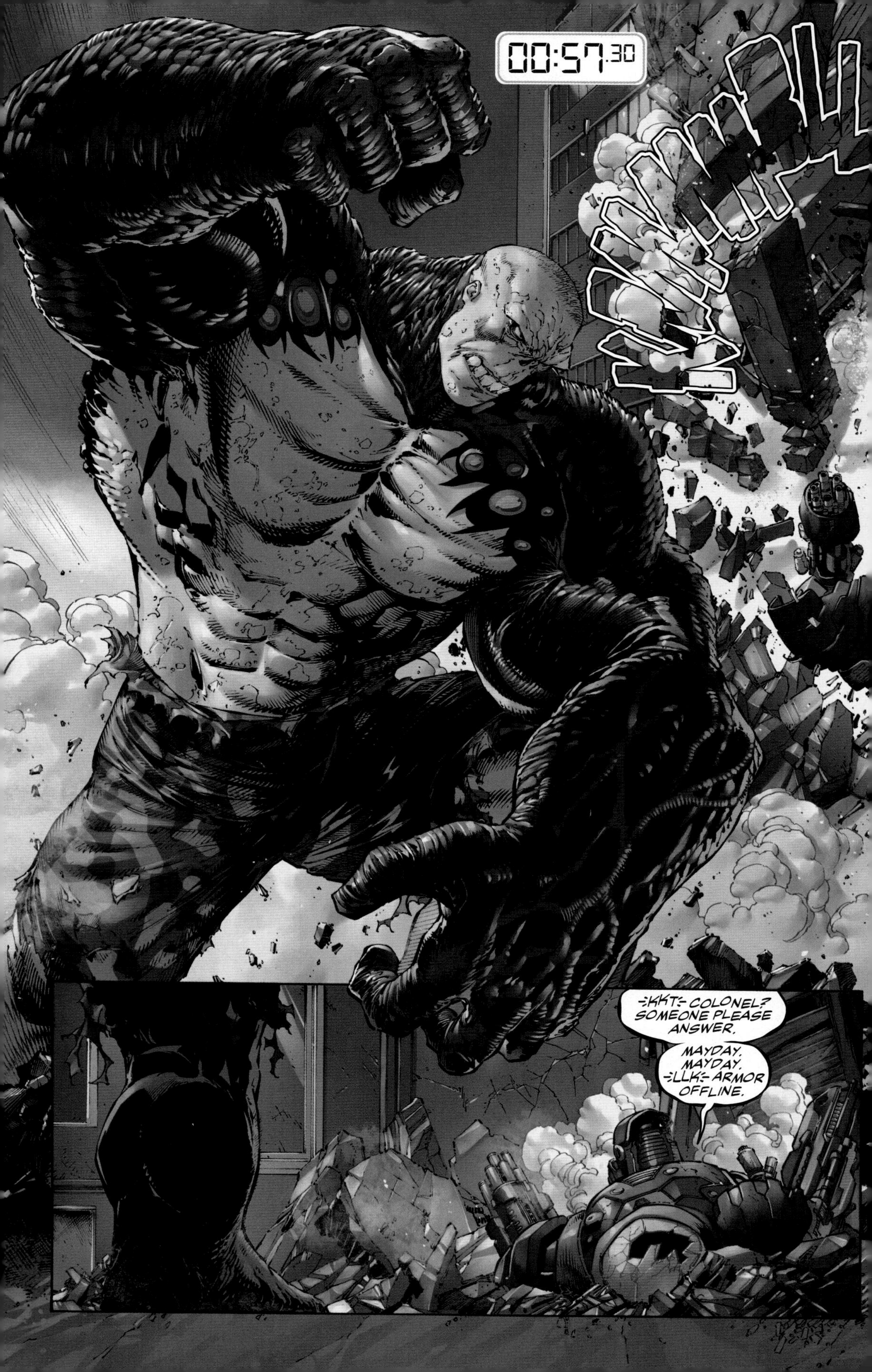
00:57.30
=KKT= COLONEL? SOMEONE PLEASE ANSWER.
MAYDAY. MAYDAY. =LLK= ARMOR OFFLINE.

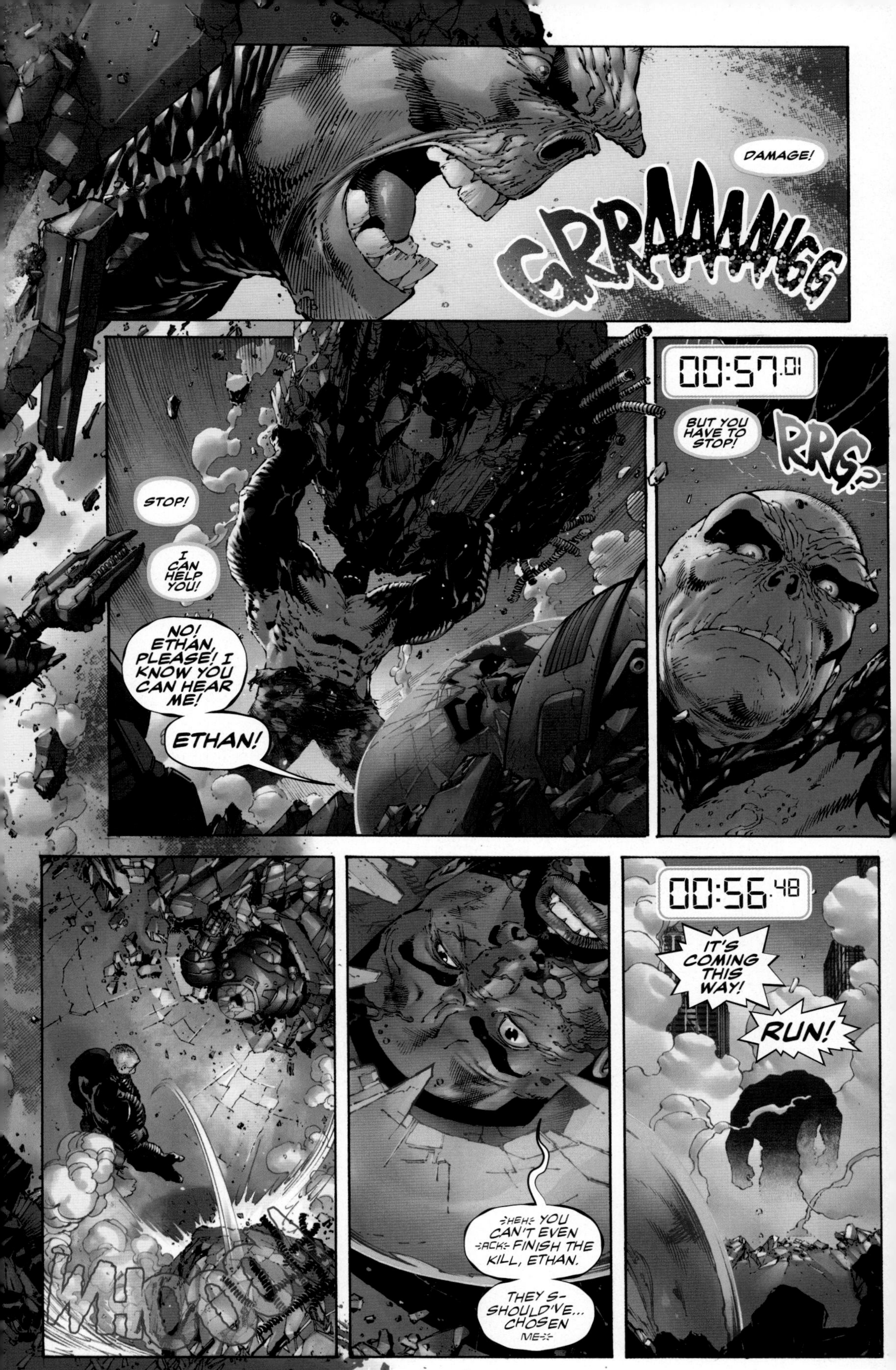
DAMAGE!
GRRAAAAUGG
STOP!
I CAN HELP YOU!
NO! ETHAN, PLEASE! I KNOW YOU CAN HEAR ME!
ETHAN!
00:57.01
BUT YOU HAVE TO STOP!
RRG?
00:56.48
IT'S COMING THIS WAY!
RUN!
HEH YOU CAN'T EVEN ACK FINISH THE KILL, ETHAN.
THEY S-SHOULD'VE... CHOSEN ME

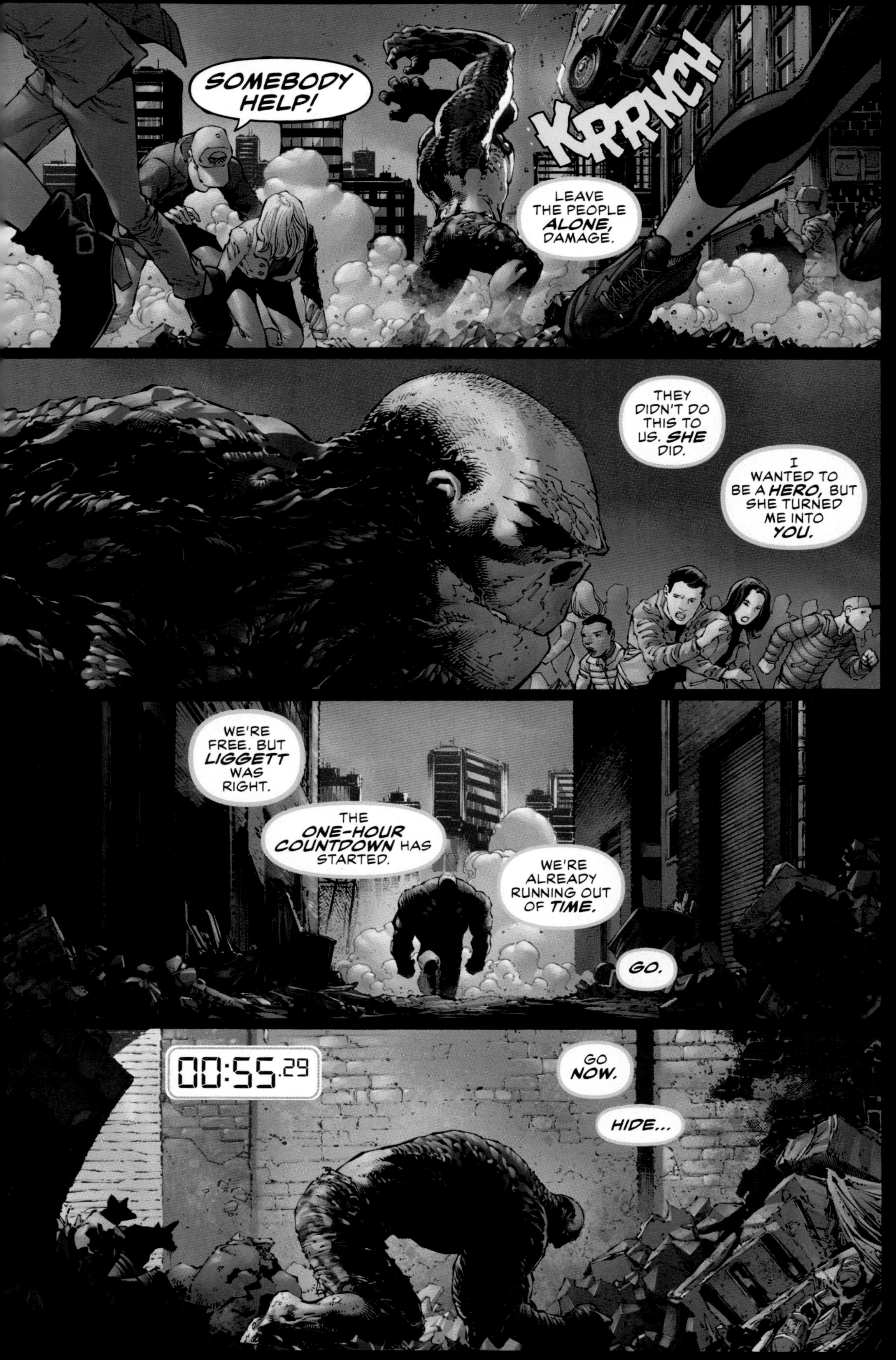
SOMEBODY HELP!
KRRNCH
LEAVE THE PEOPLE ALONE, DAMAGE.
THEY DIDN'T DO THIS TO US. SHE DID.
I WANTED TO BE A HERO, BUT SHE TURNED ME INTO YOU.
WE'RE FREE. BUT LIGGETT WAS RIGHT.
THE ONE-HOUR COUNTDOWN HAS STARTED.
WE'RE ALREADY RUNNING OUT OF TIME.
GO.
00:55.29
GO NOW.
HIDE...

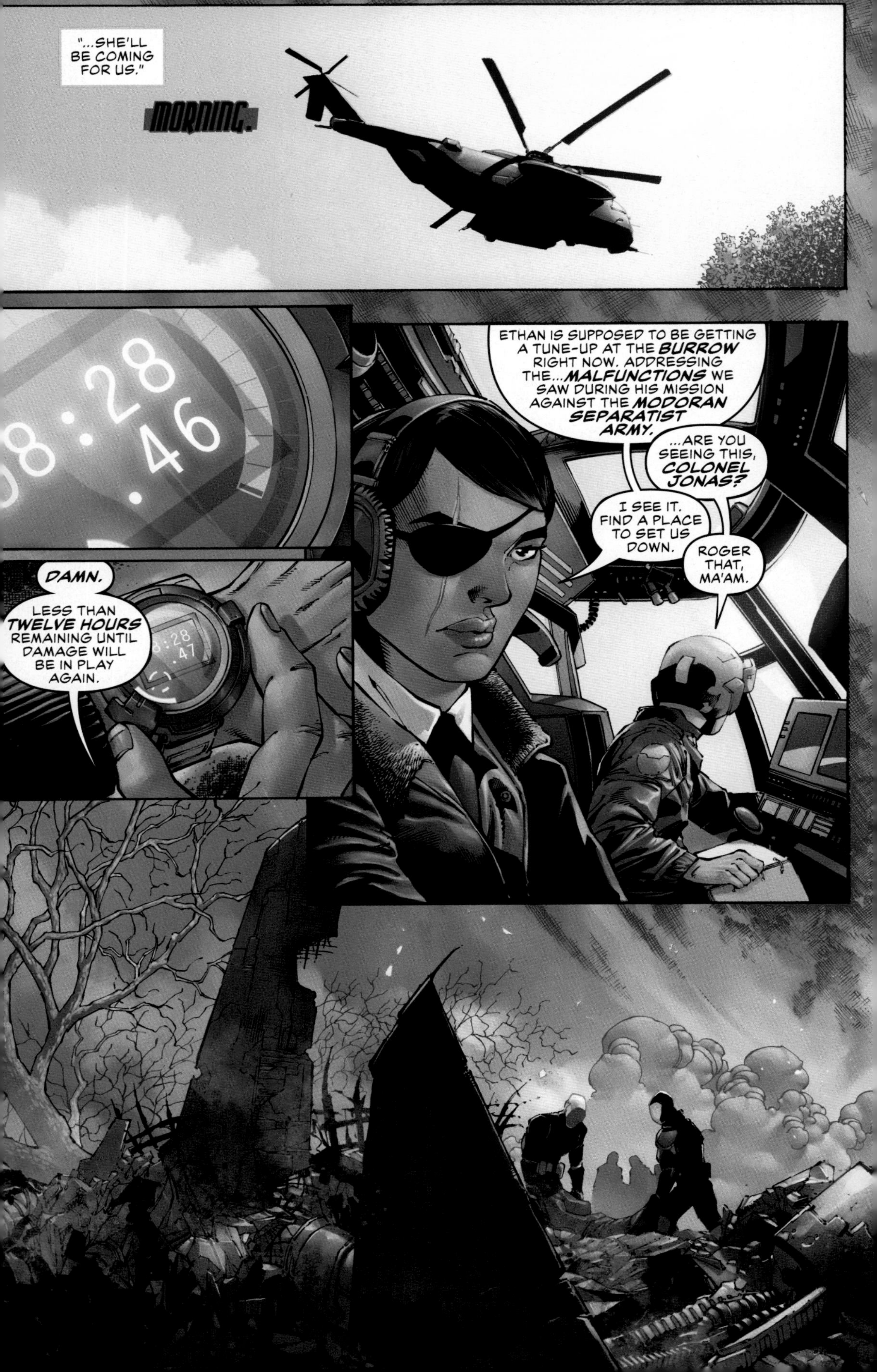
"...SHE'LL BE COMING FOR US."
MORNING.
08:28 .46
DAMN.
LESS THAN TWELVE HOURS REMAINING UNTIL DAMAGE WILL BE IN PLAY AGAIN.
8:28 .47
ETHAN IS SUPPOSED TO BE GETTING A TUNE-UP AT THE BURROW RIGHT NOW. ADDRESSING THE...MALFUNCTIONS WE SAW DURING HIS MISSION AGAINST THE MODORAN SEPARATIST ARMY.
...ARE YOU SEEING THIS, COLONEL JONAS?
I SEE IT. FIND A PLACE TO SET US DOWN.
ROGER THAT, MA'AM.

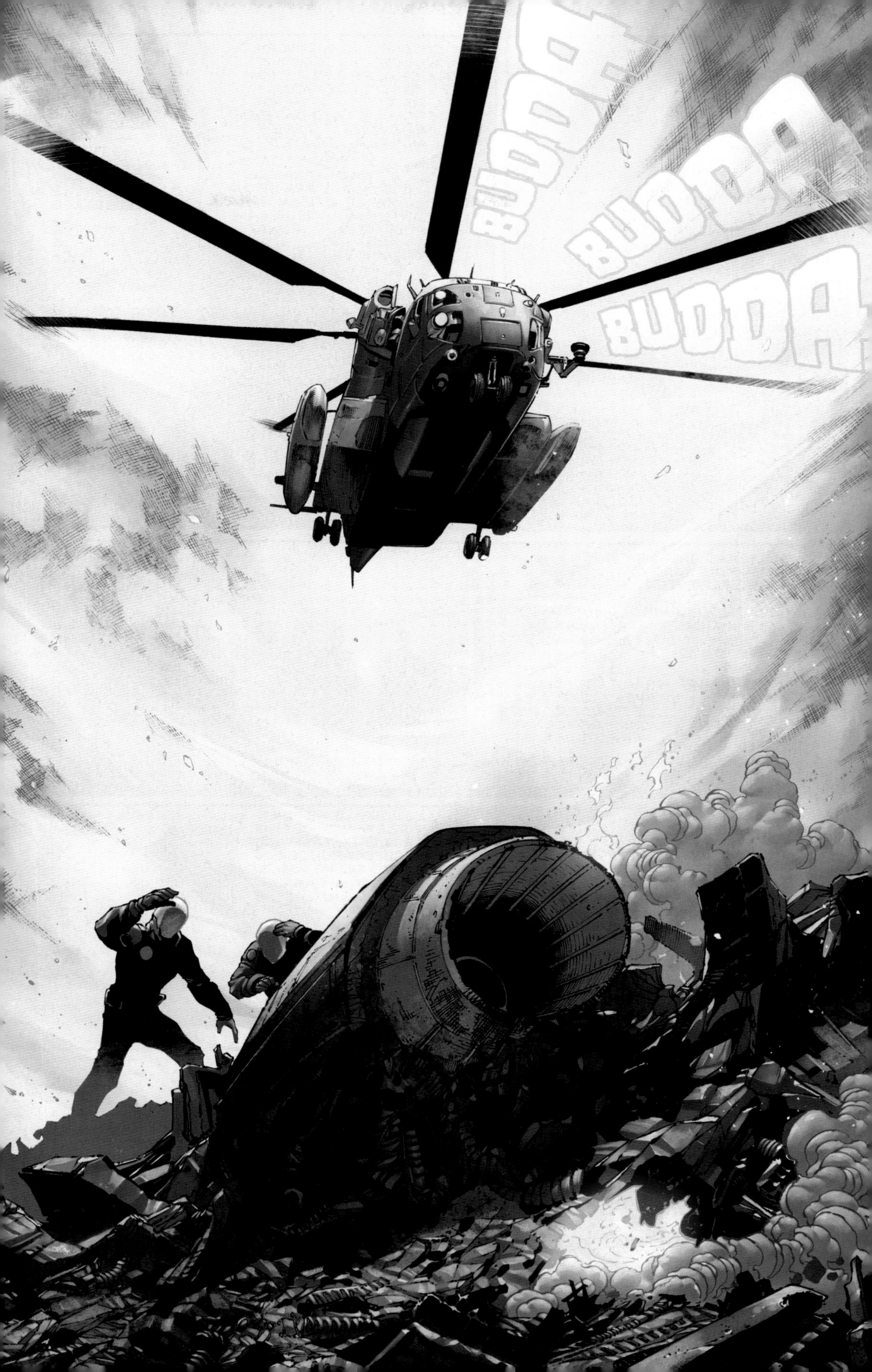
BUDDA
BUDDA
BUDDA

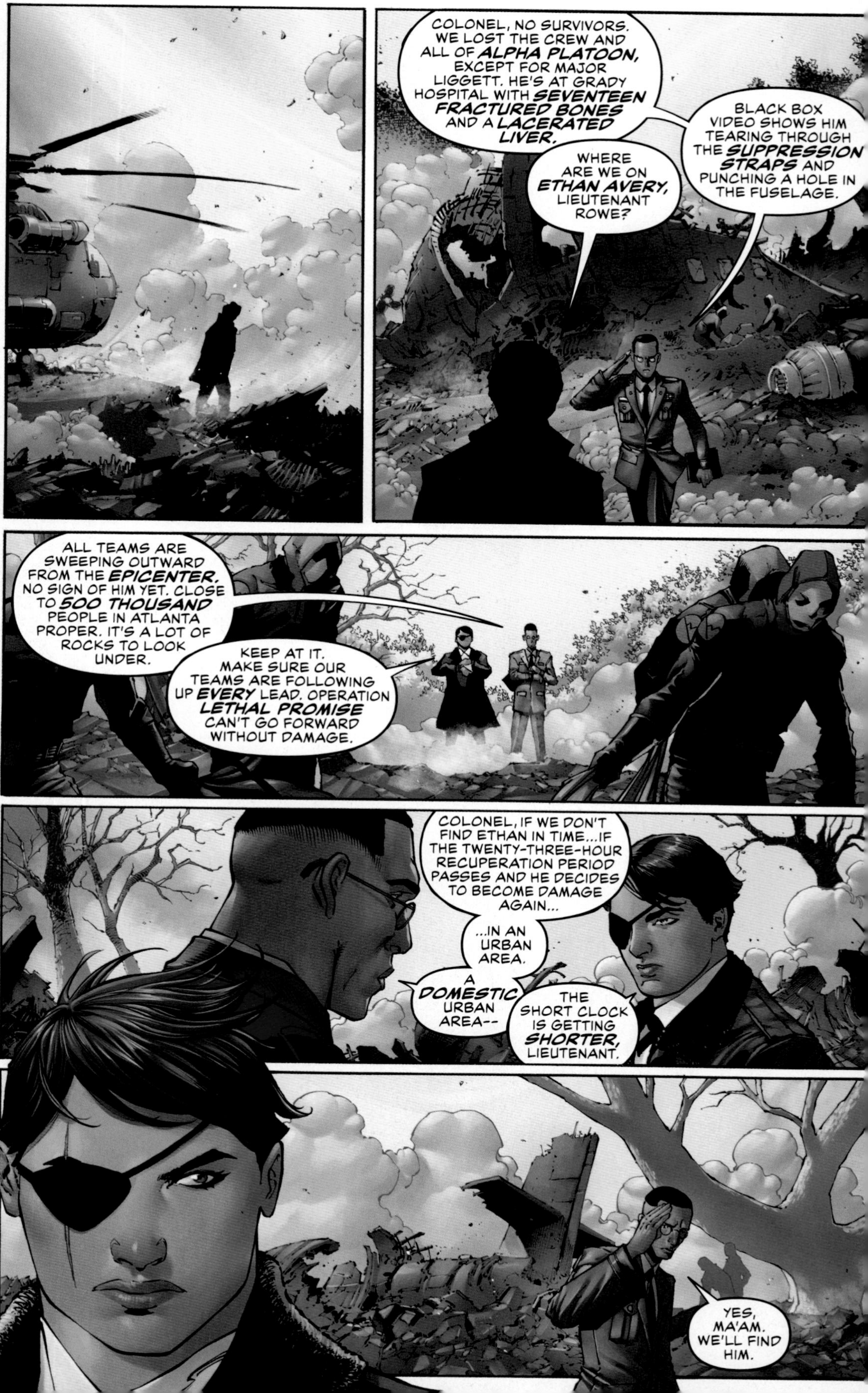
COLONEL, NO SURVIVORS. WE LOST THE CREW AND ALL OF ALPHA PLATOON, EXCEPT FOR MAJOR LIGGETT. HE'S AT GRADY HOSPITAL WITH SEVENTEEN FRACTURED BONES AND A LACERATED LIVER.
WHERE ARE WE ON ETHAN AVERY, LIEUTENANT ROWE?
BLACK BOX VIDEO SHOWS HIM TEARING THROUGH THE SUPPRESSION STRAPS AND PUNCHING A HOLE IN THE FUSELAGE.
ALL TEAMS ARE SWEEPING OUTWARD FROM THE EPICENTER. NO SIGN OF HIM YET. CLOSE TO 500 THOUSAND PEOPLE IN ATLANTA PROPER. IT'S A LOT OF ROCKS TO LOOK UNDER.
KEEP AT IT. MAKE SURE OUR TEAMS ARE FOLLOWING UP EVERY LEAD. OPERATION LETHAL PROMISE CAN'T GO FORWARD WITHOUT DAMAGE.
COLONEL, IF WE DON'T FIND ETHAN IN TIME...IF THE TWENTY-THREE-HOUR RECUPERATION PERIOD PASSES AND HE DECIDES TO BECOME DAMAGE AGAIN...
...IN AN URBAN AREA.
A DOMESTIC URBAN AREA--
THE SHORT CLOCK IS GETTING SHORTER, LIEUTENANT.
YES, MA'AM. WE'LL FIND HIM.

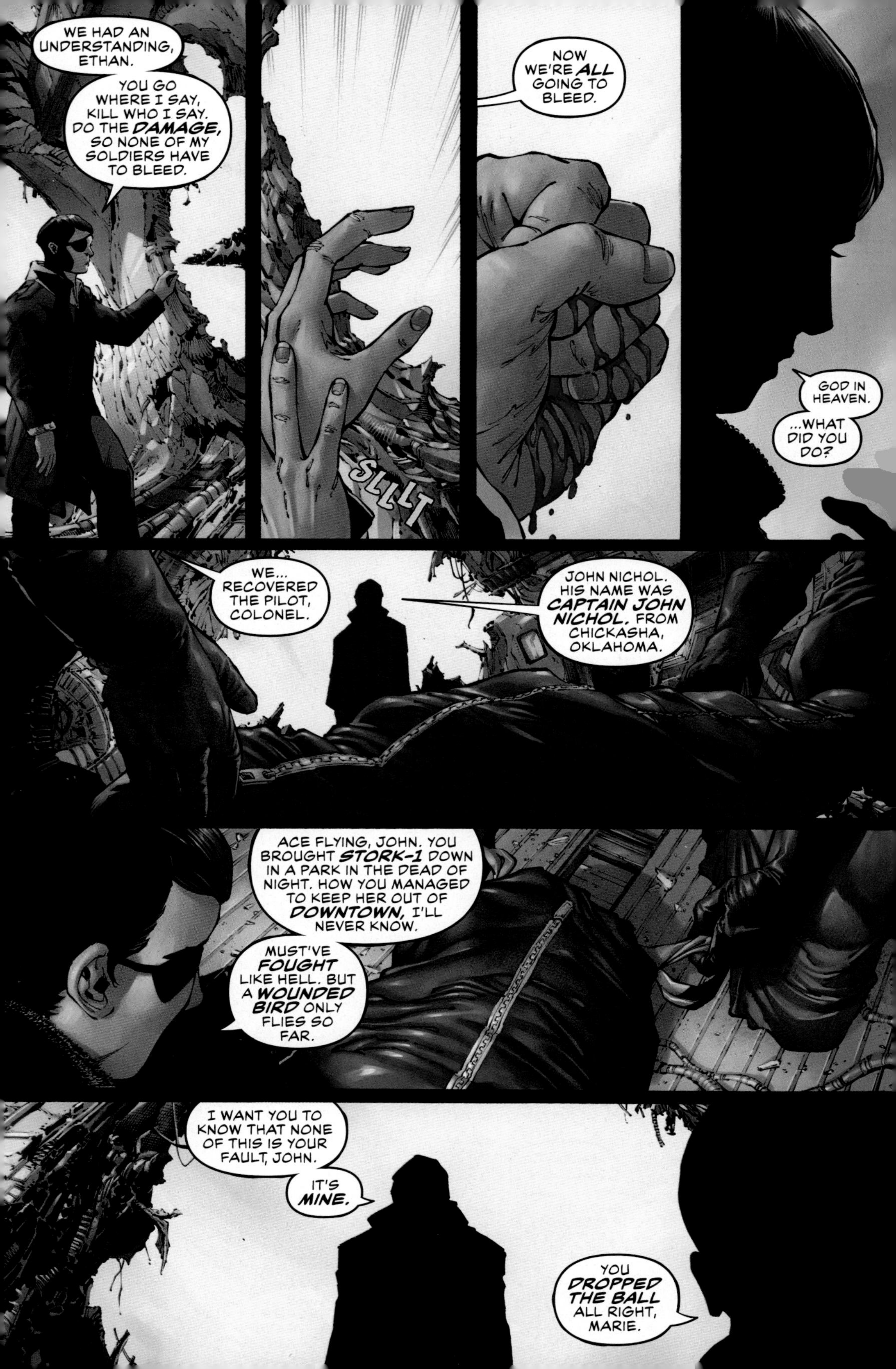
WE HAD AN UNDERSTANDING, ETHAN.
YOU GO WHERE I SAY, KILL WHO I SAY. DO THE DAMAGE, SO NONE OF MY SOLDIERS HAVE TO BLEED.
SLLLT
NOW WE'RE ALL GOING TO BLEED.
GOD IN HEAVEN.
...WHAT DID YOU DO?
WE... RECOVERED THE PILOT, COLONEL.
JOHN NICHOL. HIS NAME WAS CAPTAIN JOHN NICHOL, FROM CHICKASHA, OKLAHOMA.
ACE FLYING, JOHN. YOU BROUGHT STORK-1 DOWN IN A PARK IN THE DEAD OF NIGHT. HOW YOU MANAGED TO KEEP HER OUT OF DOWNTOWN, I'LL NEVER KNOW.
MUST'VE FOUGHT LIKE HELL. BUT A WOUNDED BIRD ONLY FLIES SO FAR.
I WANT YOU TO KNOW THAT NONE OF THIS IS YOUR FAULT, JOHN.
IT'S MINE.
YOU DROPPED THE BALL ALL RIGHT, MARIE.

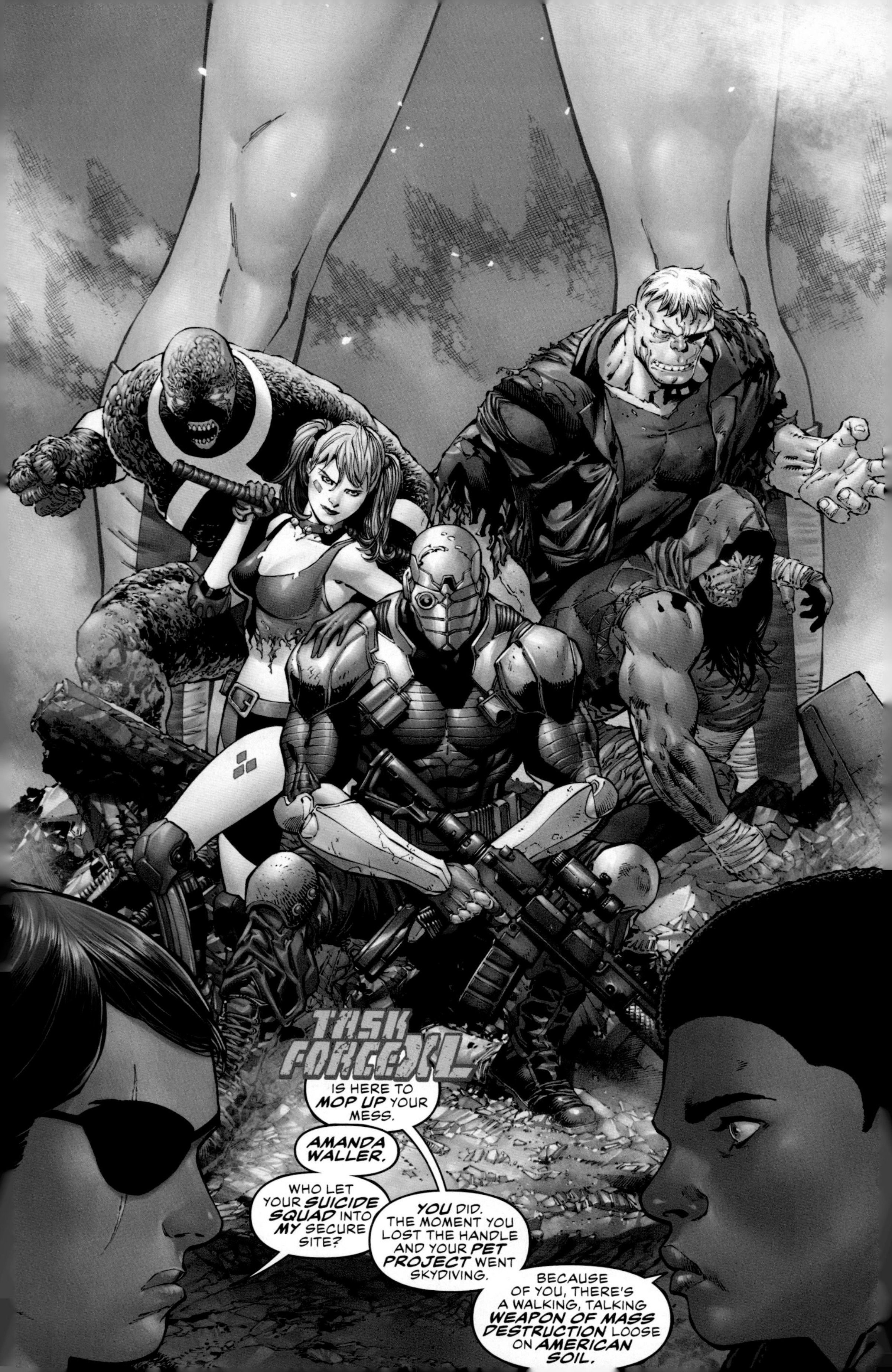
TASK FORCE XL
IS HERE TO MOP UP YOUR MESS.
AMANDA WALLER.
WHO LET YOUR SUICIDE SQUAD INTO MY SECURE SITE?
YOU DID. THE MOMENT YOU LOST THE HANDLE AND YOUR PET PROJECT WENT SKYDIVING.
BECAUSE OF YOU, THERE'S A WALKING, TALKING WEAPON OF MASS DESTRUCTION LOOSE ON AMERICAN SOIL.

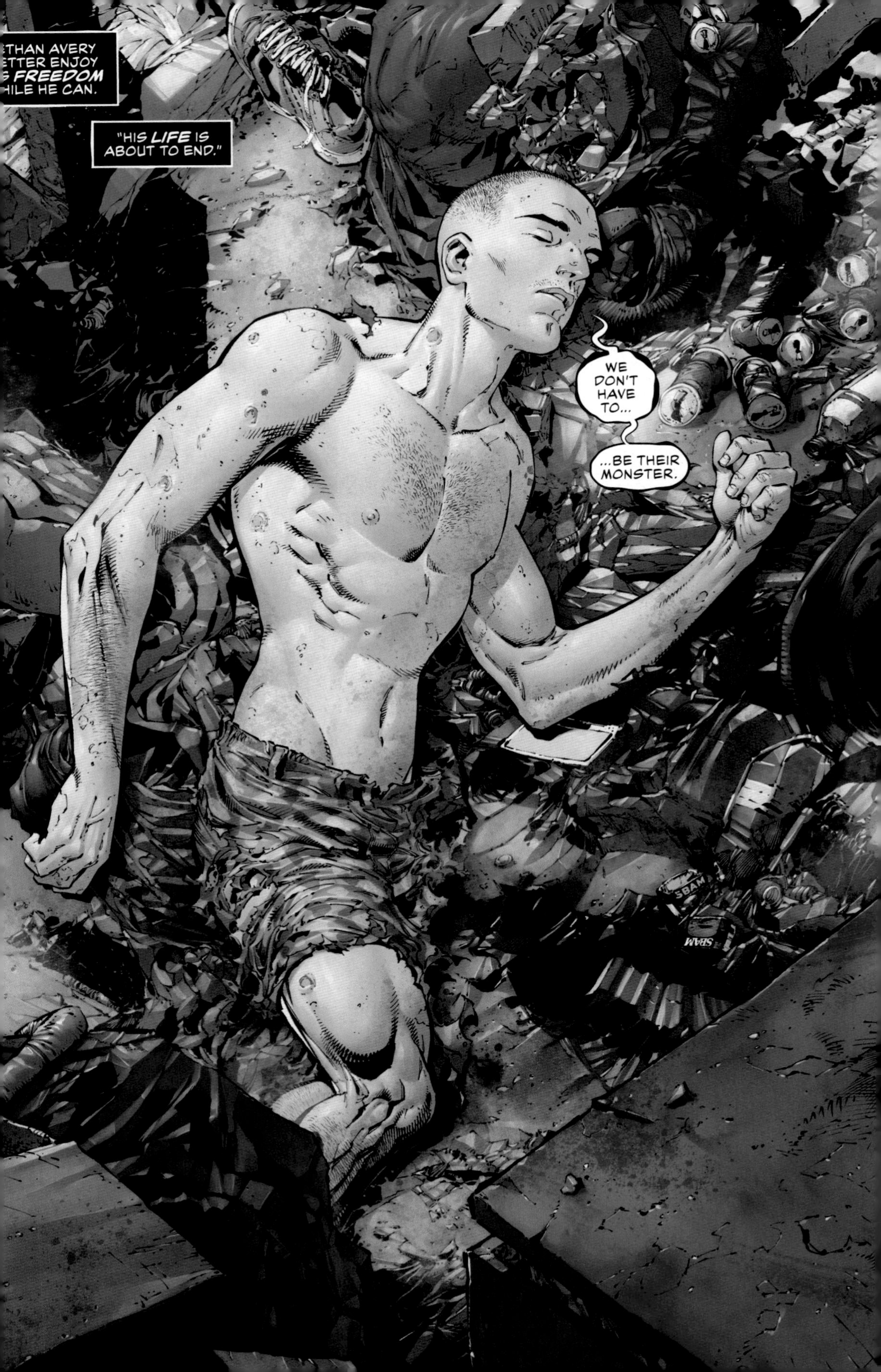
THAN AVERY
ETTER ENJOY
S FREEDOM
HILE HE CAN.
"HIS LIFE IS ABOUT TO END."
WE DON'T HAVE TO...
...BE THEIR MONSTER.
SBAM

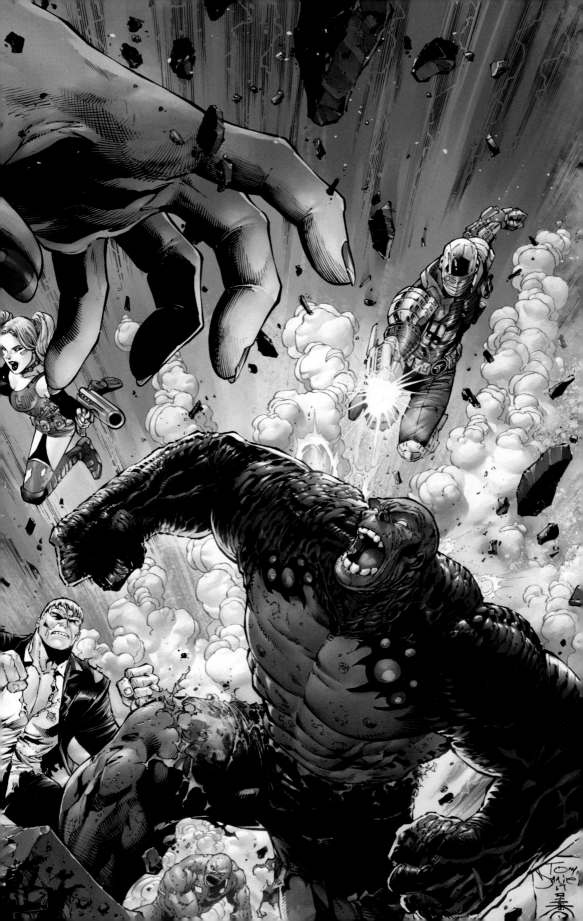

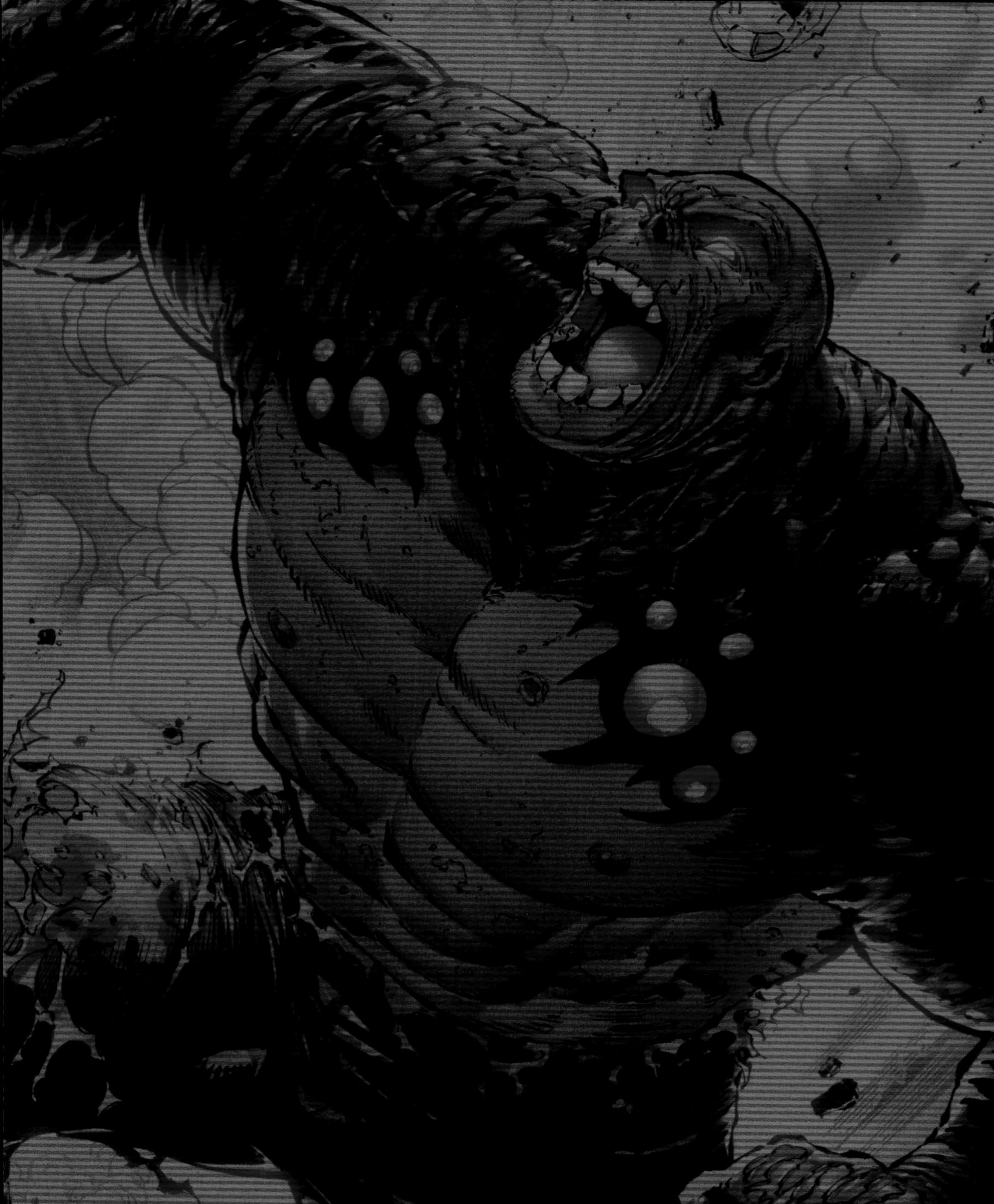

DAMAGE
#2

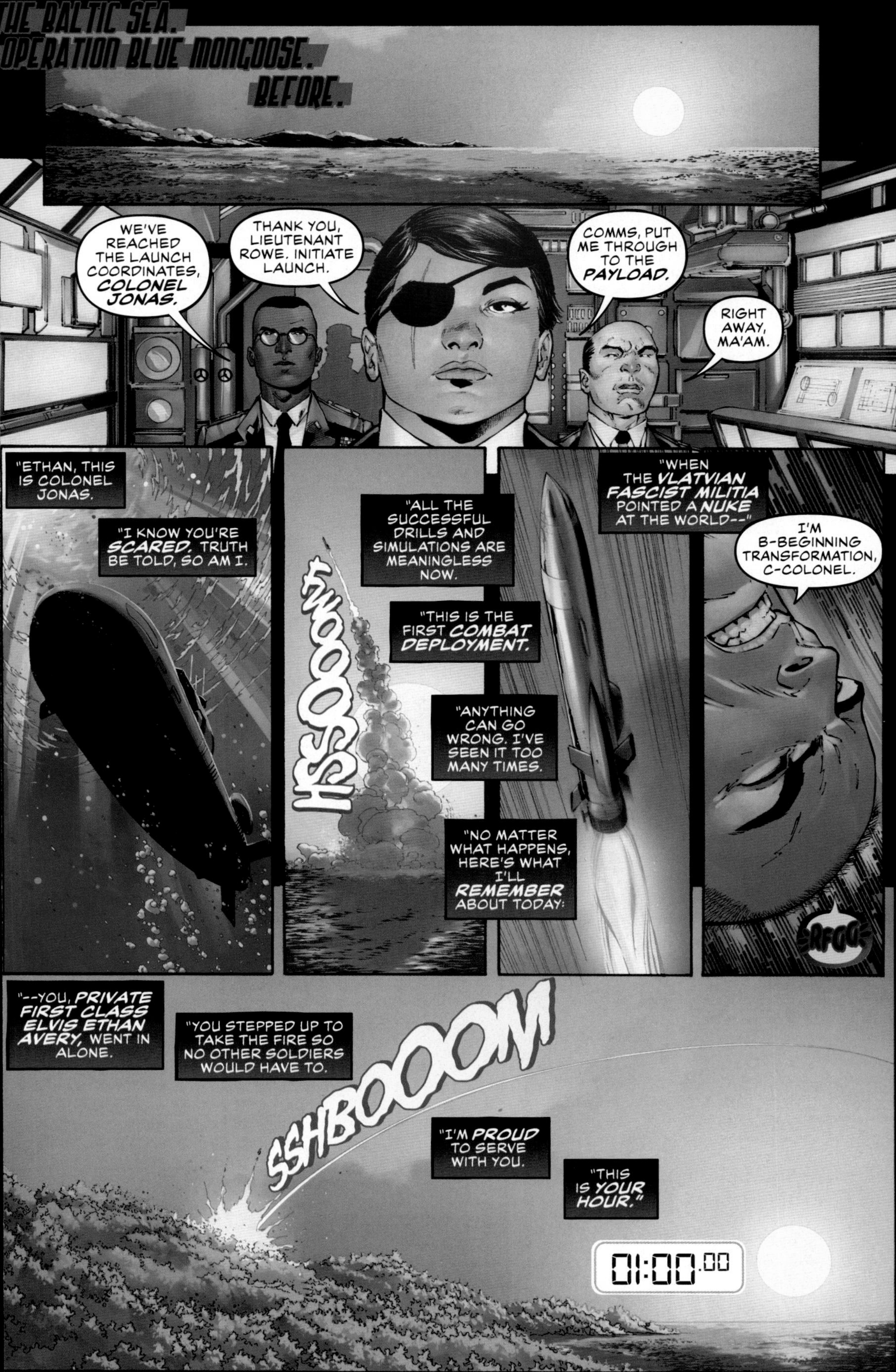
THE BALTIC SEA.
OPERATION BLUE MONGOOSE.
BEFORE.
WE'VE REACHED THE LAUNCH COORDINATES, COLONEL JONAS.
THANK YOU, LIEUTENANT ROWE. INITIATE LAUNCH.
COMMS, PUT ME THROUGH TO THE PAYLOAD.
RIGHT AWAY, MA'AM.
"ETHAN, THIS IS COLONEL JONAS.
"I KNOW YOU'RE SCARED. TRUTH BE TOLD, SO AM I.
"ALL THE SUCCESSFUL DRILLS AND SIMULATIONS ARE MEANINGLESS NOW.
HSSOOOOOOSH
"THIS IS THE FIRST COMBAT DEPLOYMENT.
"ANYTHING CAN GO WRONG. I'VE SEEN IT TOO MANY TIMES.
"NO MATTER WHAT HAPPENS, HERE'S WHAT I'LL REMEMBER ABOUT TODAY:
"WHEN THE VLATVIAN FASCIST MILITIA POINTED A NUKE AT THE WORLD--"
I'M B-BEGINNING TRANSFORMATION, C-COLONEL.
RFGG
"--YOU, PRIVATE FIRST CLASS ELVIS ETHAN AVERY, WENT IN ALONE.
"YOU STEPPED UP TO TAKE THE FIRE SO NO OTHER SOLDIERS WOULD HAVE TO.
SSHBOOOOM
"I'M PROUD TO SERVE WITH YOU.
"THIS IS YOUR HOUR."
01:00.00

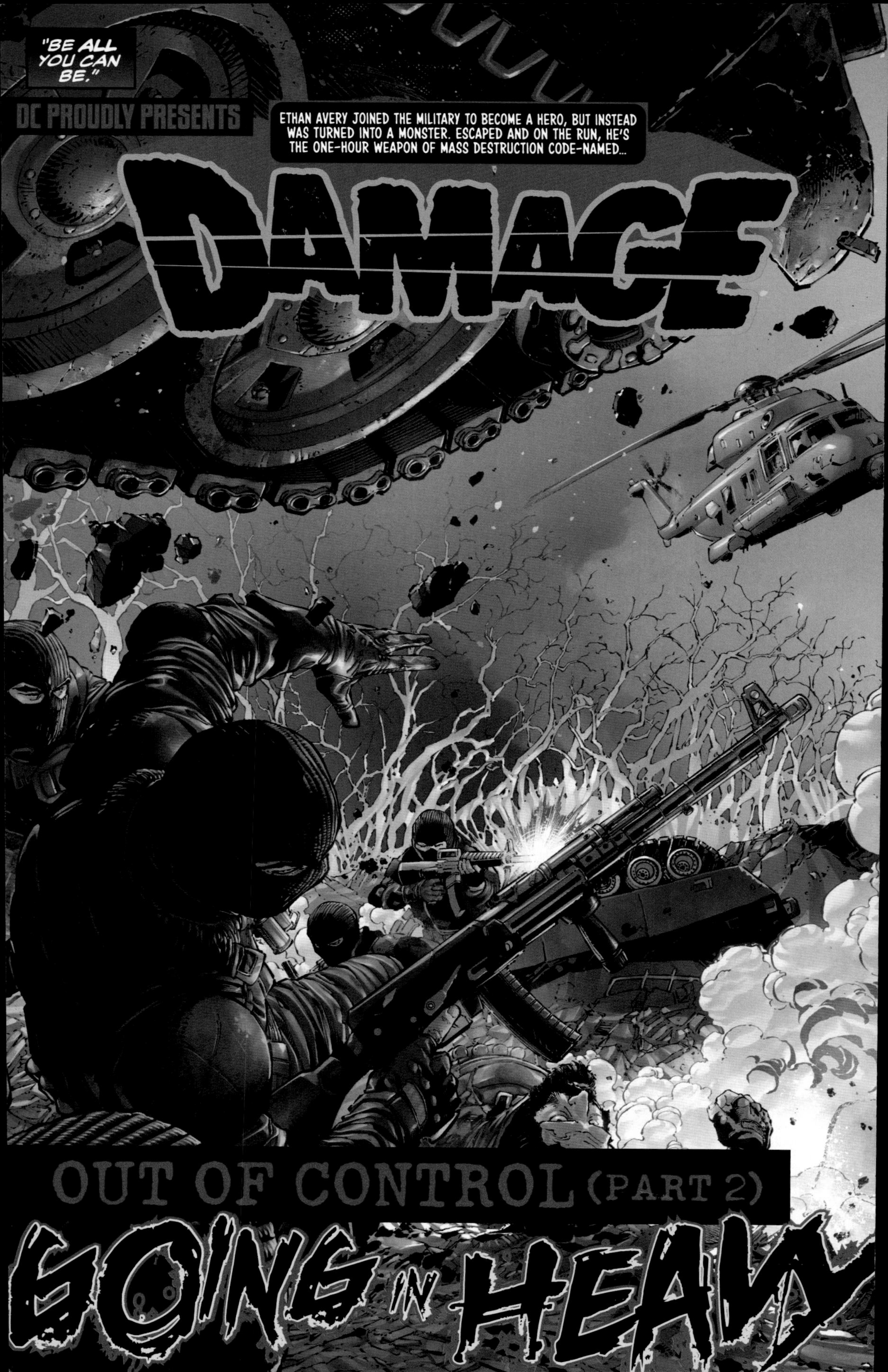
"BE ALL YOU CAN BE."
DC PROUDLY PRESENTS
ETHAN AVERY JOINED THE MILITARY TO BECOME A HERO, BUT INSTEAD WAS TURNED INTO A MONSTER. ESCAPED AND ON THE RUN, HE'S THE ONE-HOUR WEAPON OF MASS DESTRUCTION CODE-NAMED...
DAMAGE
OUT OF CONTROL (PART 2)
GOING IN HEAVY

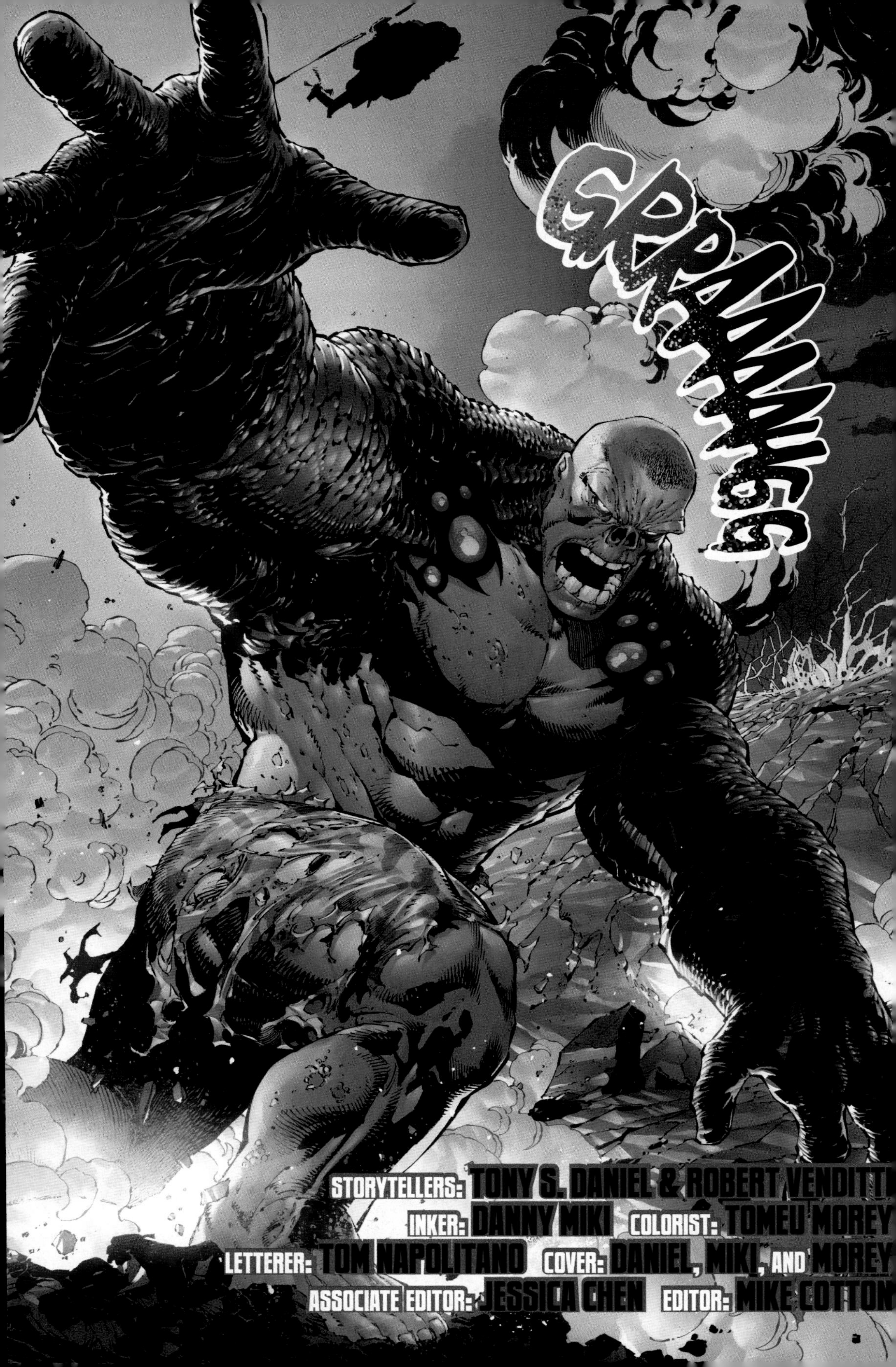
GRAAAAWGG
STORYTELLERS: TONY S. DANIEL & ROBERT VENDITTI
INKER: DANNY MIKI COLORIST: TOMEU MOREY
LETTERER: TOM NAPOLITANO COVER: DANIEL, MIKI, AND MOREY
ASSOCIATE EDITOR: JESSICA CHEN EDITOR: MIKE COTTON

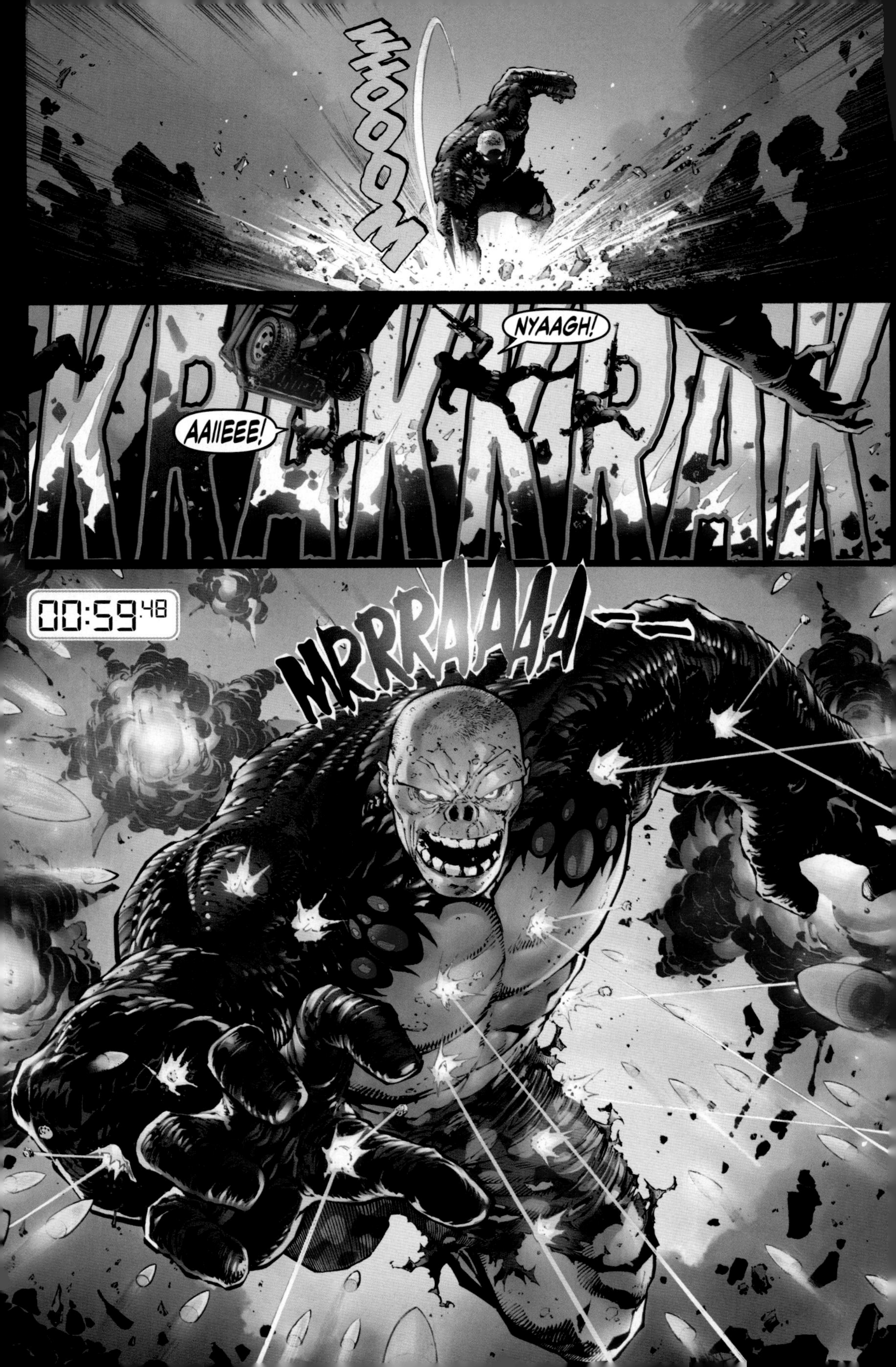
WHOOOM
NYAAGH!
AAIIEEE!
00:59.48
MRRAAAA--

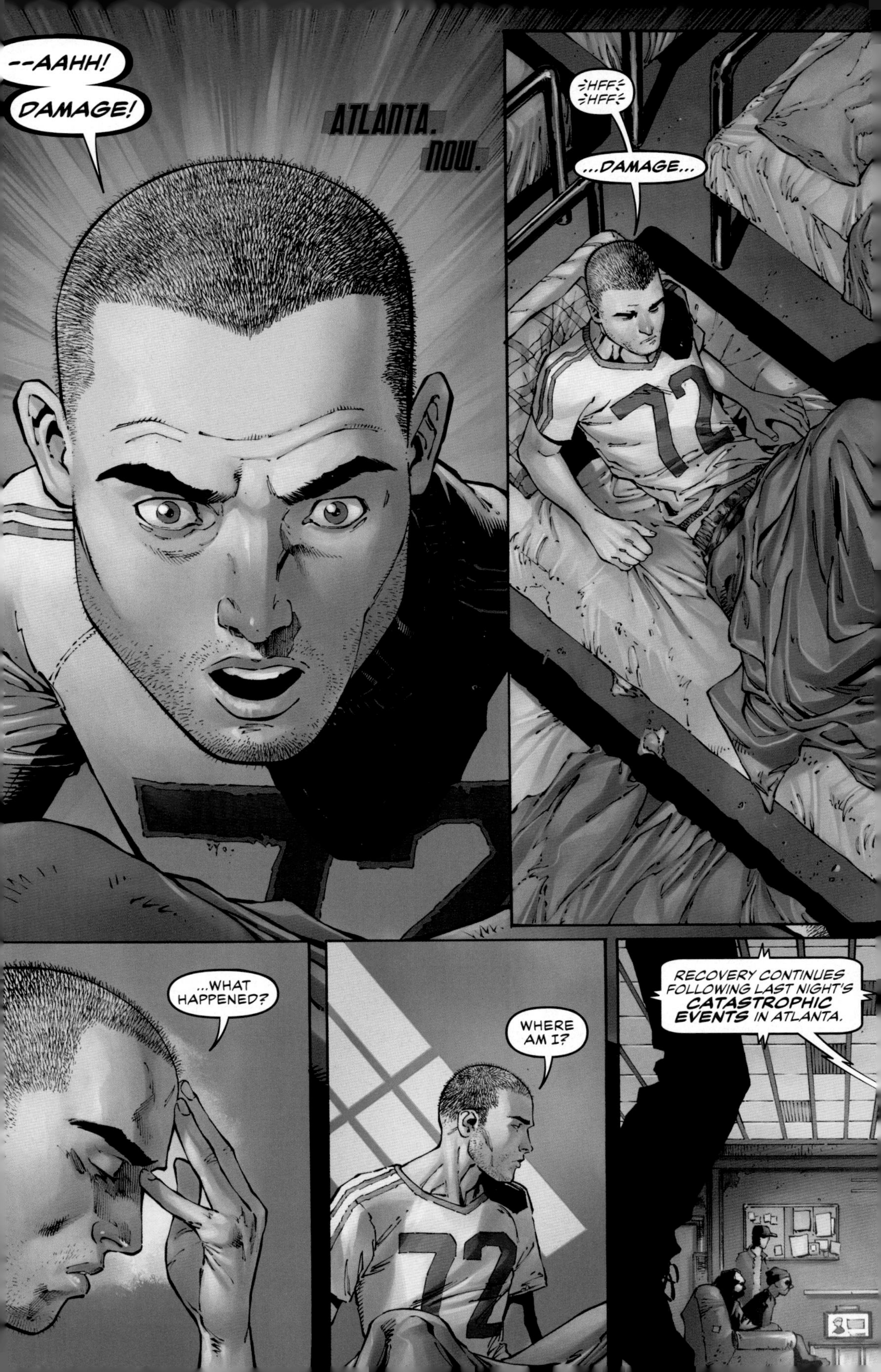
--AAHH!
DAMAGE!
ATLANTA. NOW.
HFF HFF
...DAMAGE...
...WHAT HAPPENED?
WHERE AM I?
RECOVERY CONTINUES FOLLOWING LAST NIGHT'S CATASTROPHIC EVENTS IN ATLANTA.

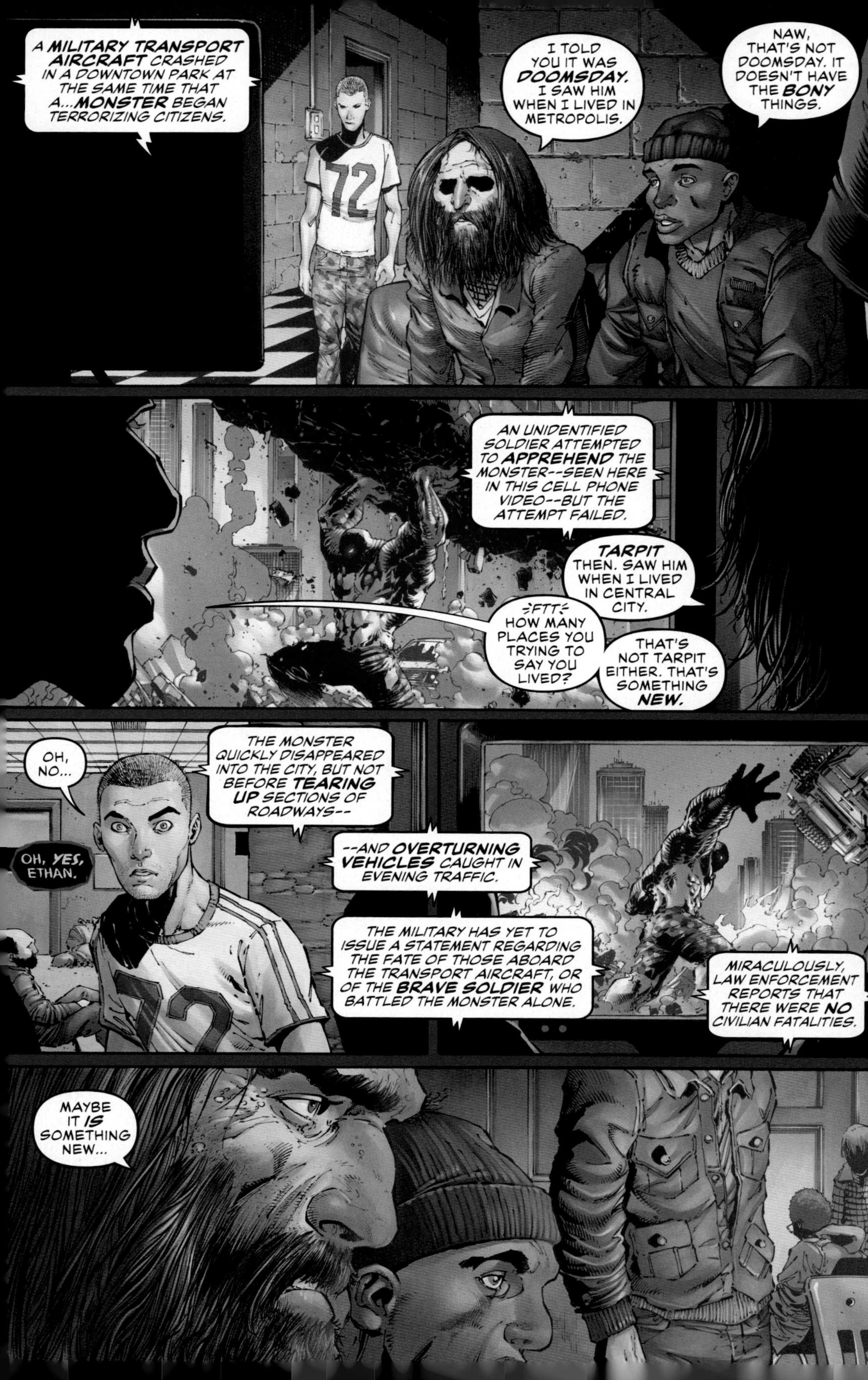
A MILITARY TRANSPORT AIRCRAFT CRASHED IN A DOWNTOWN PARK AT THE SAME TIME THAT A...MONSTER BEGAN TERRORIZING CITIZENS.
I TOLD YOU IT WAS DOOMSDAY. I SAW HIM WHEN I LIVED IN METROPOLIS.
NAW, THAT'S NOT DOOMSDAY. IT DOESN'T HAVE THE BONY THINGS.
AN UNIDENTIFIED SOLDIER ATTEMPTED TO APPREHEND THE MONSTER--SEEN HERE IN THIS CELL PHONE VIDEO--BUT THE ATTEMPT FAILED.
TARPIT THEN. SAW HIM WHEN I LIVED IN CENTRAL CITY.
FTT
HOW MANY PLACES YOU TRYING TO SAY YOU LIVED?
THAT'S NOT TARPIT EITHER. THAT'S SOMETHING NEW.
OH, NO...
THE MONSTER QUICKLY DISAPPEARED INTO THE CITY, BUT NOT BEFORE TEARING UP SECTIONS OF ROADWAYS--
OH, YES, ETHAN.
--AND OVERTURNING VEHICLES CAUGHT IN EVENING TRAFFIC.
THE MILITARY HAS YET TO ISSUE A STATEMENT REGARDING THE FATE OF THOSE ABOARD THE TRANSPORT AIRCRAFT, OR OF THE BRAVE SOLDIER WHO BATTLED THE MONSTER ALONE.
MIRACULOUSLY, LAW ENFORCEMENT REPORTS THAT THERE WERE NO CIVILIAN FATALITIES.
MAYBE IT IS SOMETHING NEW...

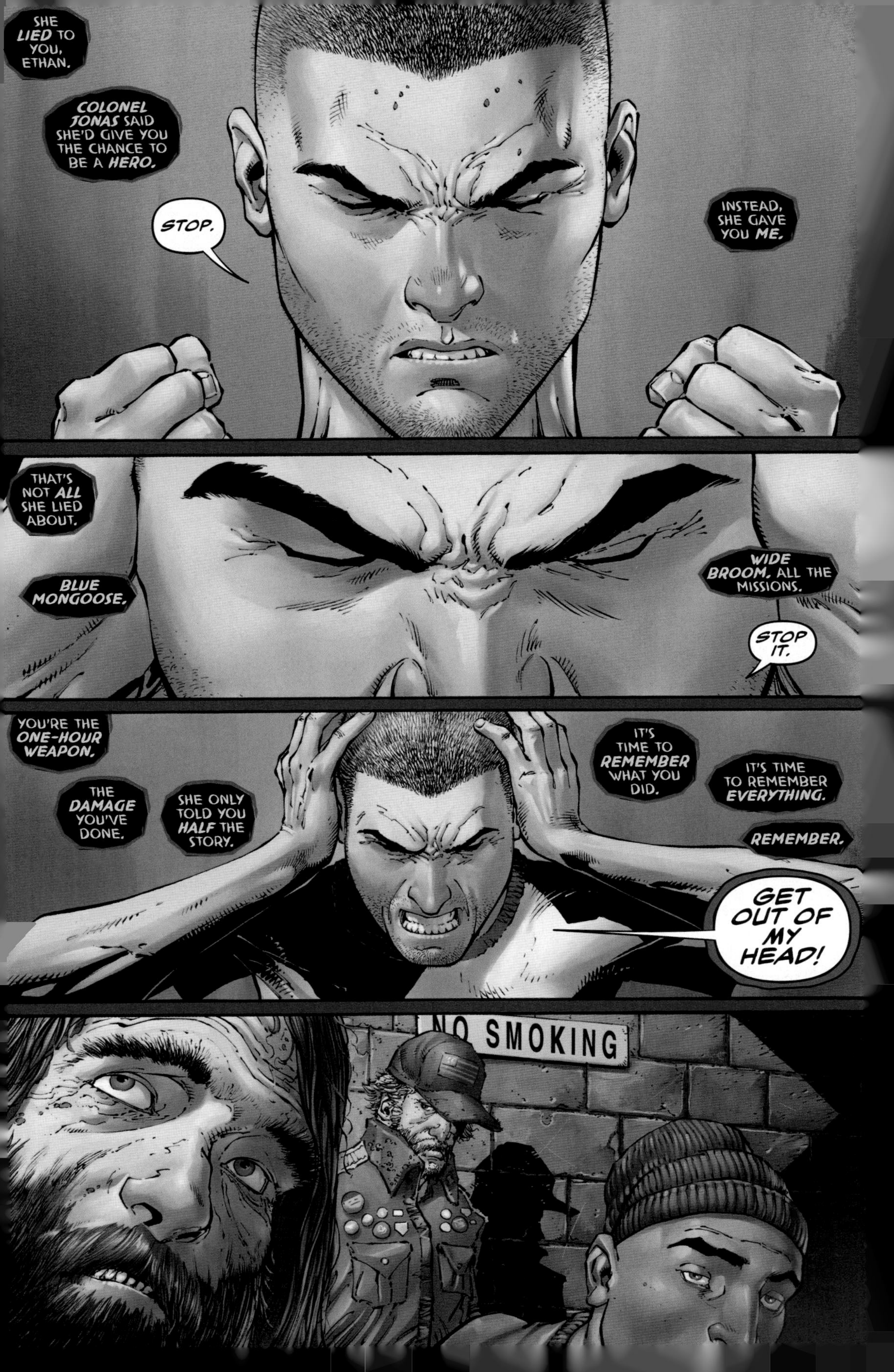
SHE LIED TO YOU, ETHAN.
COLONEL JONAS SAID SHE'D GIVE YOU THE CHANCE TO BE A HERO.
STOP.
INSTEAD, SHE GAVE YOU ME.
THAT'S NOT ALL SHE LIED ABOUT.
BLUE MONGOOSE.
WIDE BROOM. ALL THE MISSIONS.
STOP IT.
YOU'RE THE ONE-HOUR WEAPON.
THE DAMAGE YOU'VE DONE.
SHE ONLY TOLD YOU HALF THE STORY.
IT'S TIME TO REMEMBER WHAT YOU DID.
IT'S TIME TO REMEMBER EVERYTHING.
REMEMBER.
GET OUT OF MY HEAD!
NO SMOKING

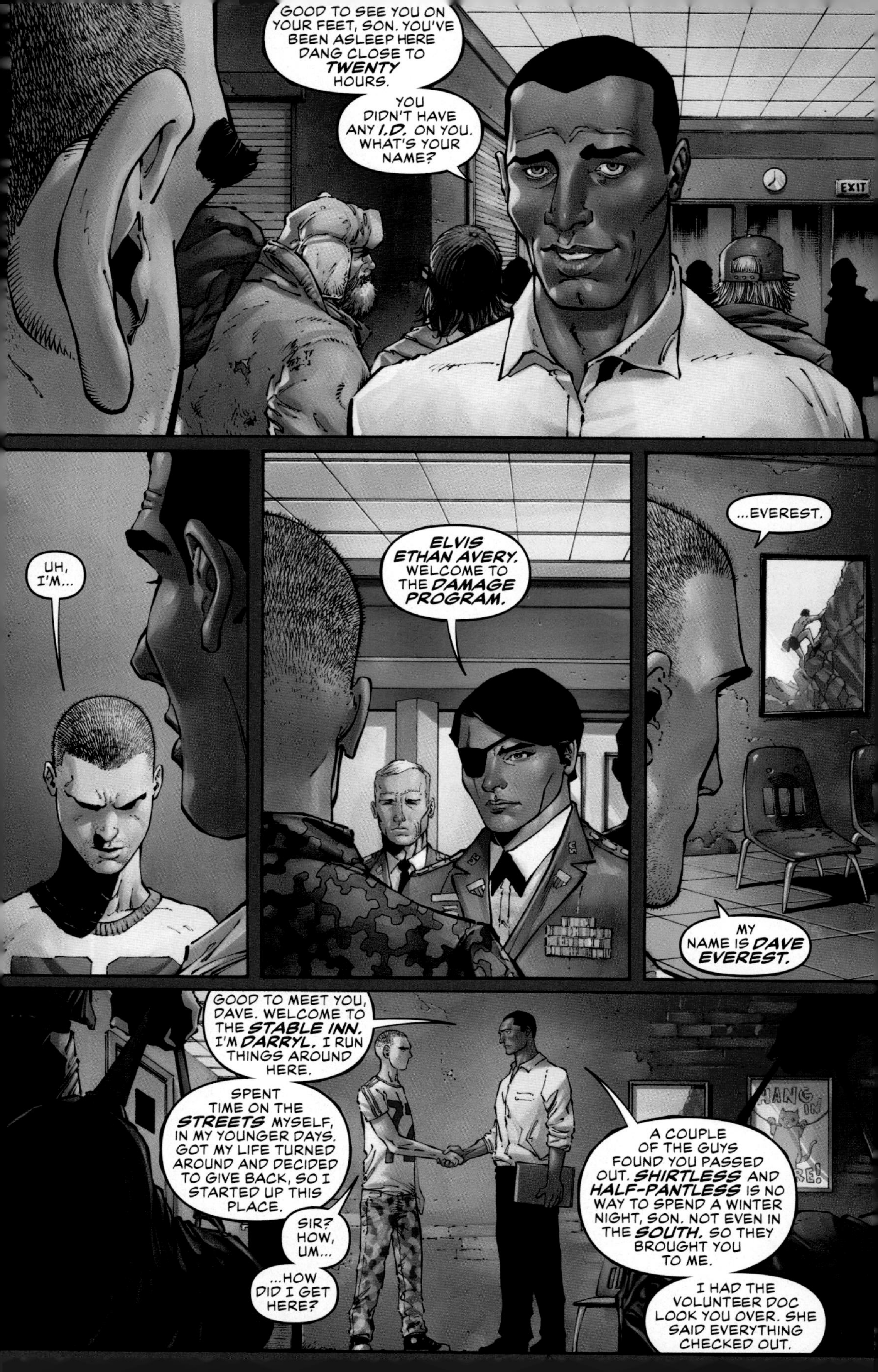
GOOD TO SEE YOU ON YOUR FEET, SON. YOU'VE BEEN ASLEEP HERE DANG CLOSE TO TWENTY HOURS.
YOU DIDN'T HAVE ANY I.D. ON YOU. WHAT'S YOUR NAME?
EXIT
UH, I'M...
ELVIS ETHAN AVERY. WELCOME TO THE DAMAGE PROGRAM.
...EVEREST.
MY NAME IS DAVE EVEREST.
GOOD TO MEET YOU, DAVE. WELCOME TO THE STABLE INN. I'M DARRYL. I RUN THINGS AROUND HERE.
SPENT TIME ON THE STREETS MYSELF, IN MY YOUNGER DAYS. GOT MY LIFE TURNED AROUND AND DECIDED TO GIVE BACK, SO I STARTED UP THIS PLACE.
SIR? HOW, UM...
...HOW DID I GET HERE?
A COUPLE OF THE GUYS FOUND YOU PASSED OUT. SHIRTLESS AND HALF-PANTLESS IS NO WAY TO SPEND A WINTER NIGHT, SON. NOT EVEN IN THE SOUTH. SO THEY BROUGHT YOU TO ME.
I HAD THE VOLUNTEER DOC LOOK YOU OVER. SHE SAID EVERYTHING CHECKED OUT.

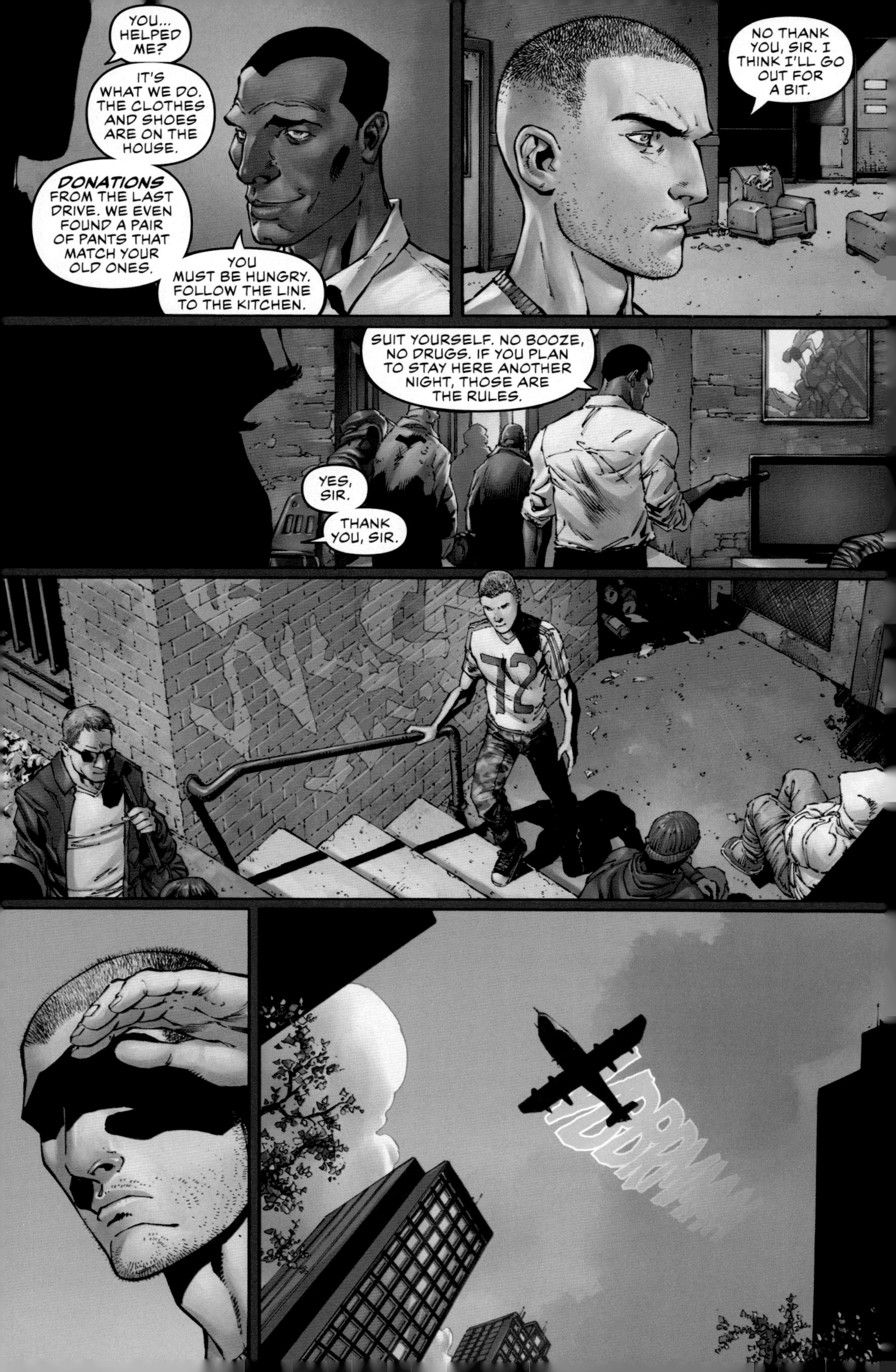
YOU... HELPED ME?
IT'S WHAT WE DO. THE CLOTHES AND SHOES ARE ON THE HOUSE.
DONATIONS FROM THE LAST DRIVE. WE EVEN FOUND A PAIR OF PANTS THAT MATCH YOUR OLD ONES.
YOU MUST BE HUNGRY. FOLLOW THE LINE TO THE KITCHEN.
NO THANK YOU, SIR. I THINK I'LL GO OUT FOR A BIT.
SUIT YOURSELF. NO BOOZE, NO DRUGS. IF YOU PLAN TO STAY HERE ANOTHER NIGHT, THOSE ARE THE RULES.
YES, SIR.
THANK YOU, SIR.
72

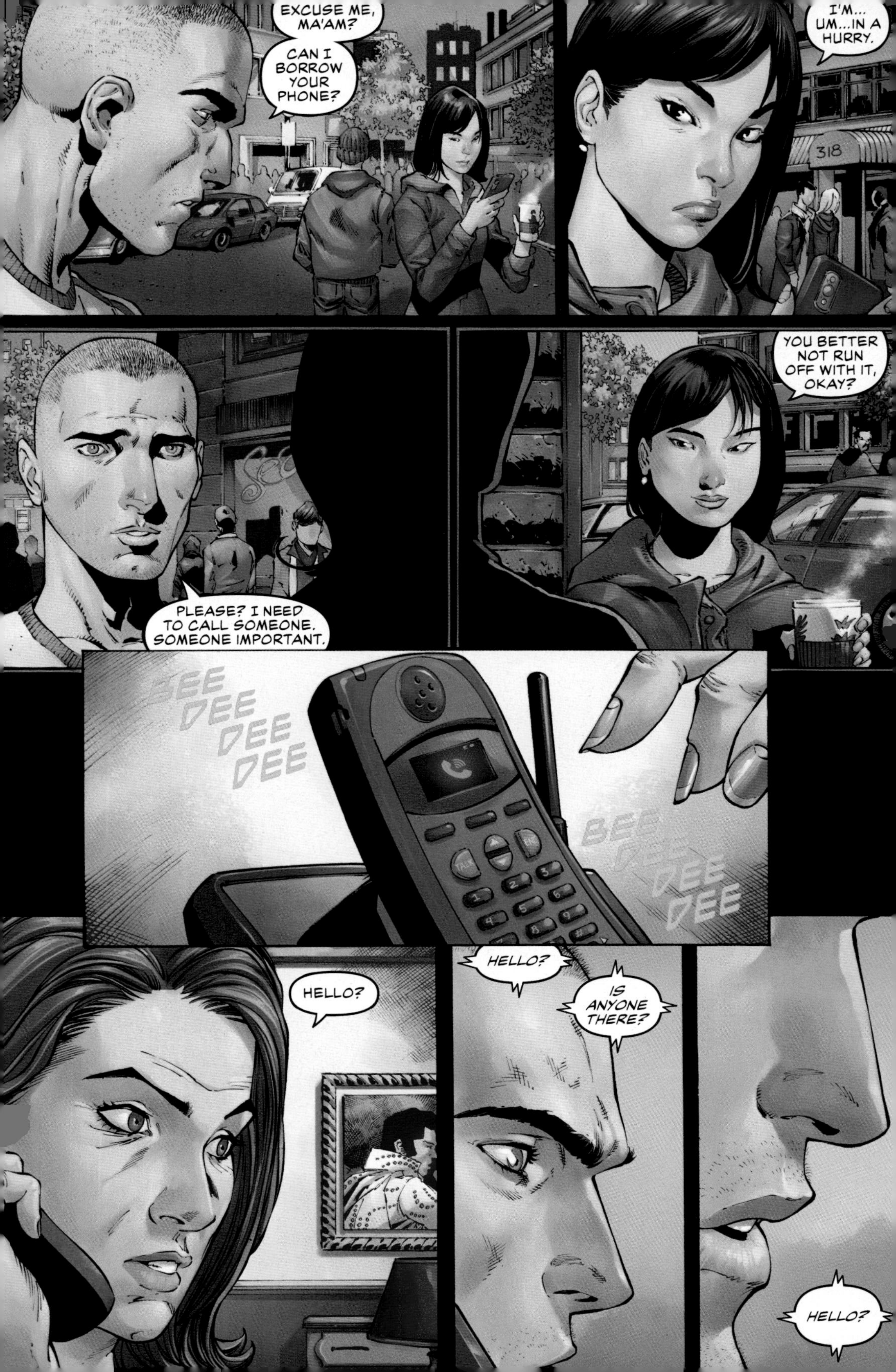
EXCUSE ME, MA'AM?
CAN I BORROW YOUR PHONE?
I'M... UM...IN A HURRY.
318
PLEASE? I NEED TO CALL SOMEONE. SOMEONE IMPORTANT.
YOU BETTER NOT RUN OFF WITH IT, OKAY?
BEE DEE DEE DEE
BEE DEE DEE DEE
HELLO?
HELLO?
IS ANYONE THERE?
HELLO?

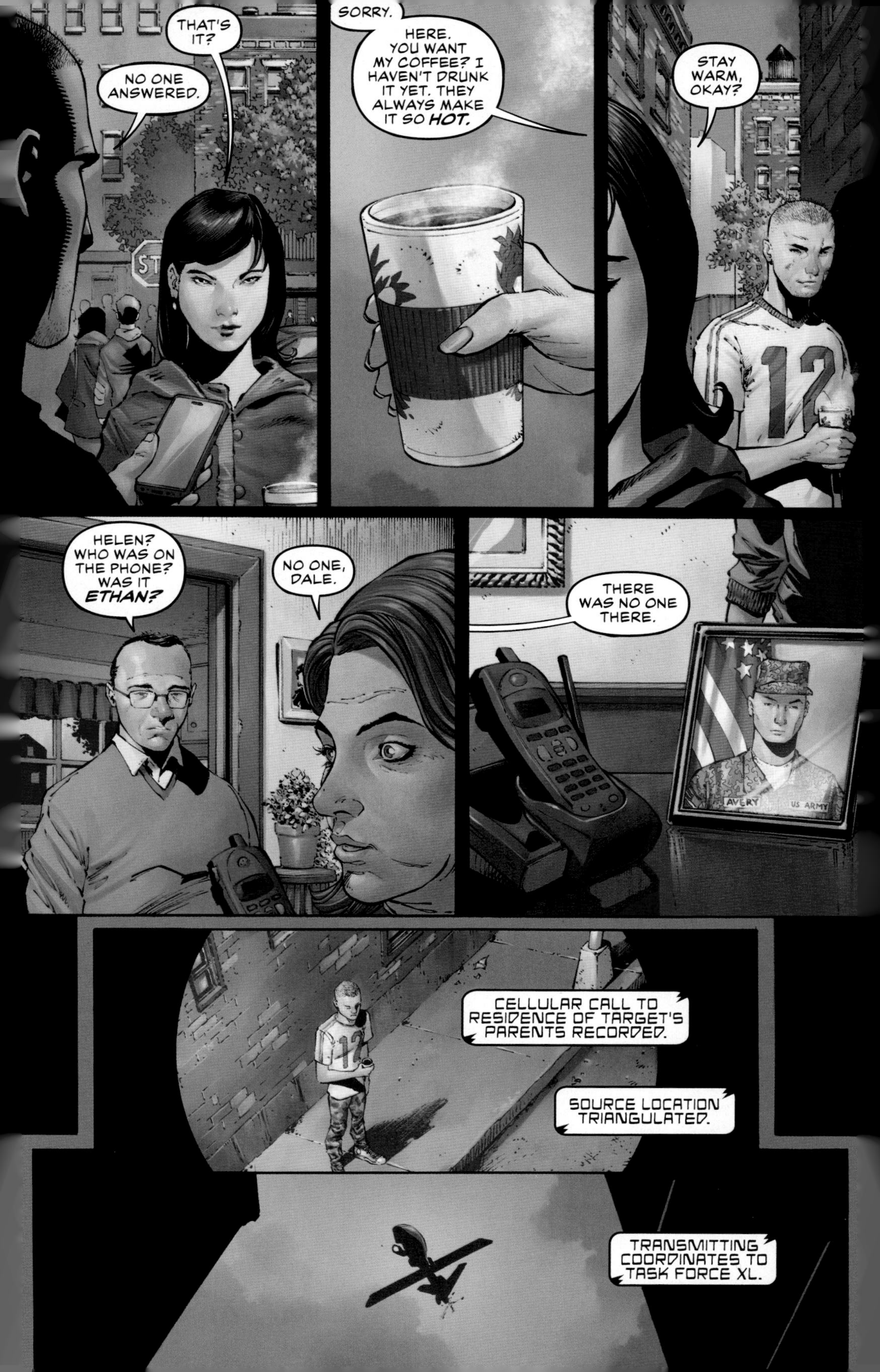
THAT'S IT?
NO ONE ANSWERED.
SORRY.
HERE. YOU WANT MY COFFEE? I HAVEN'T DRUNK IT YET. THEY ALWAYS MAKE IT SO **HOT.**
STAY WARM, OKAY?
12
HELEN? WHO WAS ON THE PHONE? WAS IT ***ETHAN?***
NO ONE, DALE.
THERE WAS NO ONE THERE.
AVERY
US ARMY
12
CELLULAR CALL TO RESIDENCE OF TARGET'S PARENTS RECORDED.
SOURCE LOCATION TRIANGULATED.
TRANSMITTING COORDINATES TO TASK FORCE XL.

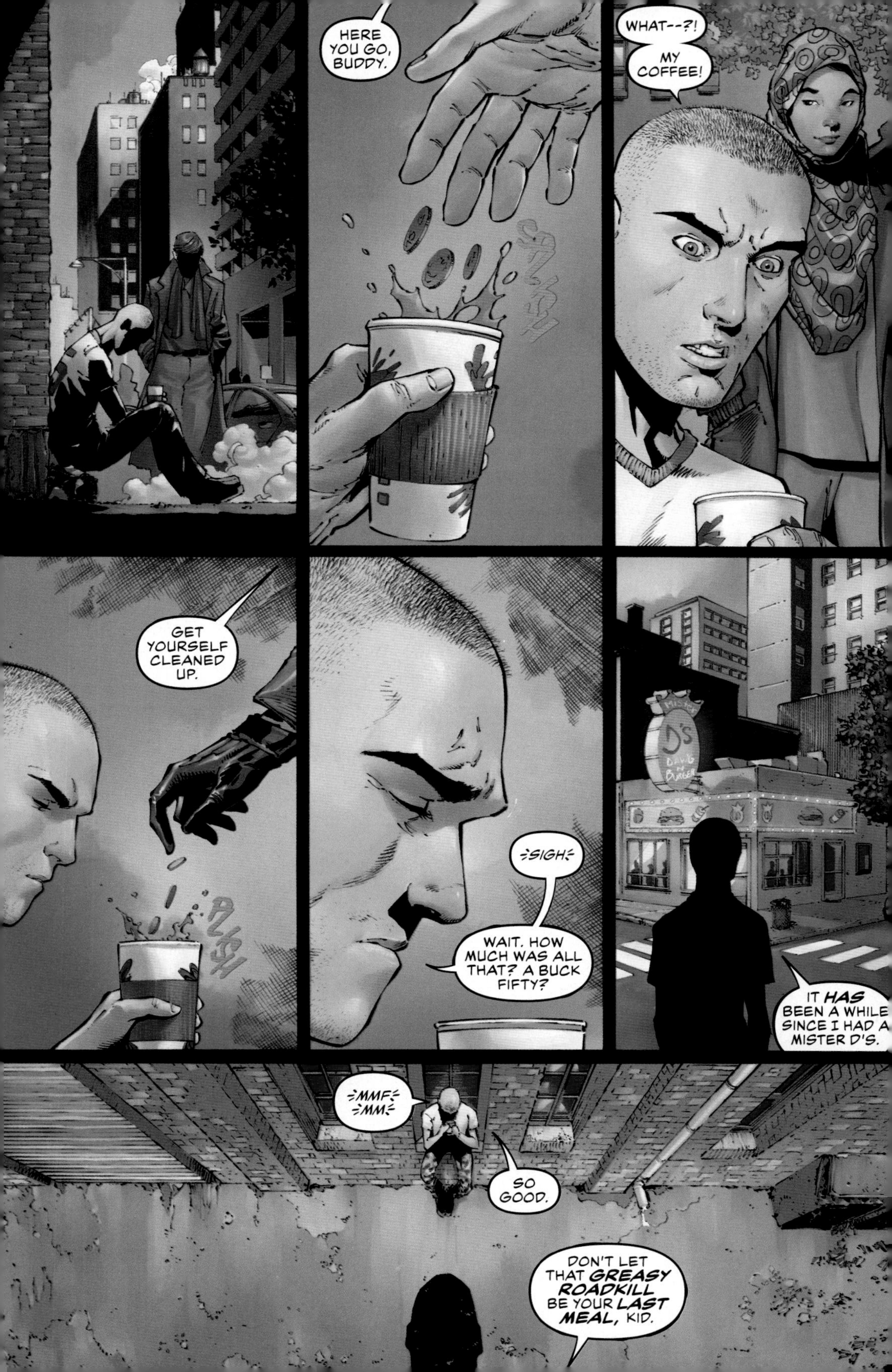
HERE YOU GO, BUDDY.
WHAT--?!
MY COFFEE!
GET YOURSELF CLEANED UP.
=SIGH=
WAIT. HOW MUCH WAS ALL THAT? A BUCK FIFTY?
D'S
IT HAS BEEN A WHILE SINCE I HAD A MISTER D'S.
=MMF= =MM=
SO GOOD.
DON'T LET THAT GREASY ROADKILL BE YOUR LAST MEAL, KID.

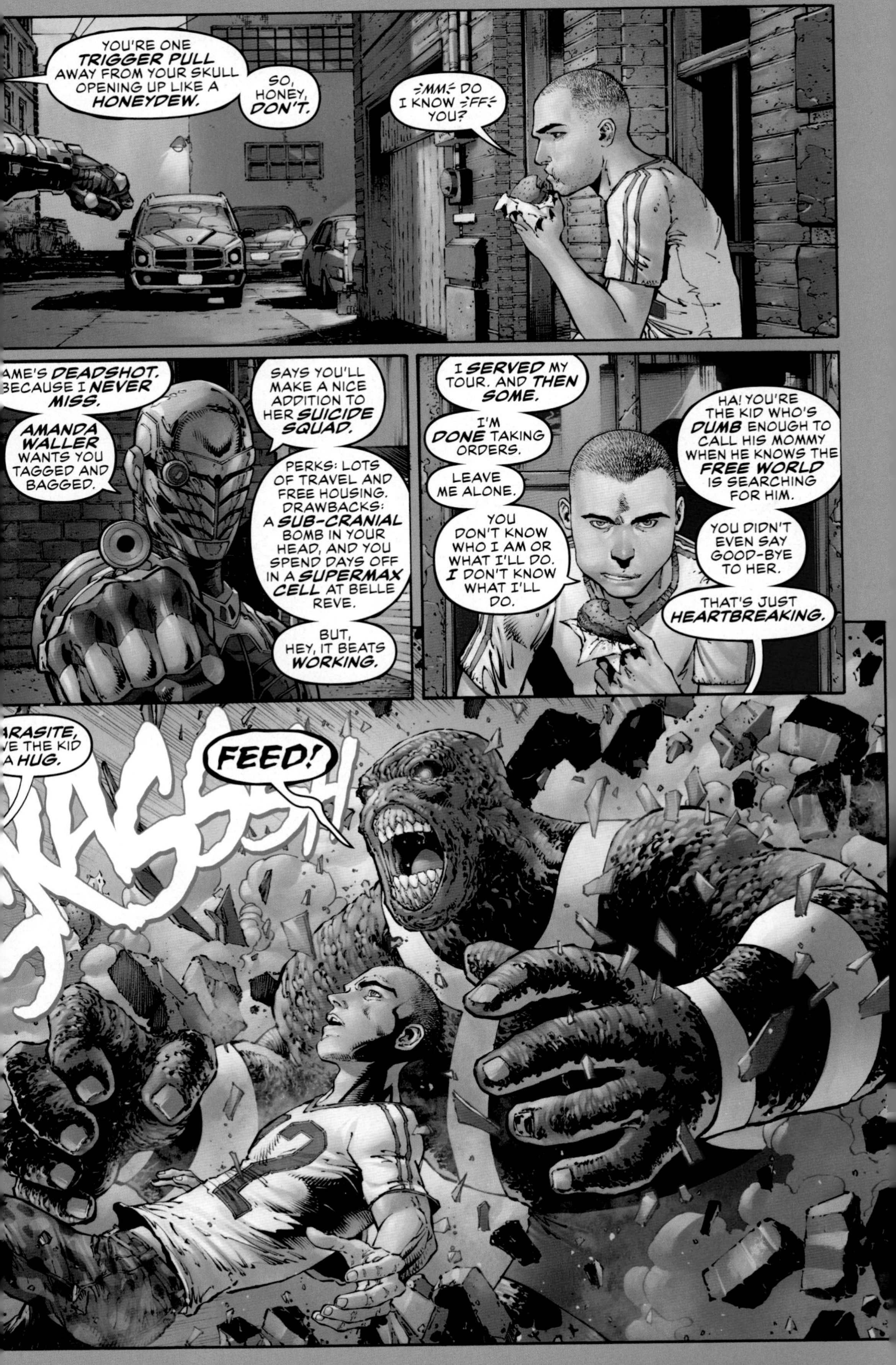

YOU'RE ONE TRIGGER PULL AWAY FROM YOUR SKULL OPENING UP LIKE A HONEYDEW.
SO, HONEY, DON'T.
=MM= DO I KNOW =FF= YOU?
AME'S DEADSHOT. BECAUSE I NEVER MISS.
AMANDA WALLER WANTS YOU TAGGED AND BAGGED.
SAYS YOU'LL MAKE A NICE ADDITION TO HER SUICIDE SQUAD.
PERKS: LOTS OF TRAVEL AND FREE HOUSING. DRAWBACKS: A SUB-CRANIAL BOMB IN YOUR HEAD, AND YOU SPEND DAYS OFF IN A SUPERMAX CELL AT BELLE REVE.
BUT, HEY, IT BEATS WORKING.
I SERVED MY TOUR. AND THEN SOME.
I'M DONE TAKING ORDERS.
LEAVE ME ALONE.
YOU DON'T KNOW WHO I AM OR WHAT I'LL DO. I DON'T KNOW WHAT I'LL DO.
HA! YOU'RE THE KID WHO'S DUMB ENOUGH TO CALL HIS MOMMY WHEN HE KNOWS THE FREE WORLD IS SEARCHING FOR HIM.
YOU DIDN'T EVEN SAY GOOD-BYE TO HER.
THAT'S JUST HEARTBREAKING.
ARASITE, VE THE KID A HUG.
FEED!

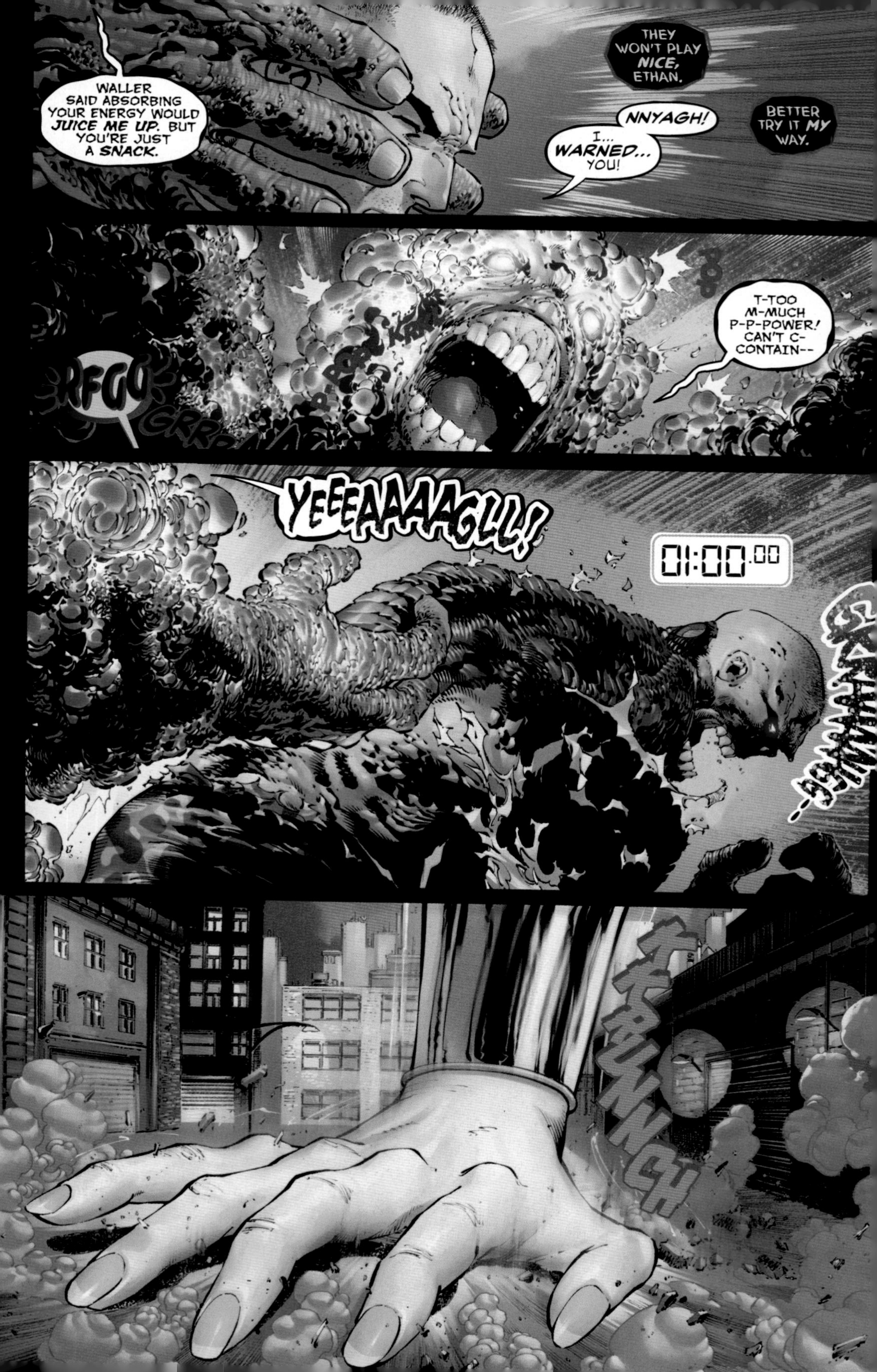
WALLER SAID ABSORBING YOUR ENERGY WOULD JUICE ME UP. BUT YOU'RE JUST A SNACK.
THEY WON'T PLAY NICE, ETHAN.
NNYAGH!
I... WARNED... YOU!
BETTER TRY IT MY WAY.
T-TOO M-MUCH P-P-POWER! CAN'T C-CONTAIN--
YEEEAAAAAGLLL!
01:00.00
KRUNNCH

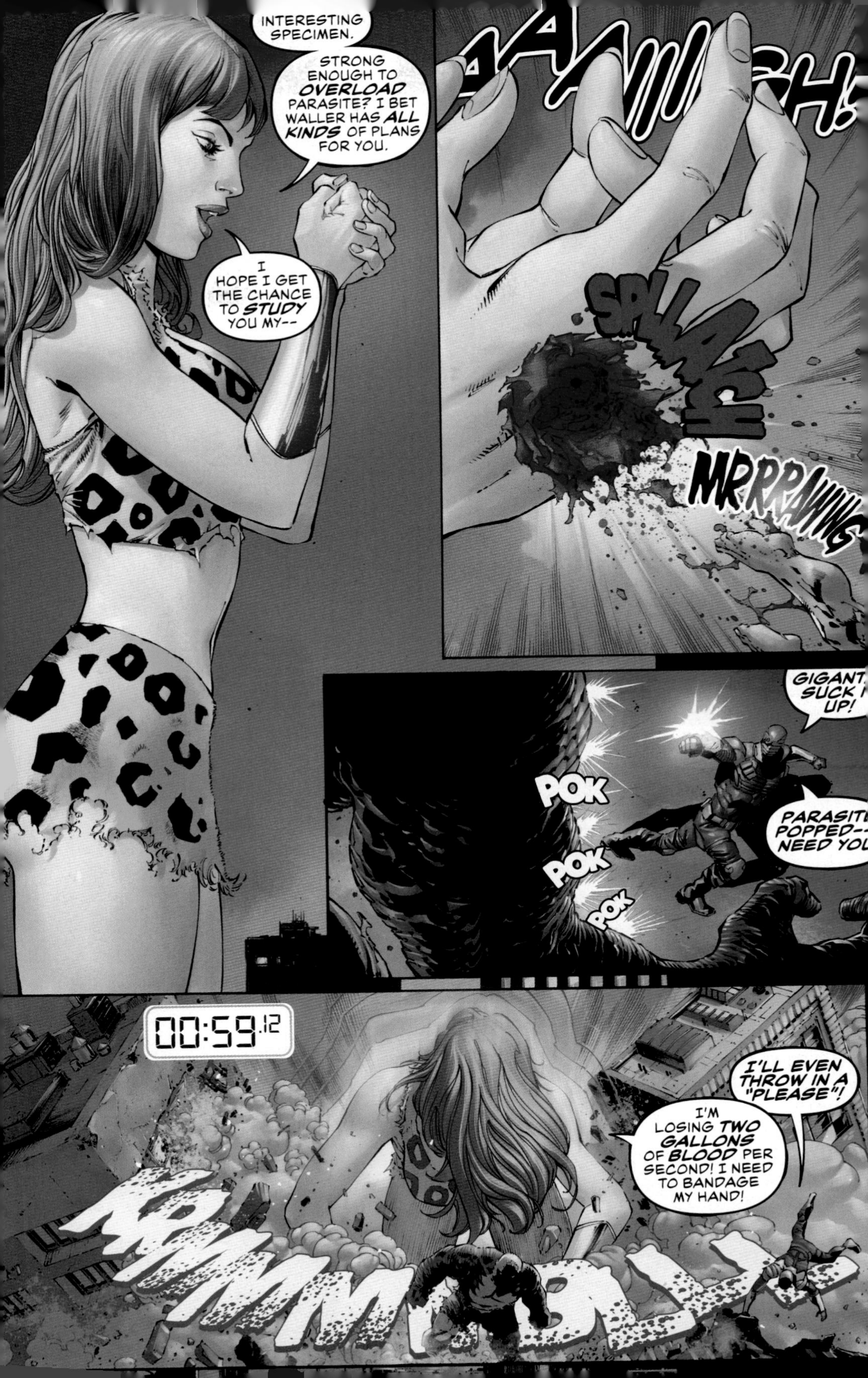
INTERESTING SPECIMEN.
STRONG ENOUGH TO OVERLOAD PARASITE? I BET WALLER HAS ALL KINDS OF PLANS FOR YOU.
I HOPE I GET THE CHANCE TO STUDY YOU MY--
AAAIIIIGH!
SPLLATCH
MRRRAWWG
GIGANT SUCK UP!
POK
POK
POK
PARASITE POPPED-- NEED YOU
00:59.12
I'LL EVEN THROW IN A "PLEASE"!
I'M LOSING TWO GALLONS OF BLOOD PER SECOND! I NEED TO BANDAGE MY HAND!

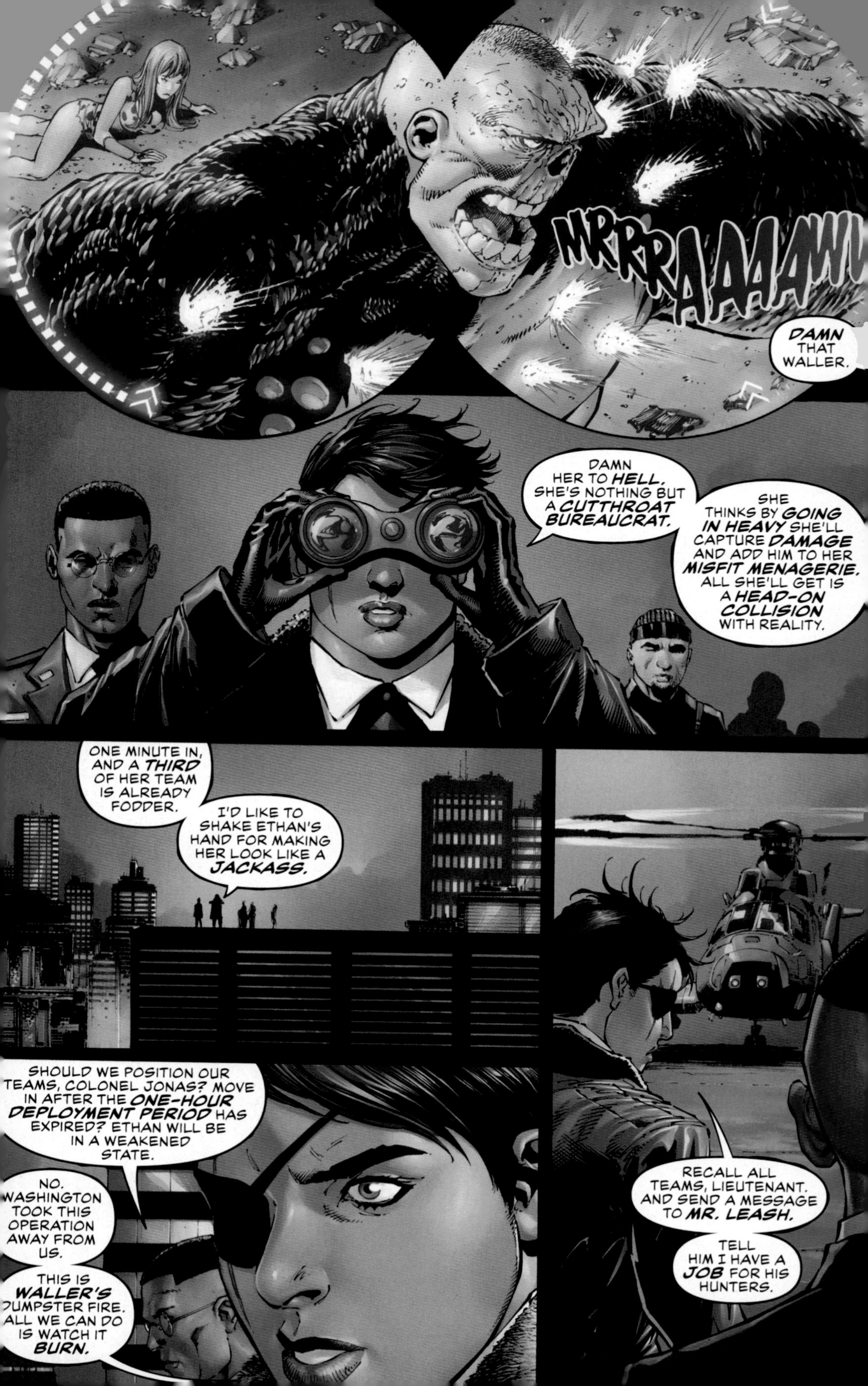
MRRRAAAAWW
DAMN THAT WALLER.
DAMN HER TO HELL. SHE'S NOTHING BUT A CUTTHROAT BUREAUCRAT.
SHE THINKS BY GOING IN HEAVY SHE'LL CAPTURE DAMAGE AND ADD HIM TO HER MISFIT MENAGERIE. ALL SHE'LL GET IS A HEAD-ON COLLISION WITH REALITY.
ONE MINUTE IN, AND A THIRD OF HER TEAM IS ALREADY FODDER.
I'D LIKE TO SHAKE ETHAN'S HAND FOR MAKING HER LOOK LIKE A JACKASS.
SHOULD WE POSITION OUR TEAMS, COLONEL JONAS? MOVE IN AFTER THE ONE-HOUR DEPLOYMENT PERIOD HAS EXPIRED? ETHAN WILL BE IN A WEAKENED STATE.
NO. WASHINGTON TOOK THIS OPERATION AWAY FROM US.
THIS IS WALLER'S DUMPSTER FIRE. ALL WE CAN DO IS WATCH IT BURN.
RECALL ALL TEAMS, LIEUTENANT. AND SEND A MESSAGE TO MR. LEASH.
TELL HIM I HAVE A JOB FOR HIS HUNTERS.

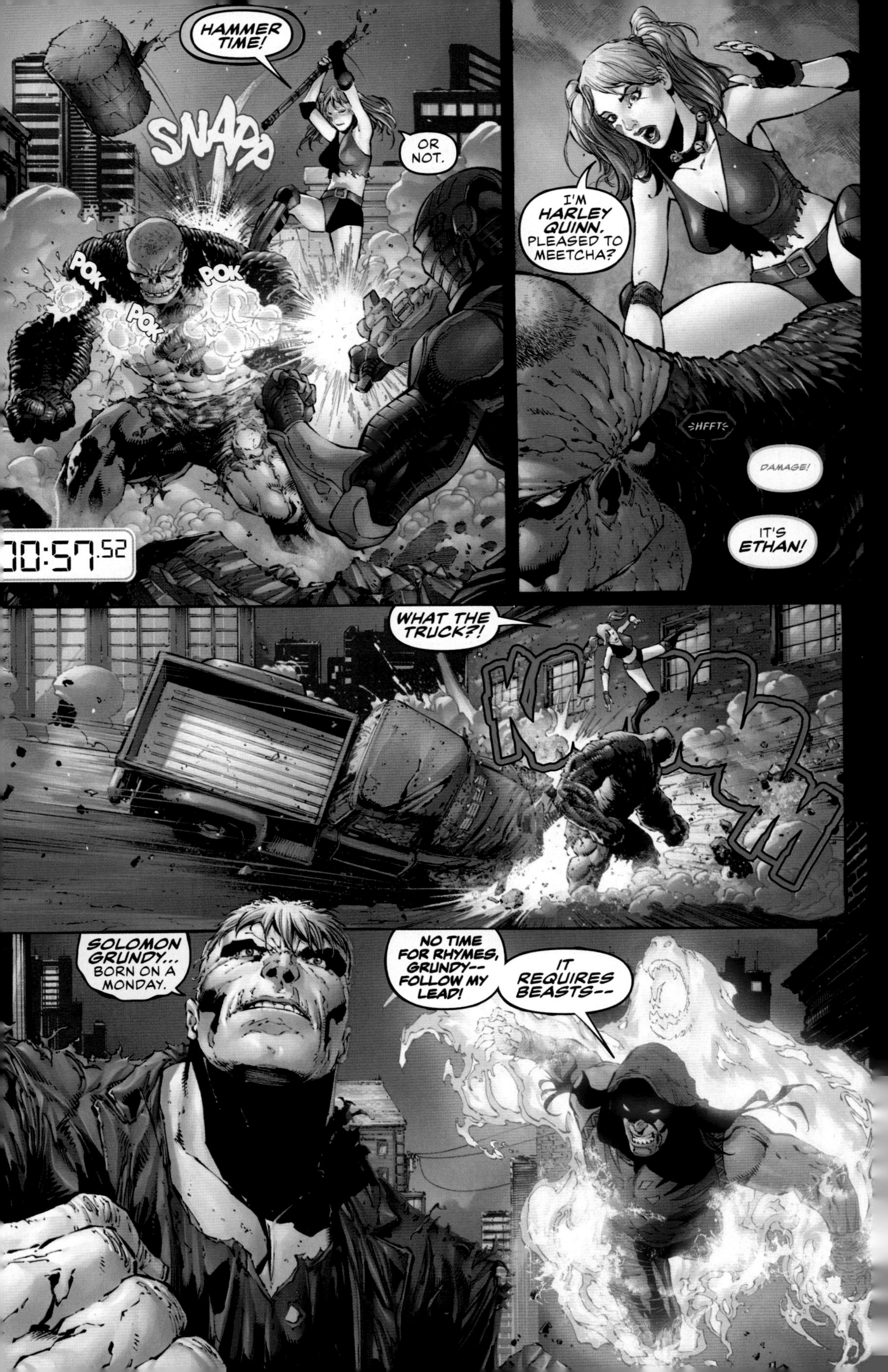
HAMMER TIME!
SNAPP
OR NOT.
POK
POK
POK
00:57.52
I'M HARLEY QUINN. PLEASED TO MEETCHA?
HFFT
DAMAGE!
IT'S ETHAN!
WHAT THE TRUCK?!
SOLOMON GRUNDY... BORN ON A MONDAY.
NO TIME FOR RHYMES, GRUNDY-- FOLLOW MY LEAD!
IT REQUIRES BEASTS--

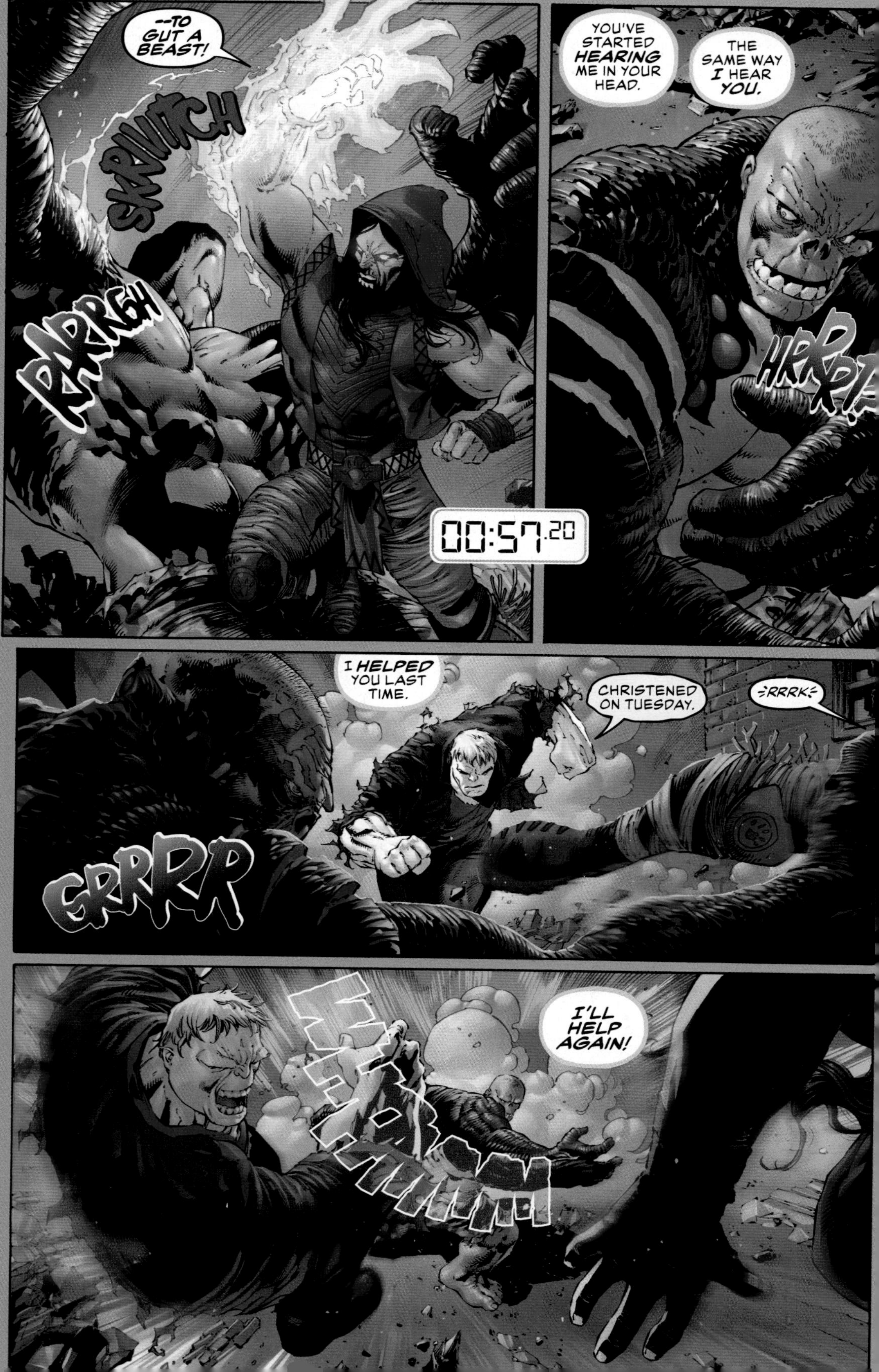
--TO GUT A BEAST!
BARRGH
00:57.20
YOU'VE STARTED HEARING ME IN YOUR HEAD.
THE SAME WAY I HEAR YOU.
I HELPED YOU LAST TIME.
CHRISTENED ON TUESDAY.
RRRK
GRRRP
I'LL HELP AGAIN!

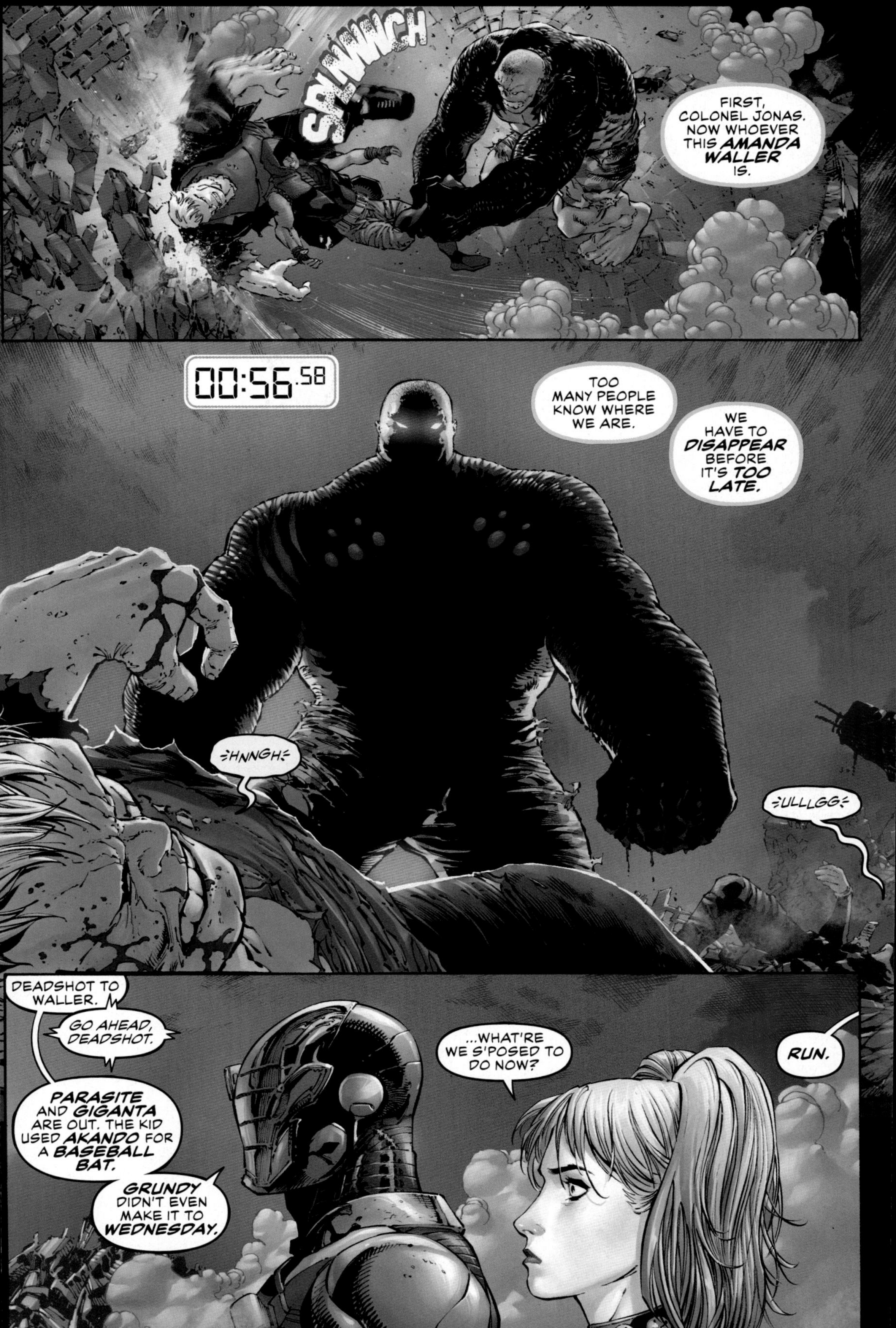

SPLNNNCH
FIRST, COLONEL JONAS. NOW WHOEVER THIS AMANDA WALLER IS.
00:56.58
TOO MANY PEOPLE KNOW WHERE WE ARE.
WE HAVE TO DISAPPEAR BEFORE IT'S TOO LATE.
HNNGH
ULLLGG
DEADSHOT TO WALLER.
GO AHEAD, DEADSHOT.
PARASITE AND GIGANTA ARE OUT. THE KID USED AKANDO FOR A BASEBALL BAT.
GRUNDY DIDN'T EVEN MAKE IT TO WEDNESDAY.
...WHAT'RE WE S'POSED TO DO NOW?
RUN.

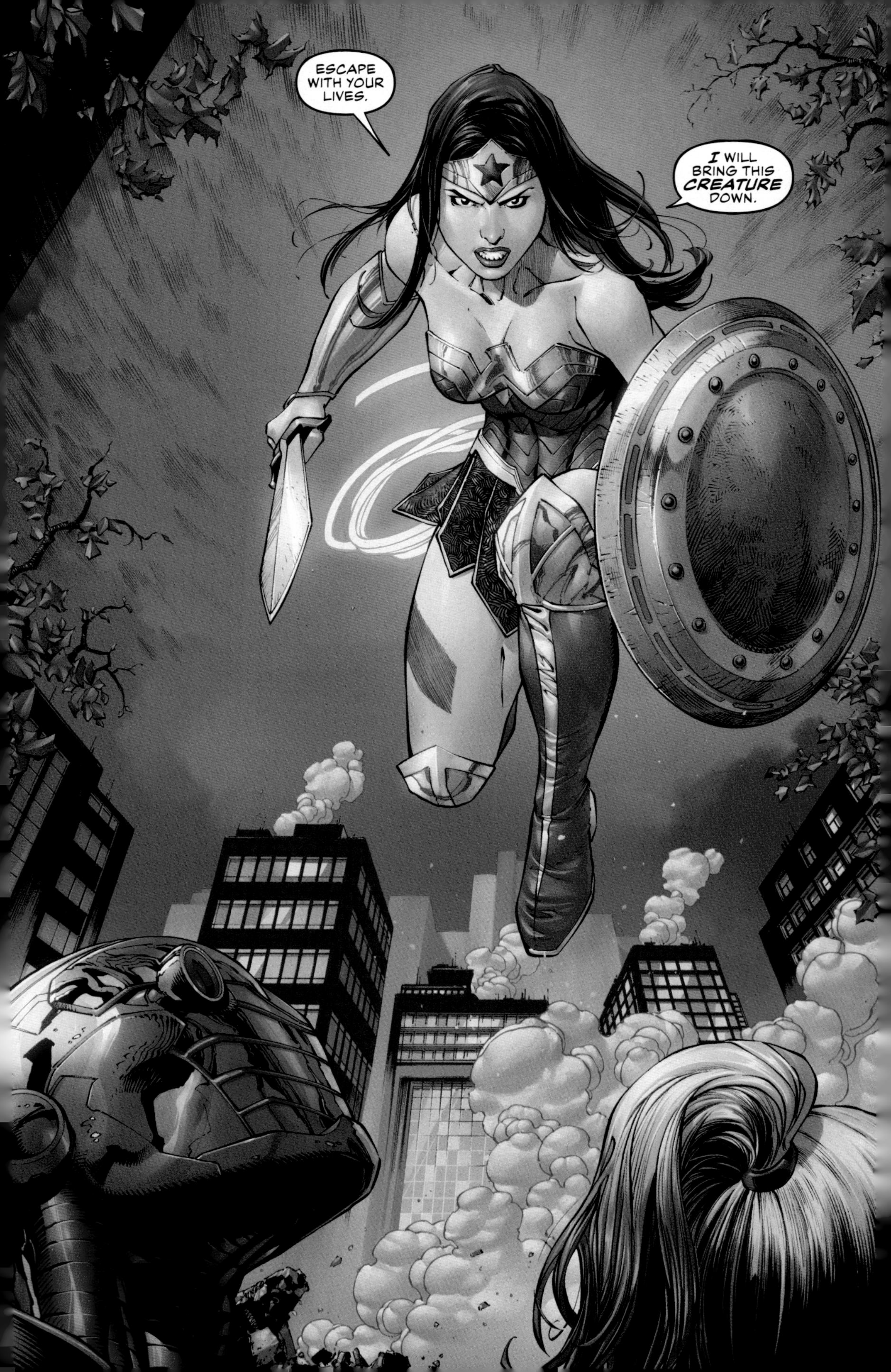
ESCAPE WITH YOUR LIVES.
I WILL BRING THIS CREATURE DOWN.

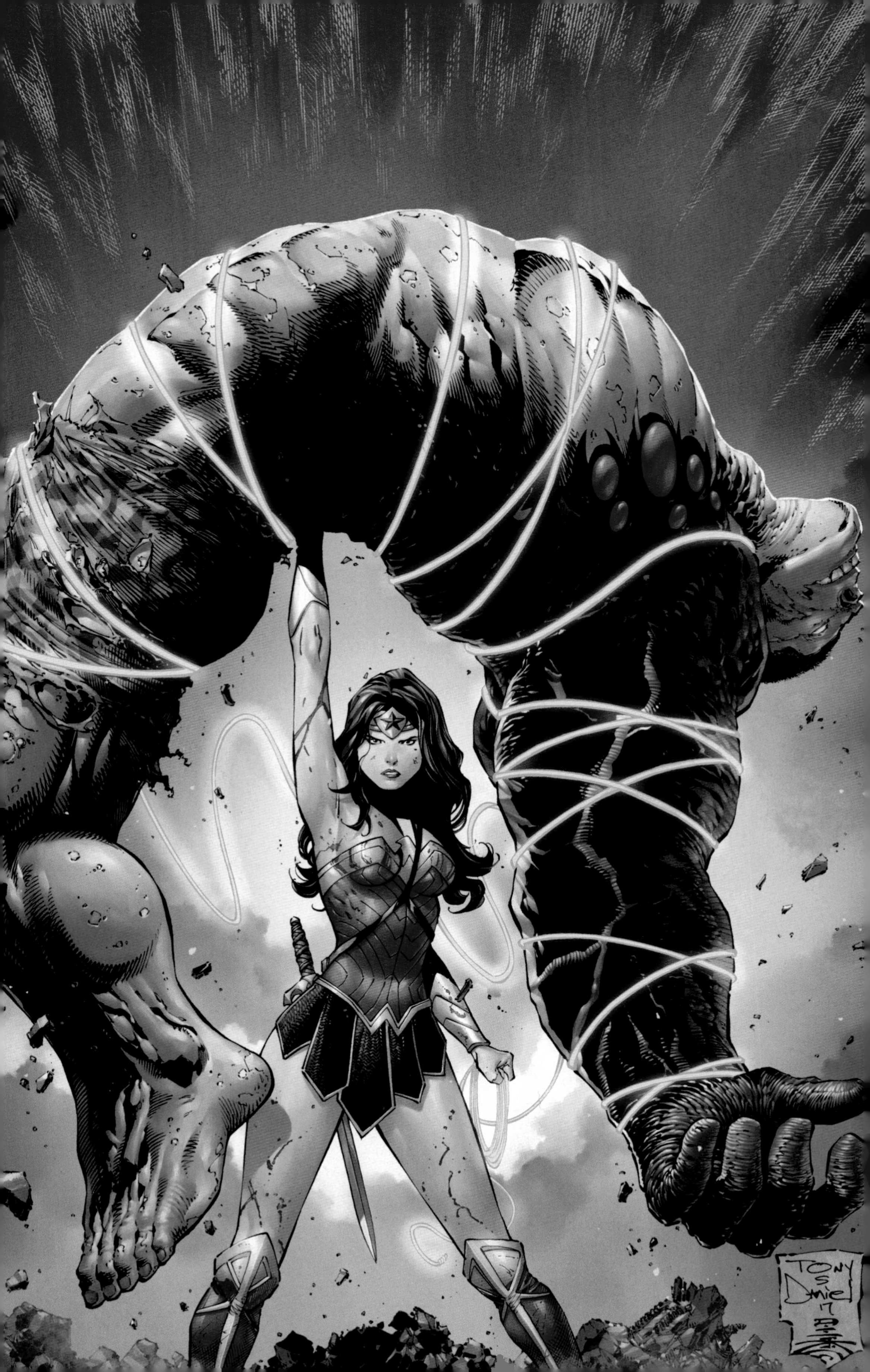

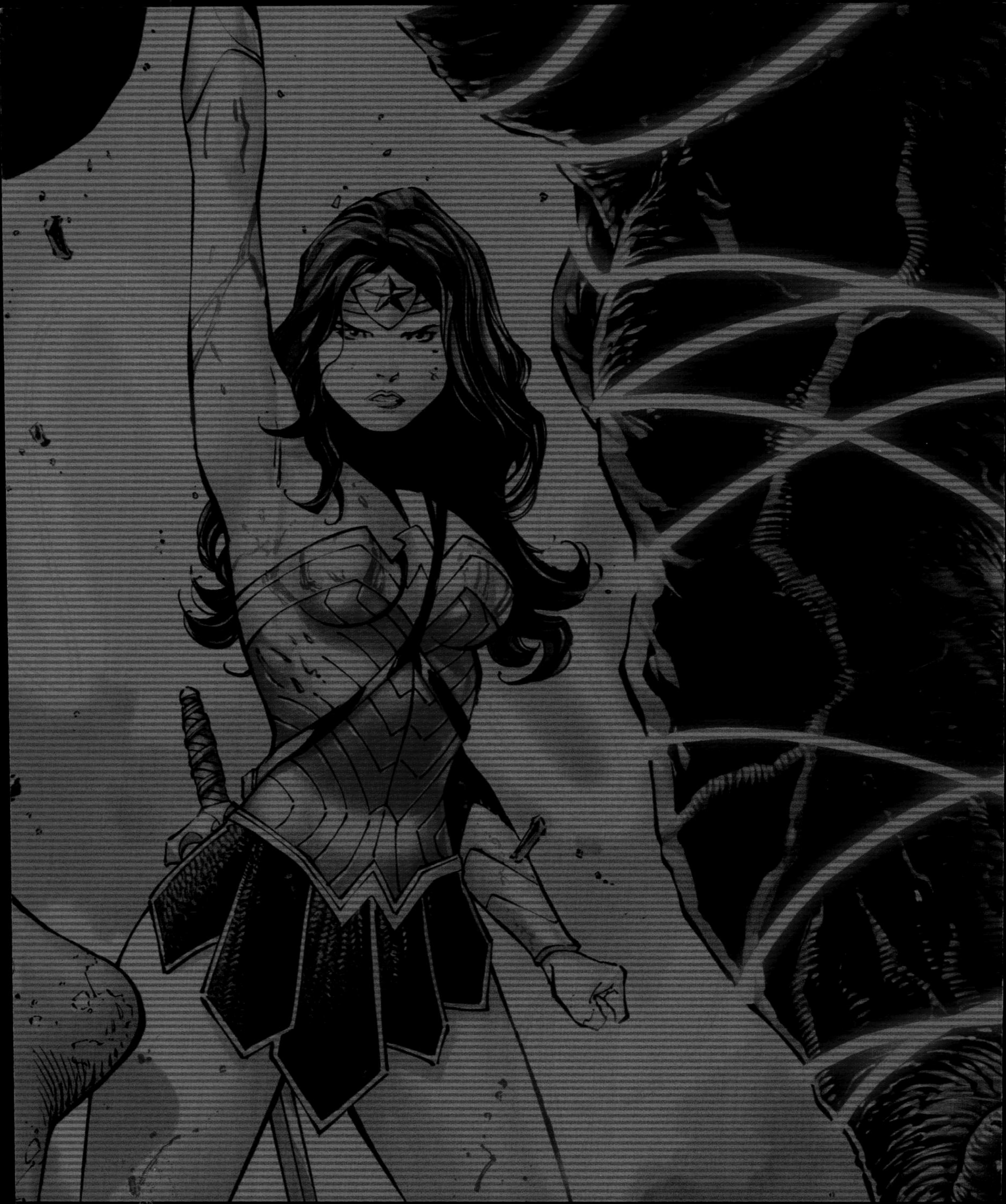

DAMAGE
#3

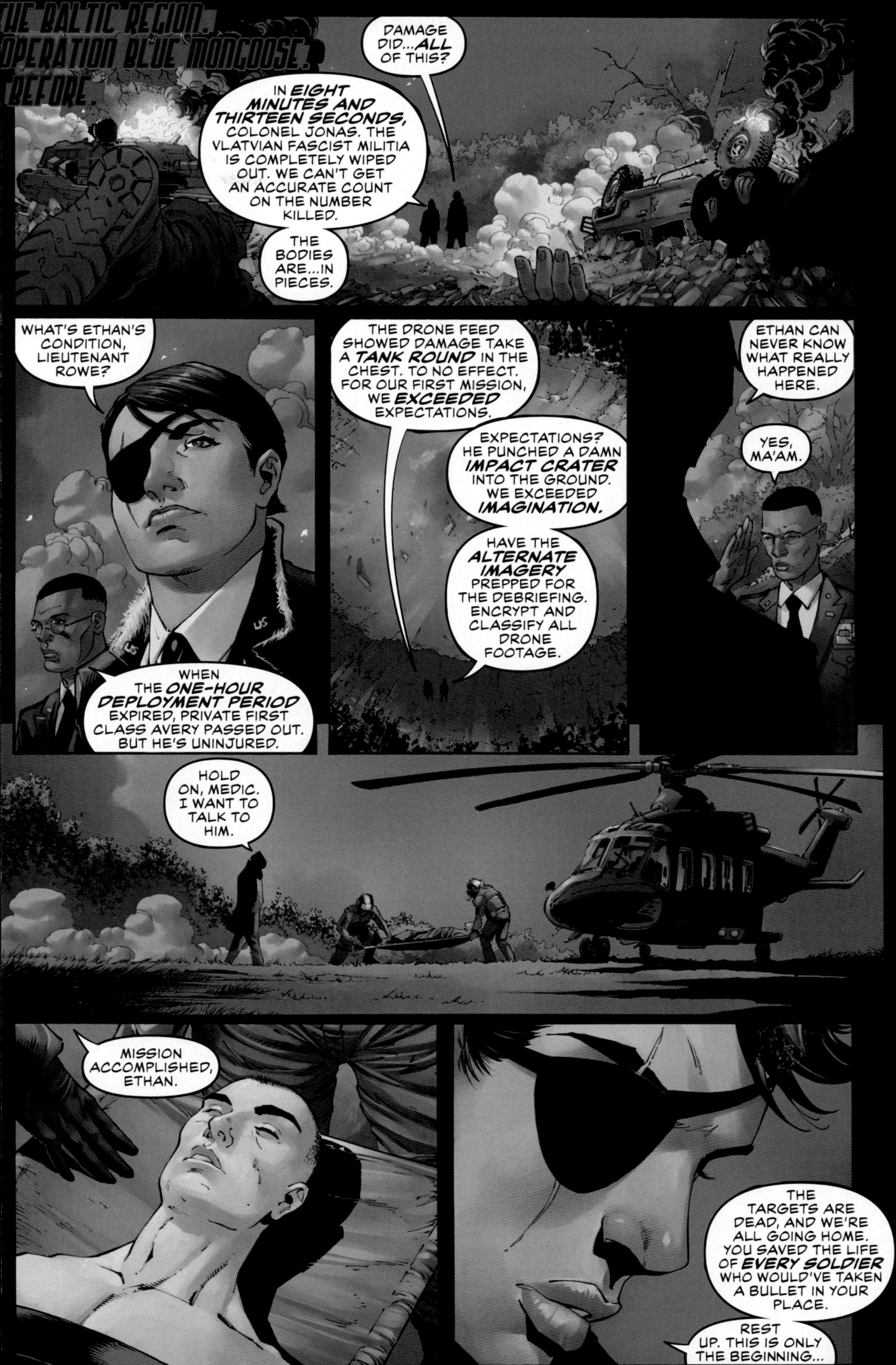

THE BALTIC REGION. OPERATION BLUE MONGOOSE. BEFORE.
DAMAGE DID...ALL OF THIS?
IN EIGHT MINUTES AND THIRTEEN SECONDS, COLONEL JONAS. THE VLATVIAN FASCIST MILITIA IS COMPLETELY WIPED OUT. WE CAN'T GET AN ACCURATE COUNT ON THE NUMBER KILLED.
THE BODIES ARE...IN PIECES.
WHAT'S ETHAN'S CONDITION, LIEUTENANT ROWE?
WHEN THE ONE-HOUR DEPLOYMENT PERIOD EXPIRED, PRIVATE FIRST CLASS AVERY PASSED OUT. BUT HE'S UNINJURED.
THE DRONE FEED SHOWED DAMAGE TAKE A TANK ROUND IN THE CHEST. TO NO EFFECT. FOR OUR FIRST MISSION, WE EXCEEDED EXPECTATIONS.
EXPECTATIONS? HE PUNCHED A DAMN IMPACT CRATER INTO THE GROUND. WE EXCEEDED IMAGINATION.
HAVE THE ALTERNATE IMAGERY PREPPED FOR THE DEBRIEFING. ENCRYPT AND CLASSIFY ALL DRONE FOOTAGE.
ETHAN CAN NEVER KNOW WHAT REALLY HAPPENED HERE.
YES, MA'AM.
HOLD ON, MEDIC. I WANT TO TALK TO HIM.
MISSION ACCOMPLISHED, ETHAN.
THE TARGETS ARE DEAD, AND WE'RE ALL GOING HOME. YOU SAVED THE LIFE OF EVERY SOLDIER WHO WOULD'VE TAKEN A BULLET IN YOUR PLACE.
REST UP. THIS IS ONLY THE BEGINNING...

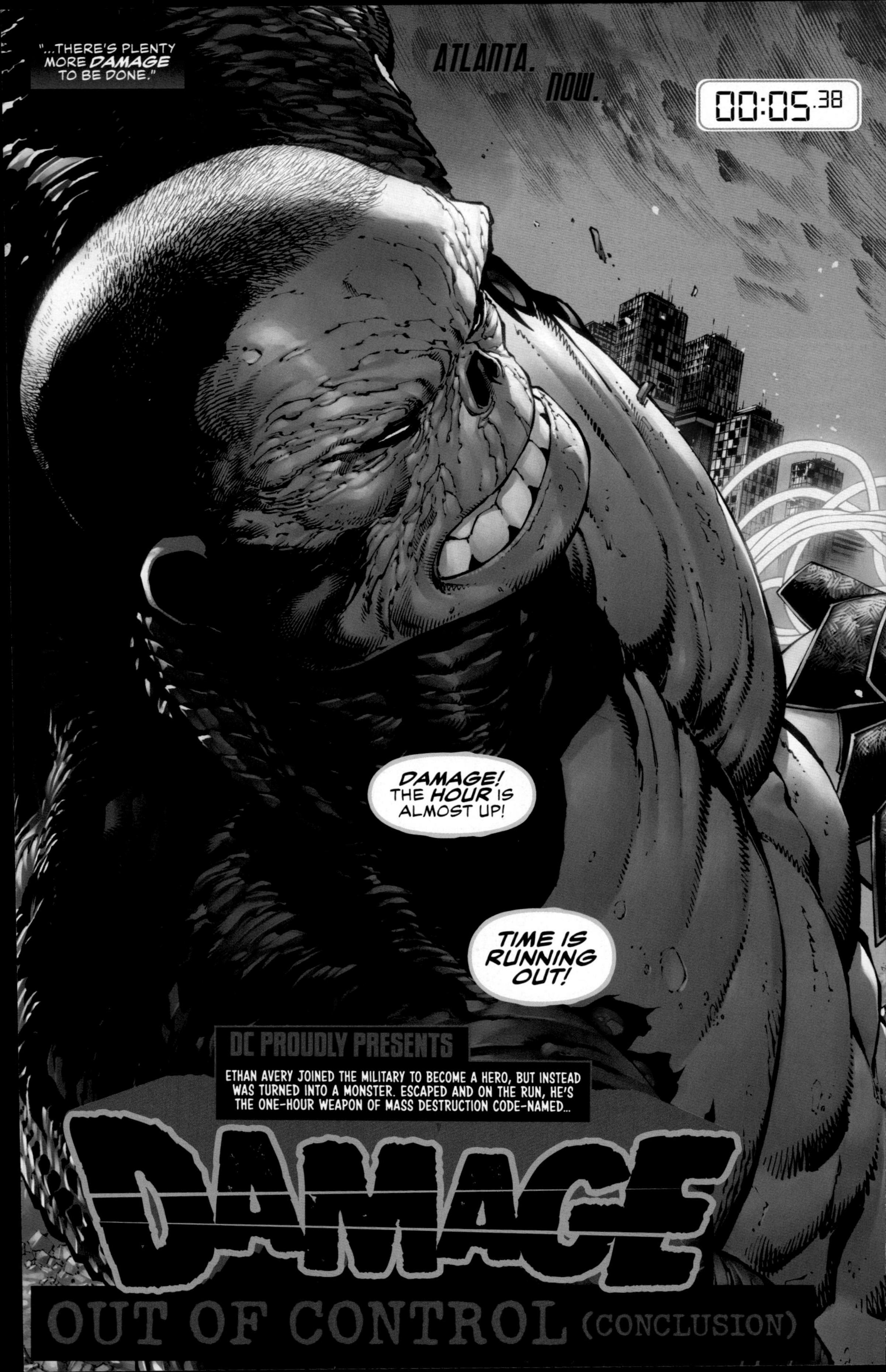
"...THERE'S PLENTY MORE DAMAGE TO BE DONE."
ATLANTA. NOW.
00:05.38
DAMAGE! THE HOUR IS ALMOST UP!
TIME IS RUNNING OUT!
DC PROUDLY PRESENTS
ETHAN AVERY JOINED THE MILITARY TO BECOME A HERO, BUT INSTEAD WAS TURNED INTO A MONSTER. ESCAPED AND ON THE RUN, HE'S THE ONE-HOUR WEAPON OF MASS DESTRUCTION CODE-NAMED...
DAMAGE
OUT OF CONTROL (CONCLUSION)

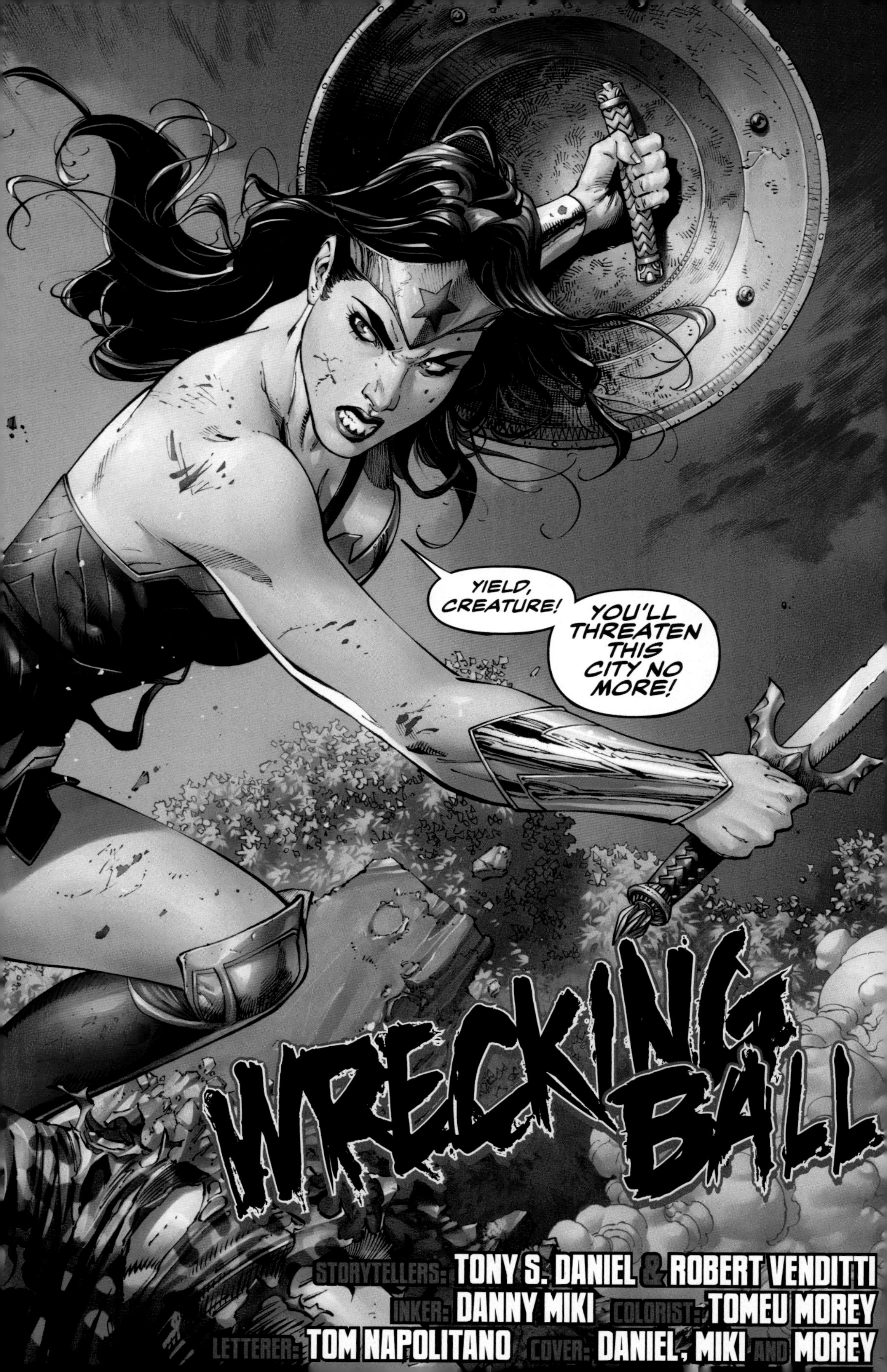

YIELD, CREATURE!
YOU'LL THREATEN THIS CITY NO MORE!
WRECKING BALL
STORYTELLERS: TONY S. DANIEL & ROBERT VENDITTI
INKER: DANNY MIKI COLORIST: TOMEU MOREY
LETTERER: TOM NAPOLITANO COVER: DANIEL, MIKI AND MOREY

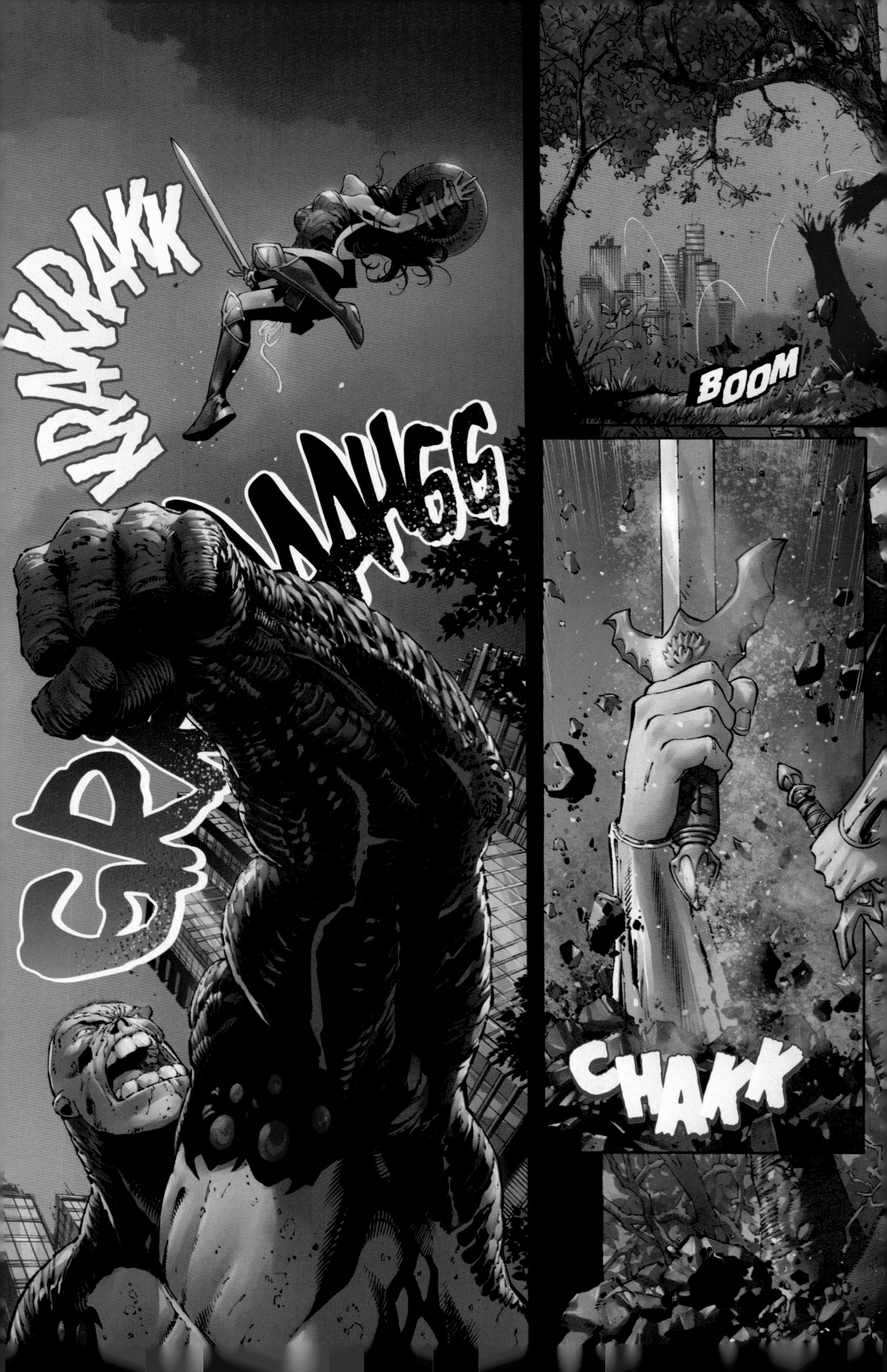
KRAKK
BOOM
CHAKK

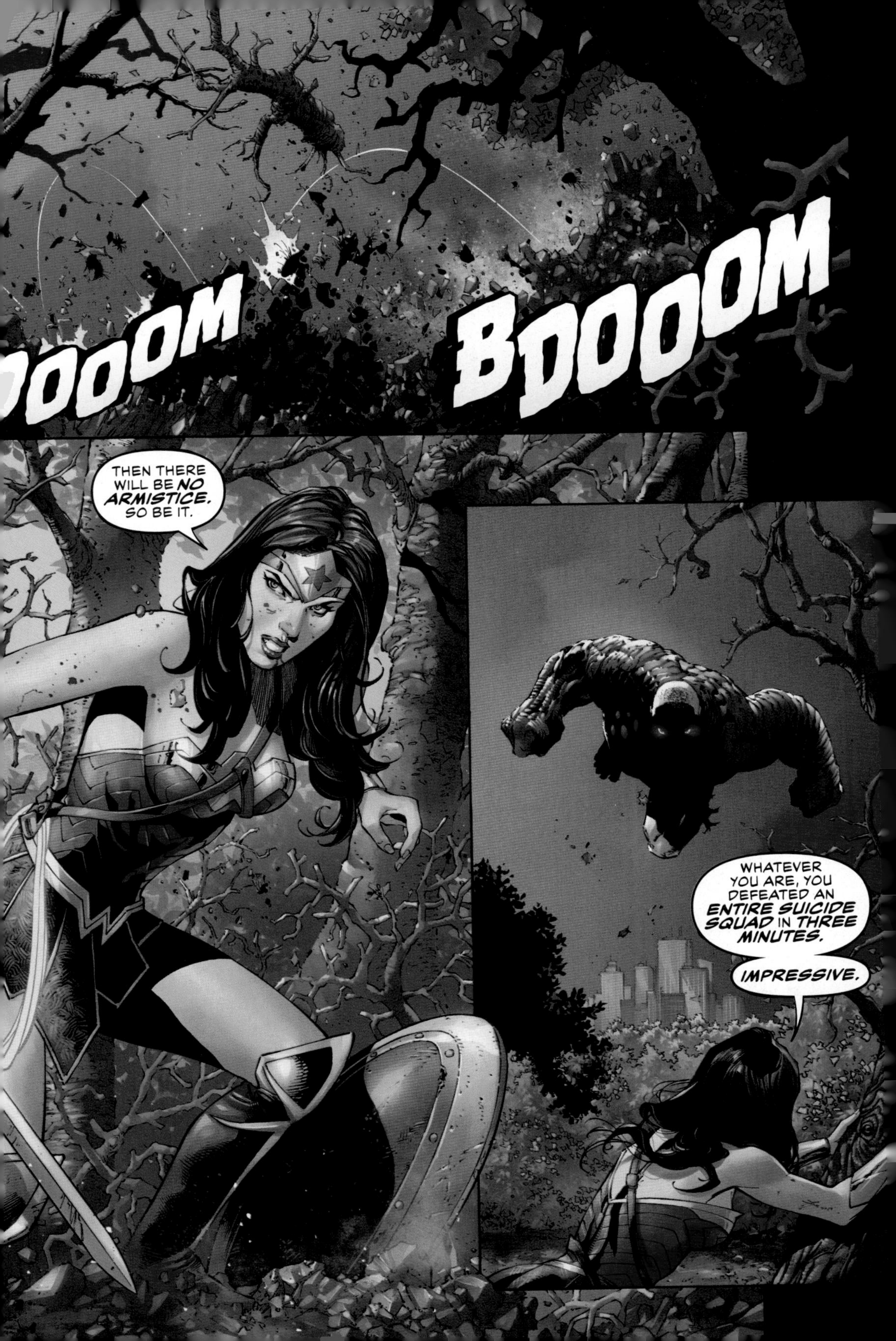
OOOOM
BOOOOM
THEN THERE WILL BE NO ARMISTICE. SO BE IT.
WHATEVER YOU ARE, YOU DEFEATED AN ENTIRE SUICIDE SQUAD IN THREE MINUTES.
IMPRESSIVE.

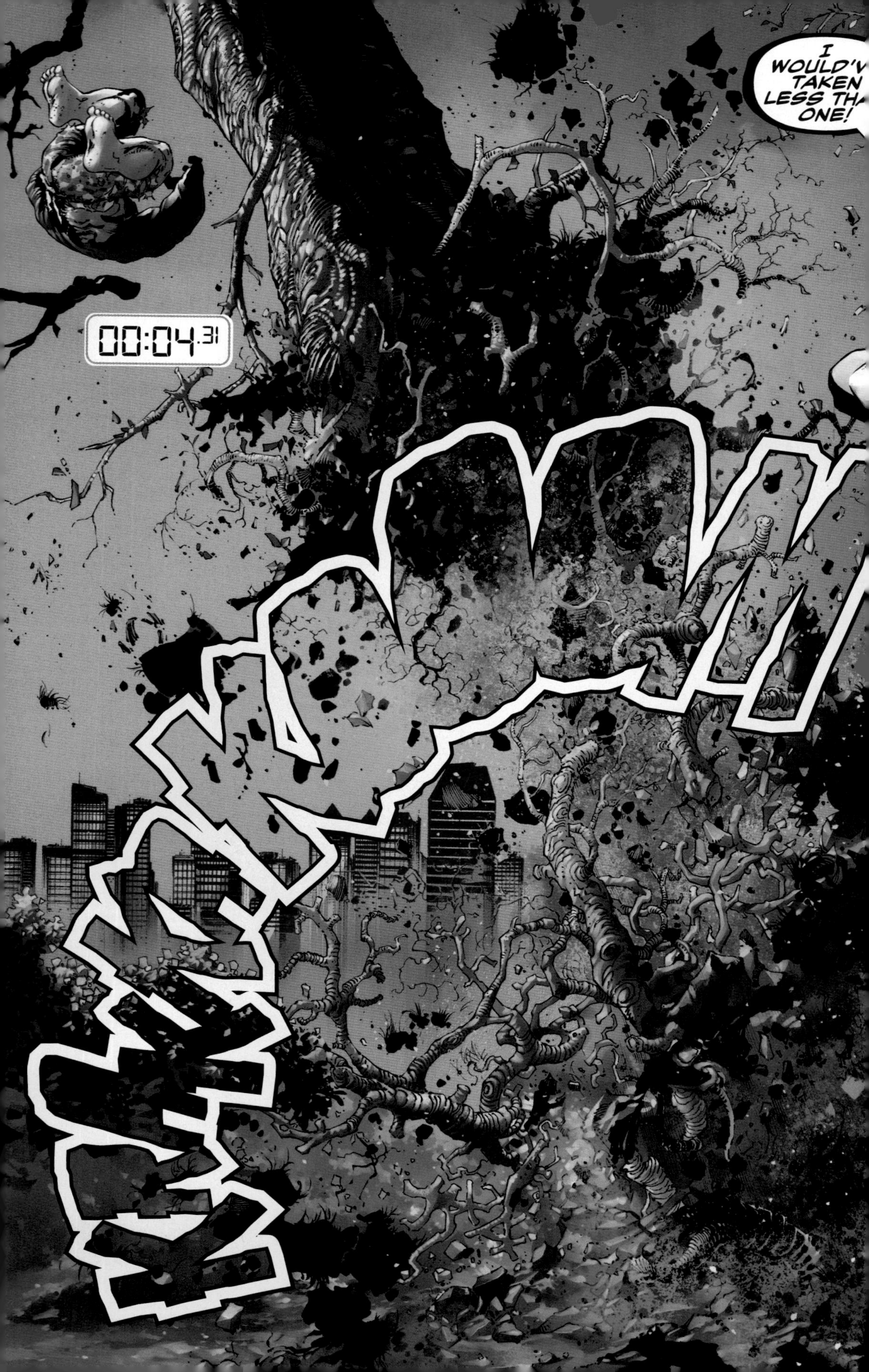

I WOULD'V TAKEN LESS THA ONE!
00:04.31

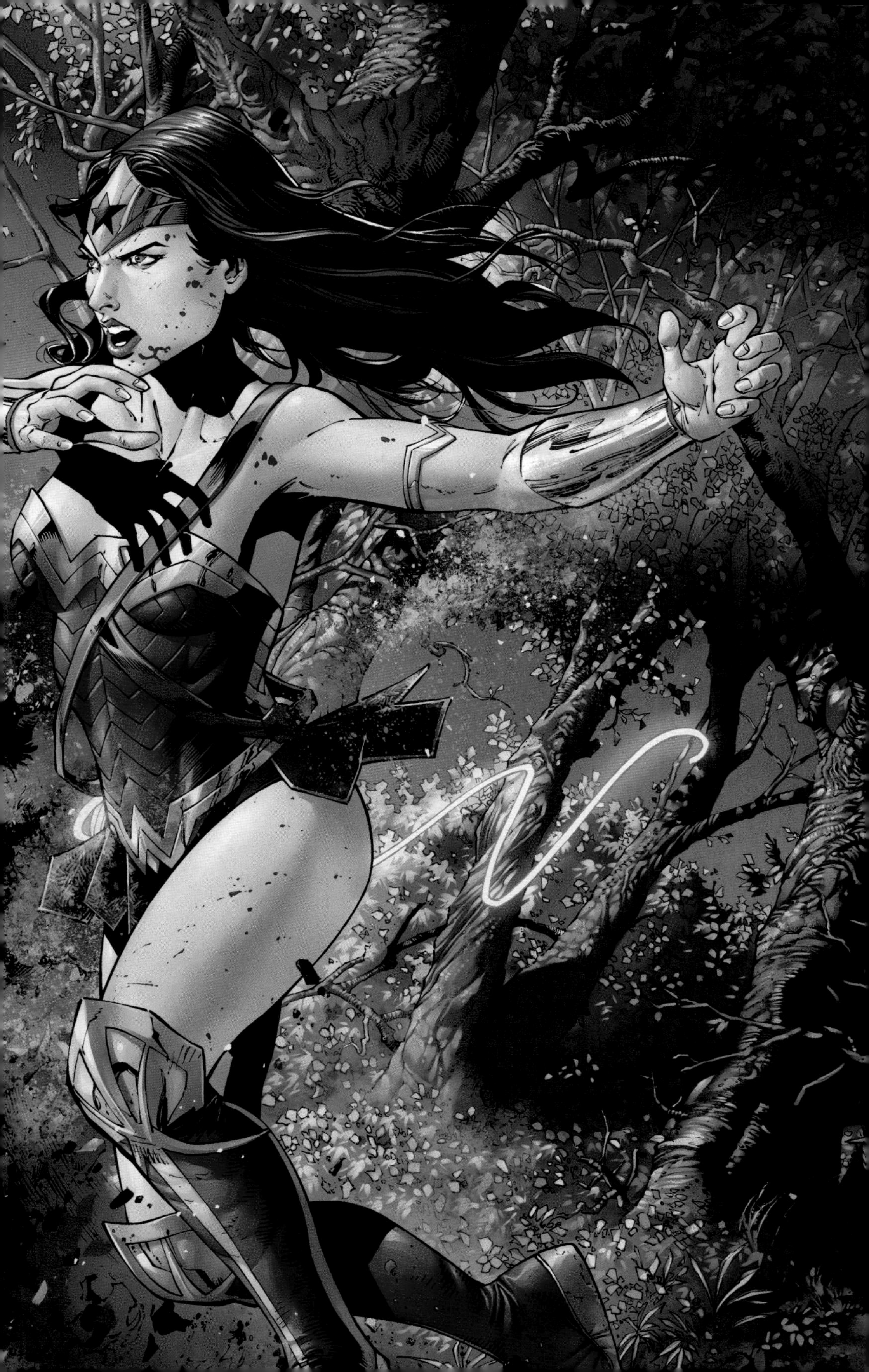

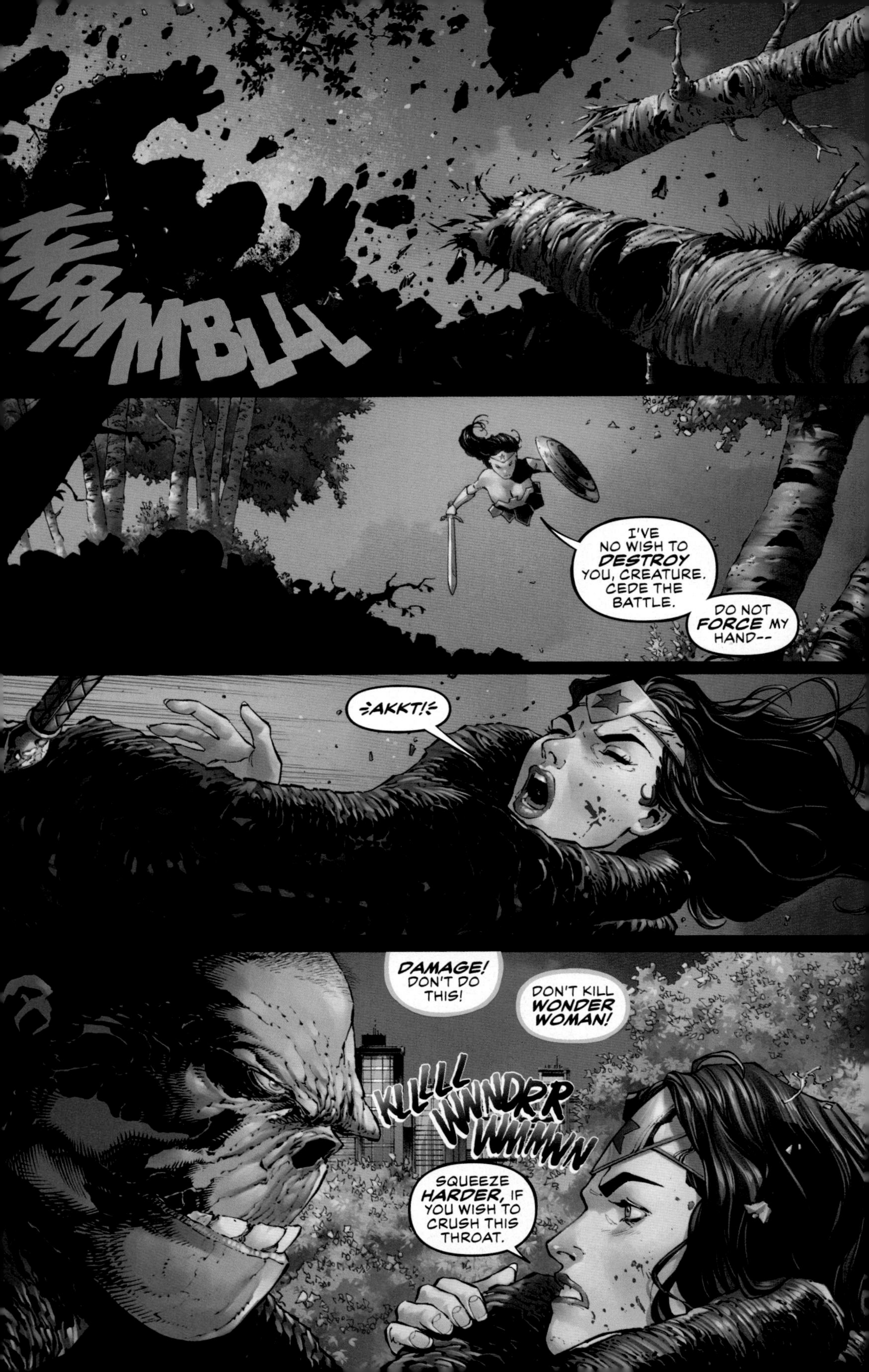
KRAMMBLLL
I'VE NO WISH TO DESTROY YOU, CREATURE. CEDE THE BATTLE.
DO NOT FORCE MY HAND--
AKKT!
DAMAGE! DON'T DO THIS!
DON'T KILL WONDER WOMAN!
KLLLLL WWNDER WMMMN
SQUEEZE HARDER, IF YOU WISH TO CRUSH THIS THROAT.

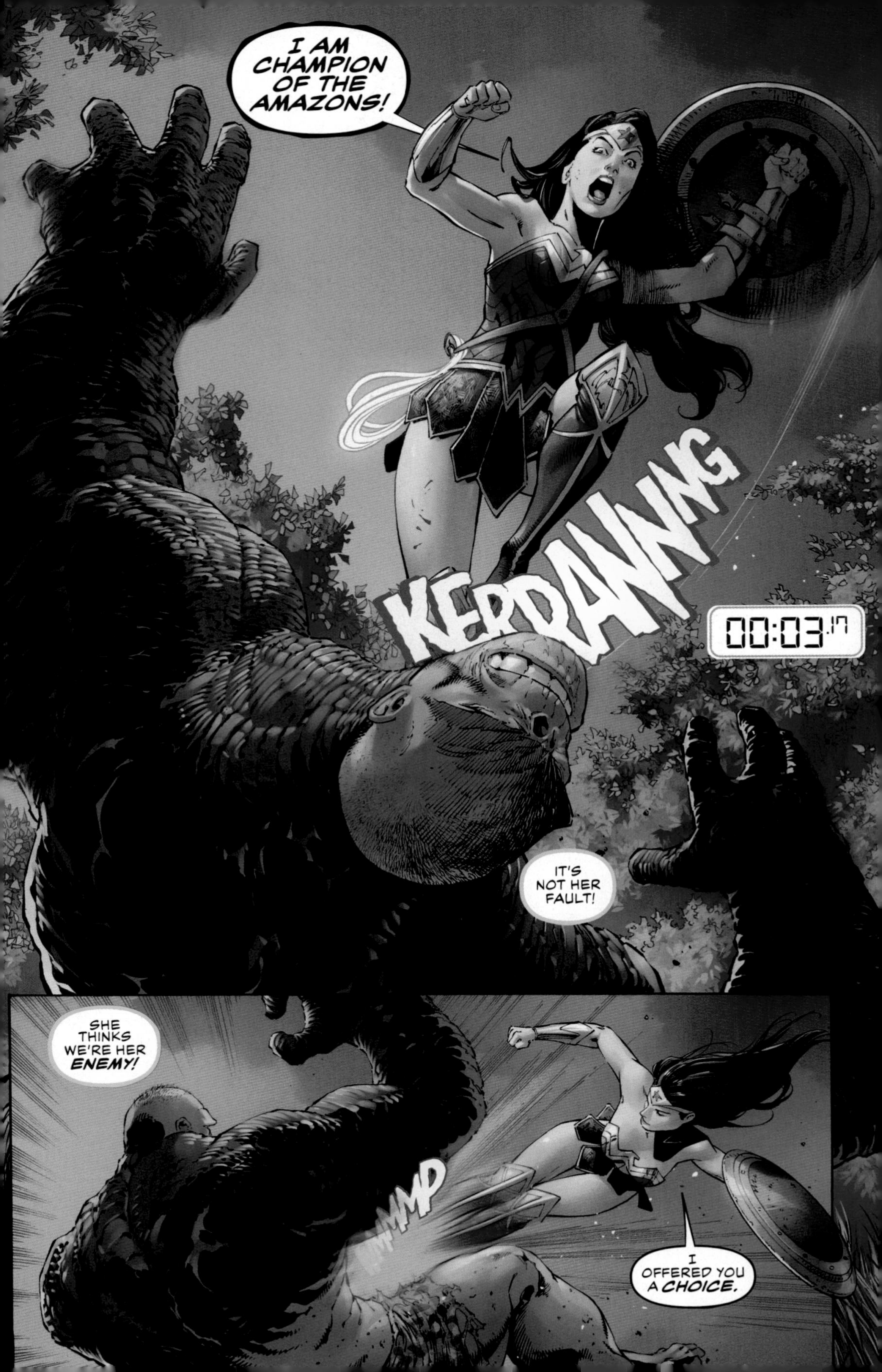
I AM CHAMPION OF THE AMAZONS!
KERRANNNG
00:03.17
IT'S NOT HER FAULT!
SHE THINKS WE'RE HER ENEMY!
WHAMMP
I OFFERED YOU A CHOICE.

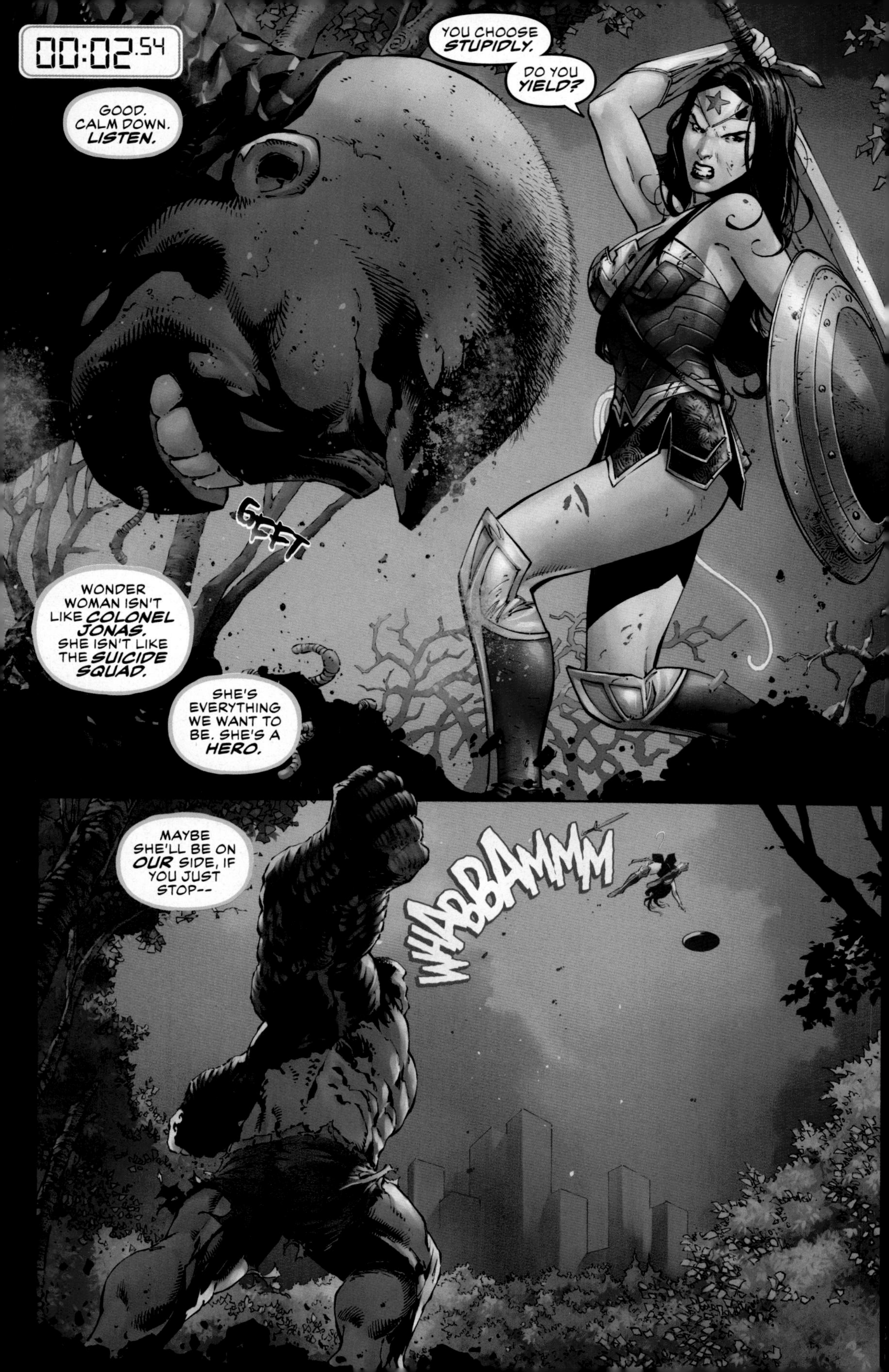

00:02.54
GOOD. CALM DOWN. LISTEN.
YOU CHOOSE STUPIDLY.
DO YOU YIELD?
GFFT
WONDER WOMAN ISN'T LIKE COLONEL JONAS. SHE ISN'T LIKE THE SUICIDE SQUAD.
SHE'S EVERYTHING WE WANT TO BE. SHE'S A HERO.
MAYBE SHE'LL BE ON OUR SIDE, IF YOU JUST STOP--
WHABBAMMM

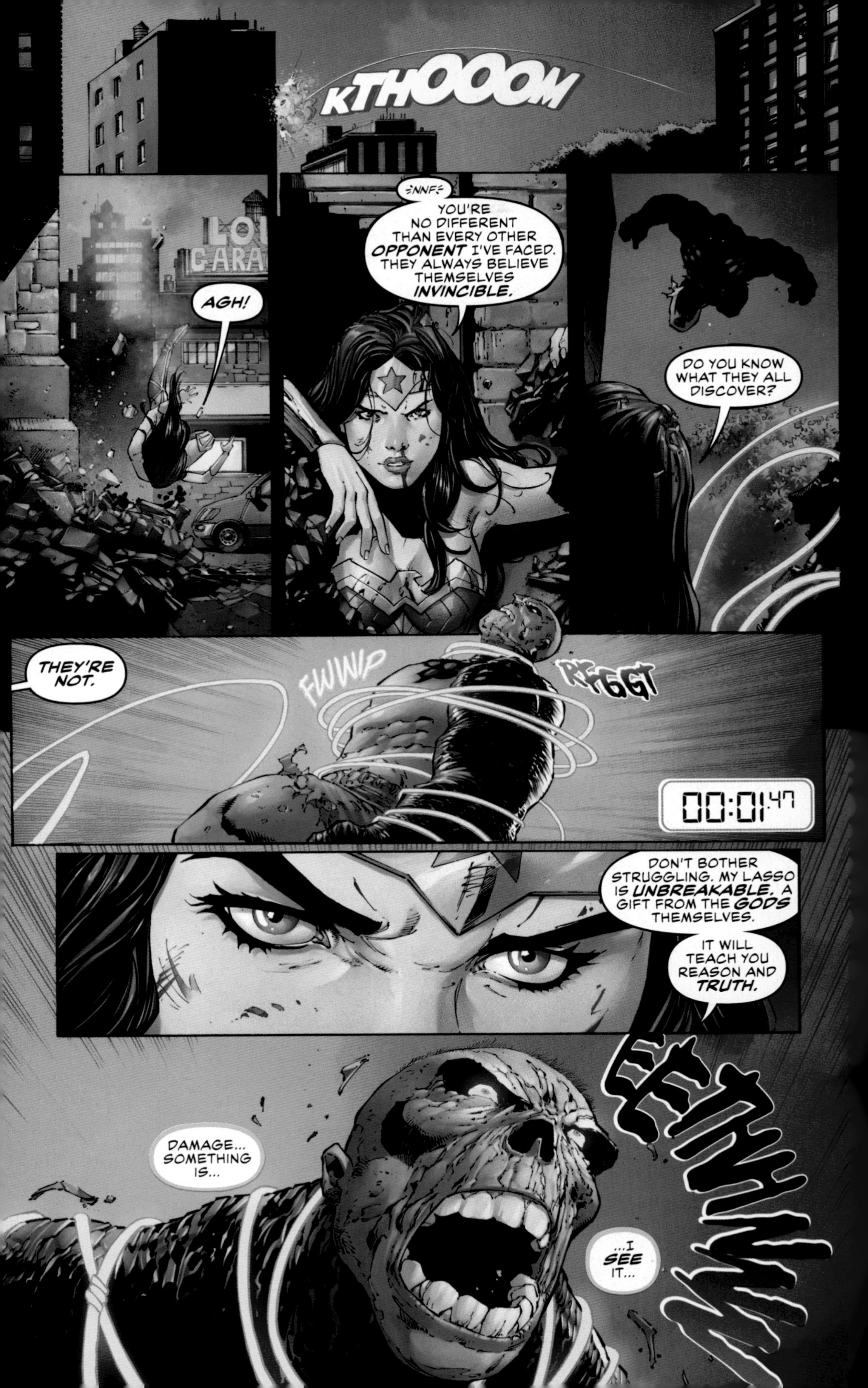
KTHOOOM
AGH!
NNF
YOU'RE NO DIFFERENT THAN EVERY OTHER OPPONENT I'VE FACED. THEY ALWAYS BELIEVE THEMSELVES INVINCIBLE.
DO YOU KNOW WHAT THEY ALL DISCOVER?
THEY'RE NOT.
FWWIP
RRGGT
00:01.47
DON'T BOTHER STRUGGLING. MY LASSO IS UNBREAKABLE. A GIFT FROM THE GODS THEMSELVES.
IT WILL TEACH YOU REASON AND TRUTH.
DAMAGE... SOMETHING IS...
...I SEE IT...

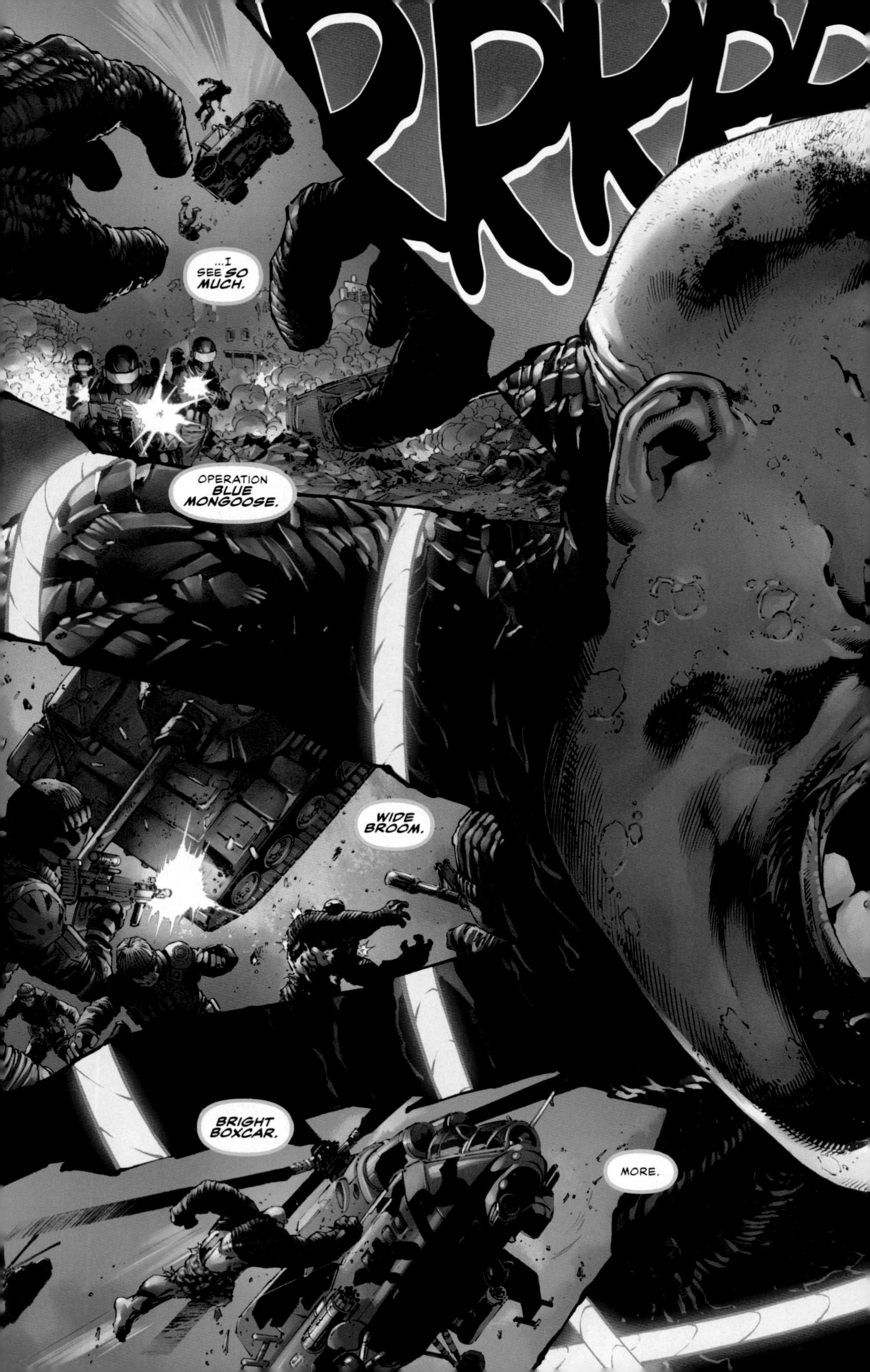
...I SEE SO MUCH.
OPERATION BLUE MONGOOSE.
WIDE BROOM.
BRIGHT BOXCAR.
MORE.

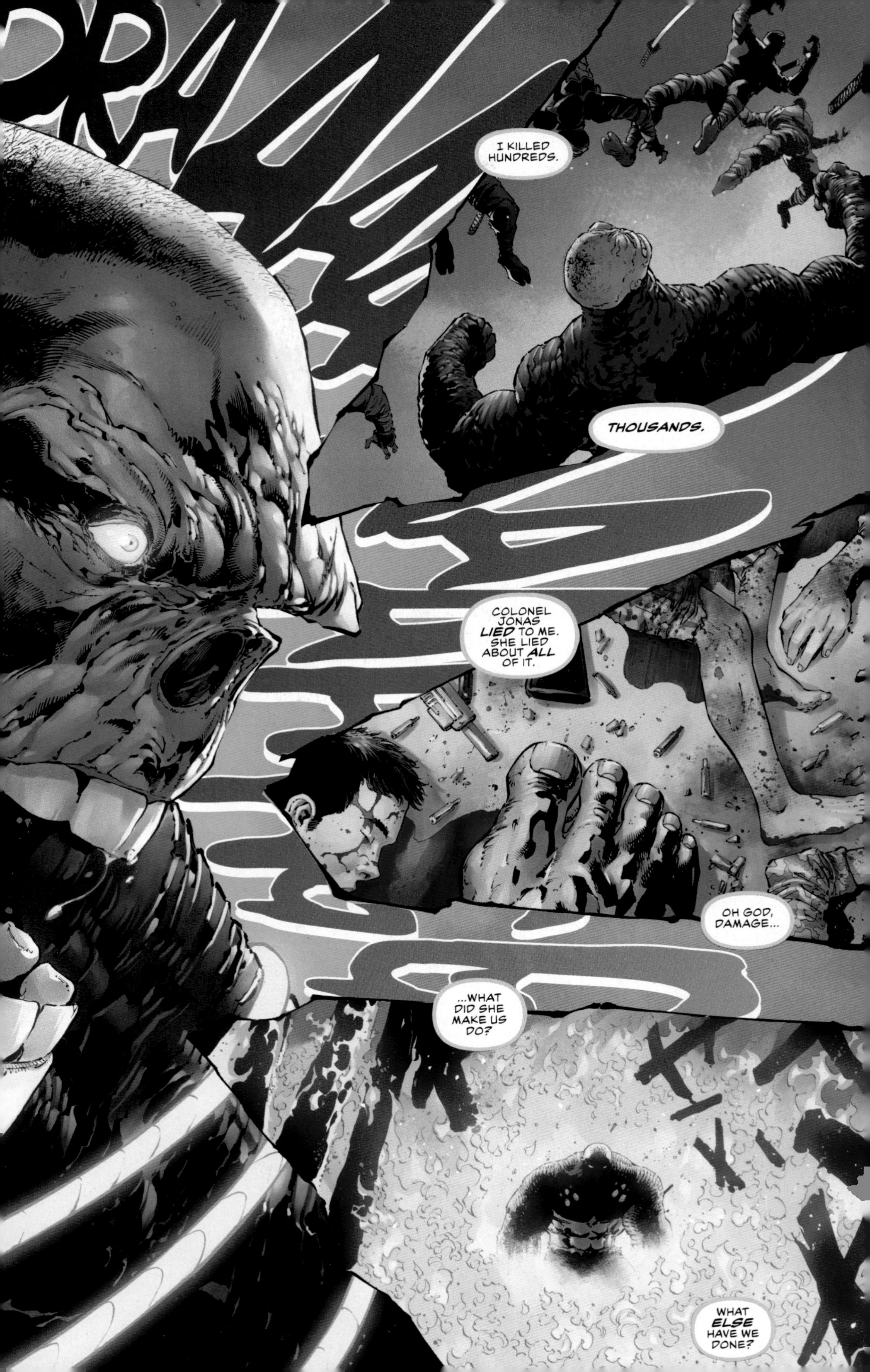
DRAAA
I KILLED HUNDREDS.
THOUSANDS.
COLONEL JONAS LIED TO ME. SHE LIED ABOUT ALL OF IT.
OH GOD, DAMAGE...
...WHAT DID SHE MAKE US DO?
WHAT ELSE HAVE WE DONE?

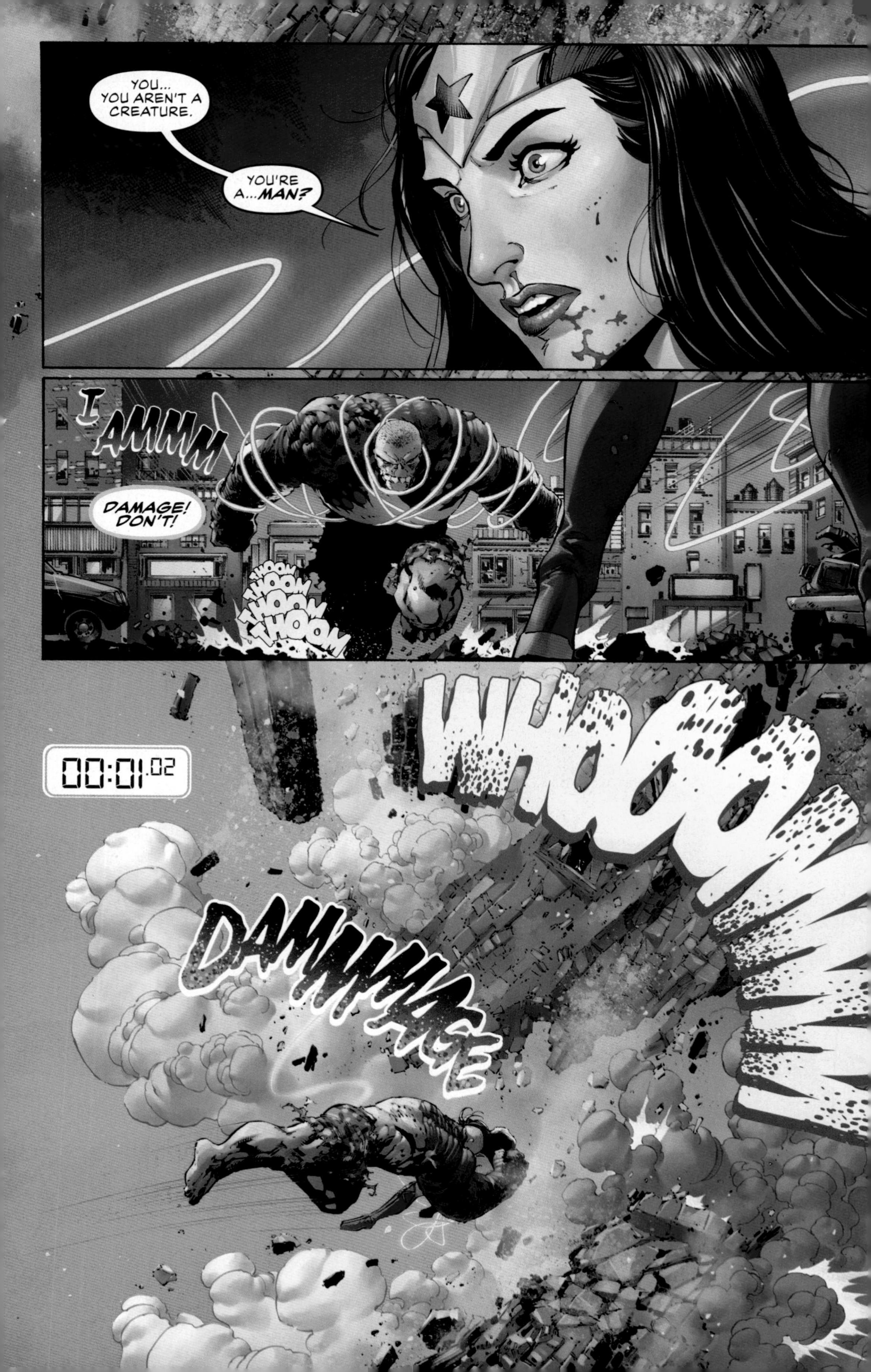

YOU... YOU AREN'T A CREATURE.
YOU'RE A...MAN?
I AMMM
DAMAGE! DON'T!
THOOM THOOM THOOM THOOM
00:01.02
WHOOM
DAMMMAGE

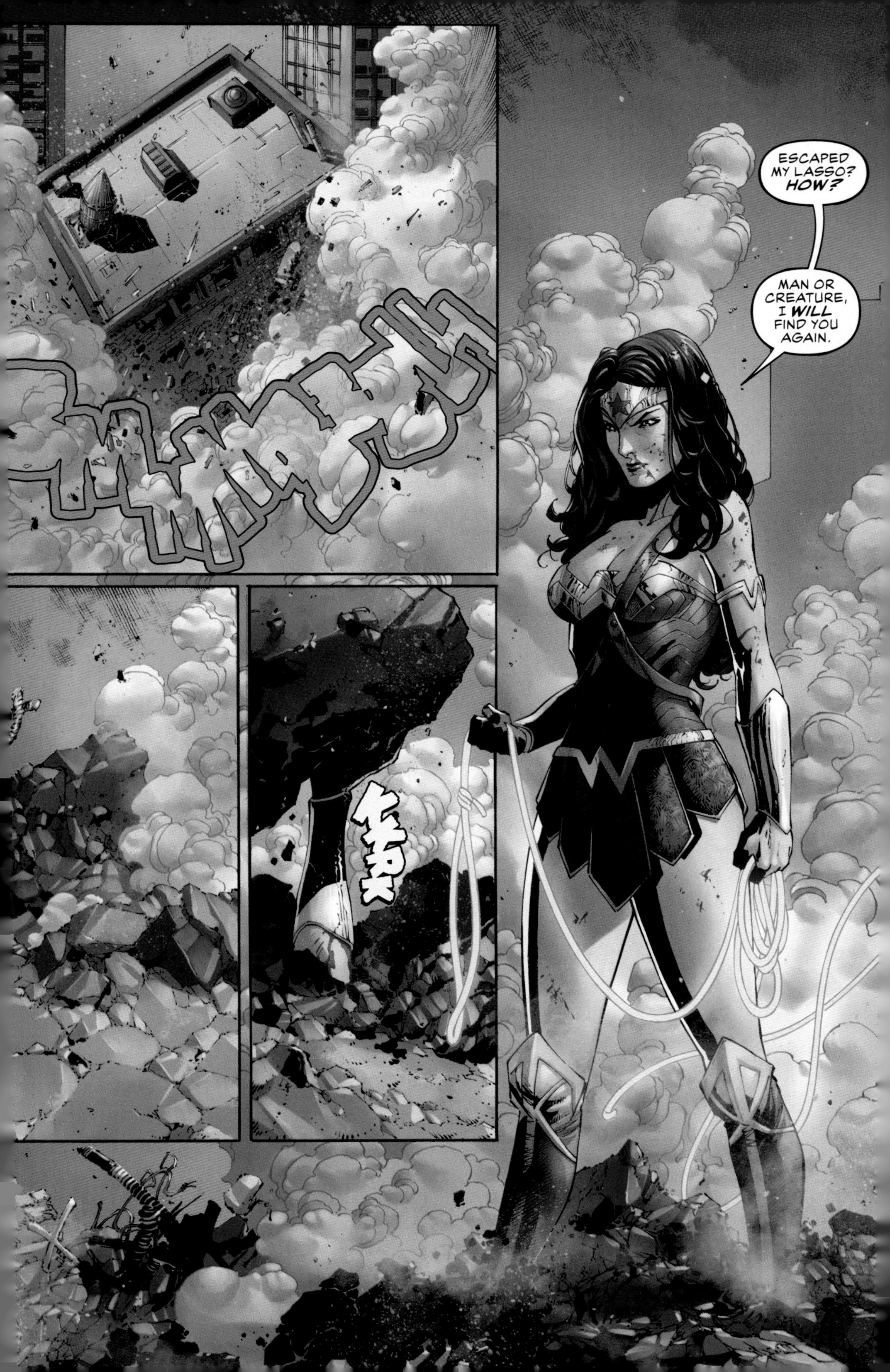
ESCAPED MY LASSO? *HOW?*
MAN OR CREATURE, I *WILL* FIND YOU AGAIN.

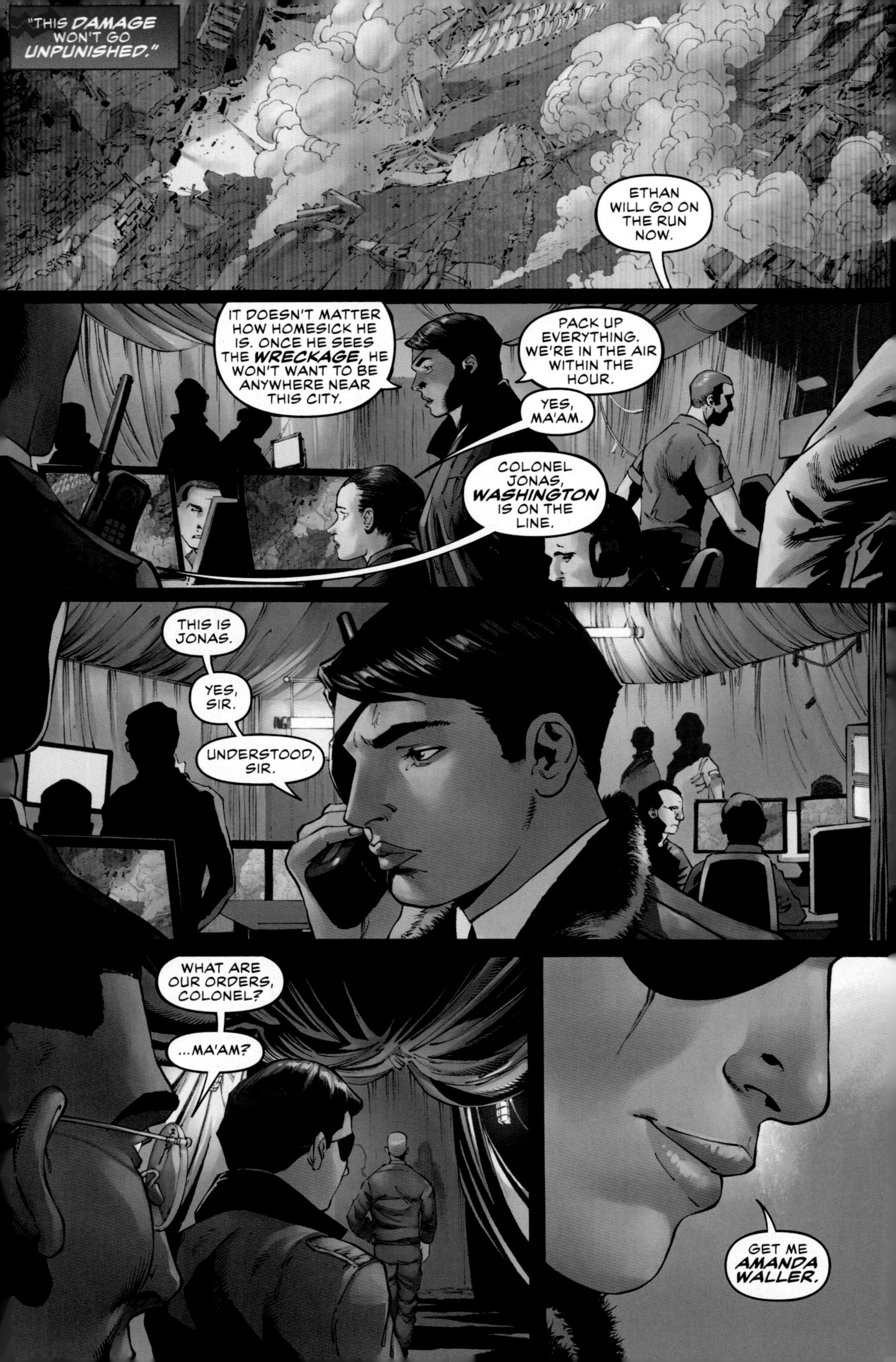
"THIS DAMAGE WON'T GO UNPUNISHED."
ETHAN WILL GO ON THE RUN NOW.
IT DOESN'T MATTER HOW HOMESICK HE IS. ONCE HE SEES THE WRECKAGE, HE WON'T WANT TO BE ANYWHERE NEAR THIS CITY.
PACK UP EVERYTHING. WE'RE IN THE AIR WITHIN THE HOUR.
YES, MA'AM.
COLONEL JONAS, WASHINGTON IS ON THE LINE.
THIS IS JONAS.
YES, SIR.
UNDERSTOOD, SIR.
WHAT ARE OUR ORDERS, COLONEL?
...MA'AM?
GET ME AMANDA WALLER.

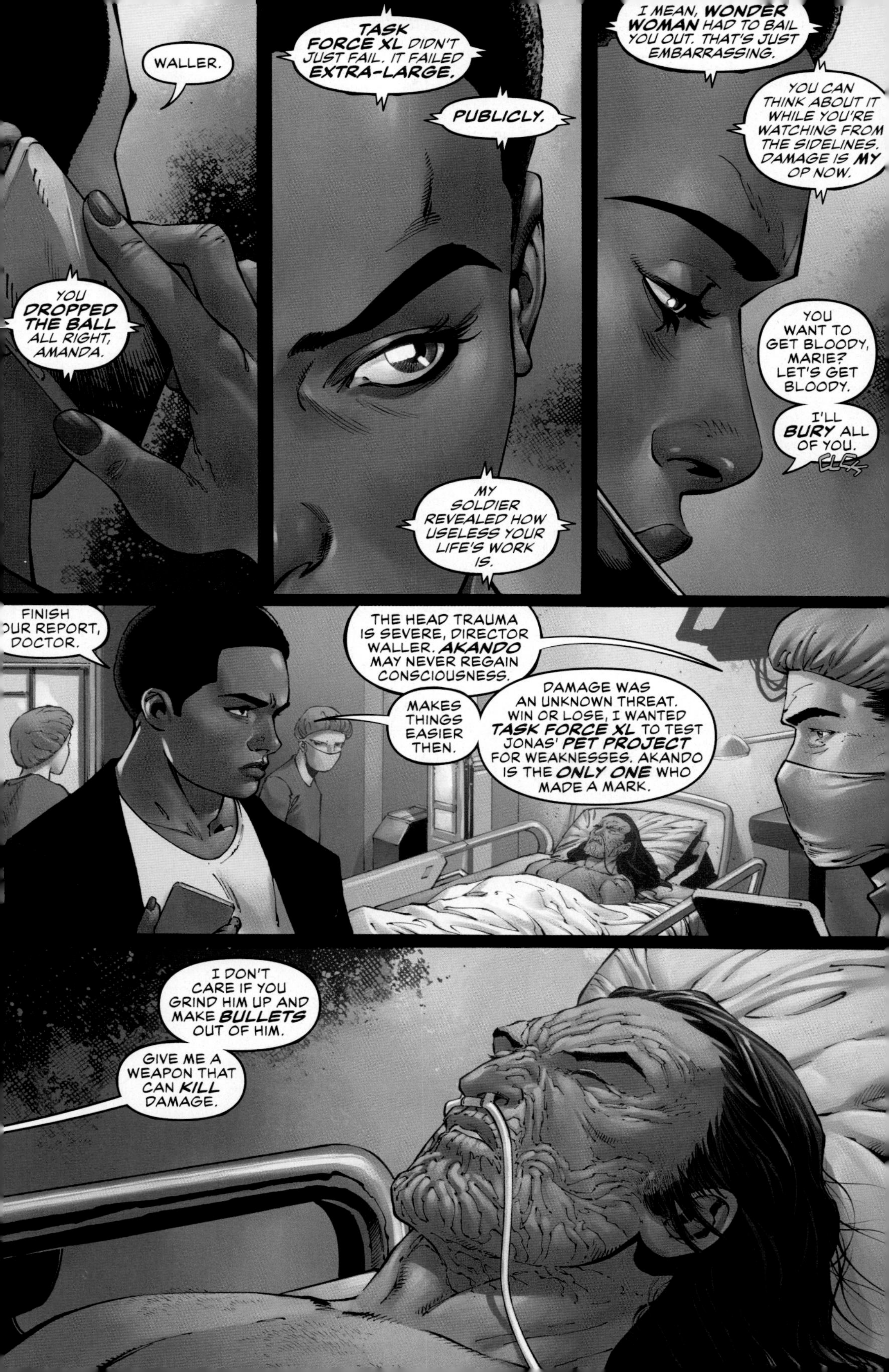
WALLER.
YOU DROPPED THE BALL ALL RIGHT, AMANDA.
TASK FORCE XL DIDN'T JUST FAIL. IT FAILED EXTRA-LARGE.
PUBLICLY.
MY SOLDIER REVEALED HOW USELESS YOUR LIFE'S WORK IS.
I MEAN, WONDER WOMAN HAD TO BAIL YOU OUT. THAT'S JUST EMBARRASSING.
YOU CAN THINK ABOUT IT WHILE YOU'RE WATCHING FROM THE SIDELINES. DAMAGE IS MY OP NOW.
YOU WANT TO GET BLOODY, MARIE? LET'S GET BLOODY.
I'LL BURY ALL OF YOU.
FINISH OUR REPORT, DOCTOR.
THE HEAD TRAUMA IS SEVERE, DIRECTOR WALLER. AKANDO MAY NEVER REGAIN CONSCIOUSNESS.
MAKES THINGS EASIER THEN.
DAMAGE WAS AN UNKNOWN THREAT. WIN OR LOSE, I WANTED TASK FORCE XL TO TEST JONAS' PET PROJECT FOR WEAKNESSES. AKANDO IS THE ONLY ONE WHO MADE A MARK.
I DON'T CARE IF YOU GRIND HIM UP AND MAKE BULLETS OUT OF HIM.
GIVE ME A WEAPON THAT CAN KILL DAMAGE.

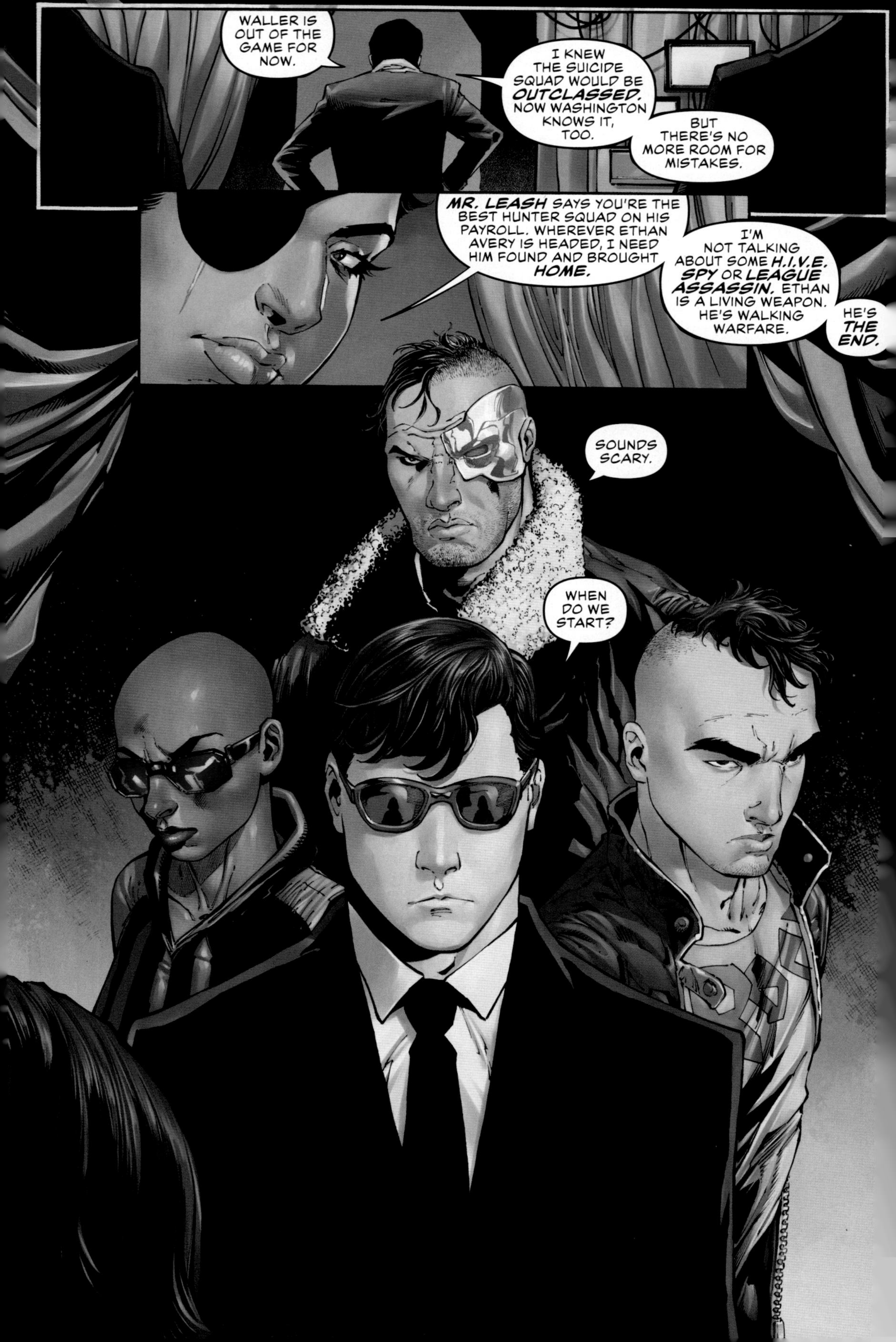
WALLER IS OUT OF THE GAME FOR NOW.
I KNEW THE SUICIDE SQUAD WOULD BE OUTCLASSED. NOW WASHINGTON KNOWS IT, TOO.
BUT THERE'S NO MORE ROOM FOR MISTAKES.
MR. LEASH SAYS YOU'RE THE BEST HUNTER SQUAD ON HIS PAYROLL. WHEREVER ETHAN AVERY IS HEADED, I NEED HIM FOUND AND BROUGHT HOME.
I'M NOT TALKING ABOUT SOME H.I.V.E. SPY OR LEAGUE ASSASSIN. ETHAN IS A LIVING WEAPON. HE'S WALKING WARFARE.
HE'S THE END.
SOUNDS SCARY.
WHEN DO WE START?

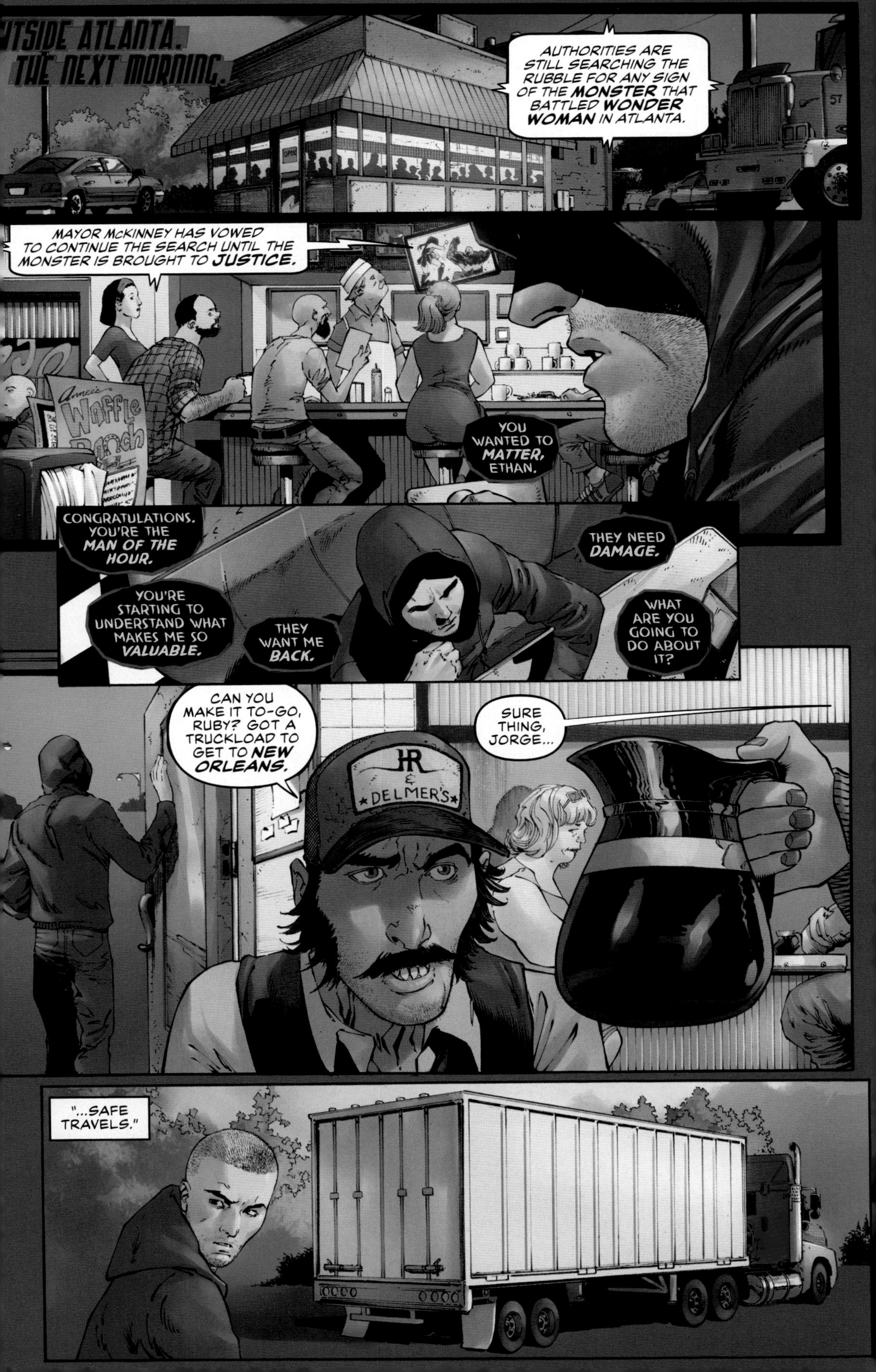

...UTSIDE ATLANTA. THE NEXT MORNING.
AUTHORITIES ARE STILL SEARCHING THE RUBBLE FOR ANY SIGN OF THE MONSTER THAT BATTLED WONDER WOMAN IN ATLANTA.
MAYOR McKINNEY HAS VOWED TO CONTINUE THE SEARCH UNTIL THE MONSTER IS BROUGHT TO JUSTICE.
YOU WANTED TO MATTER, ETHAN.
CONGRATULATIONS. YOU'RE THE MAN OF THE HOUR.
YOU'RE STARTING TO UNDERSTAND WHAT MAKES ME SO VALUABLE.
THEY WANT ME BACK.
THEY NEED DAMAGE.
WHAT ARE YOU GOING TO DO ABOUT IT?
CAN YOU MAKE IT TO-GO, RUBY? GOT A TRUCKLOAD TO GET TO NEW ORLEANS.
SURE THING, JORGE...
"...SAFE TRAVELS."

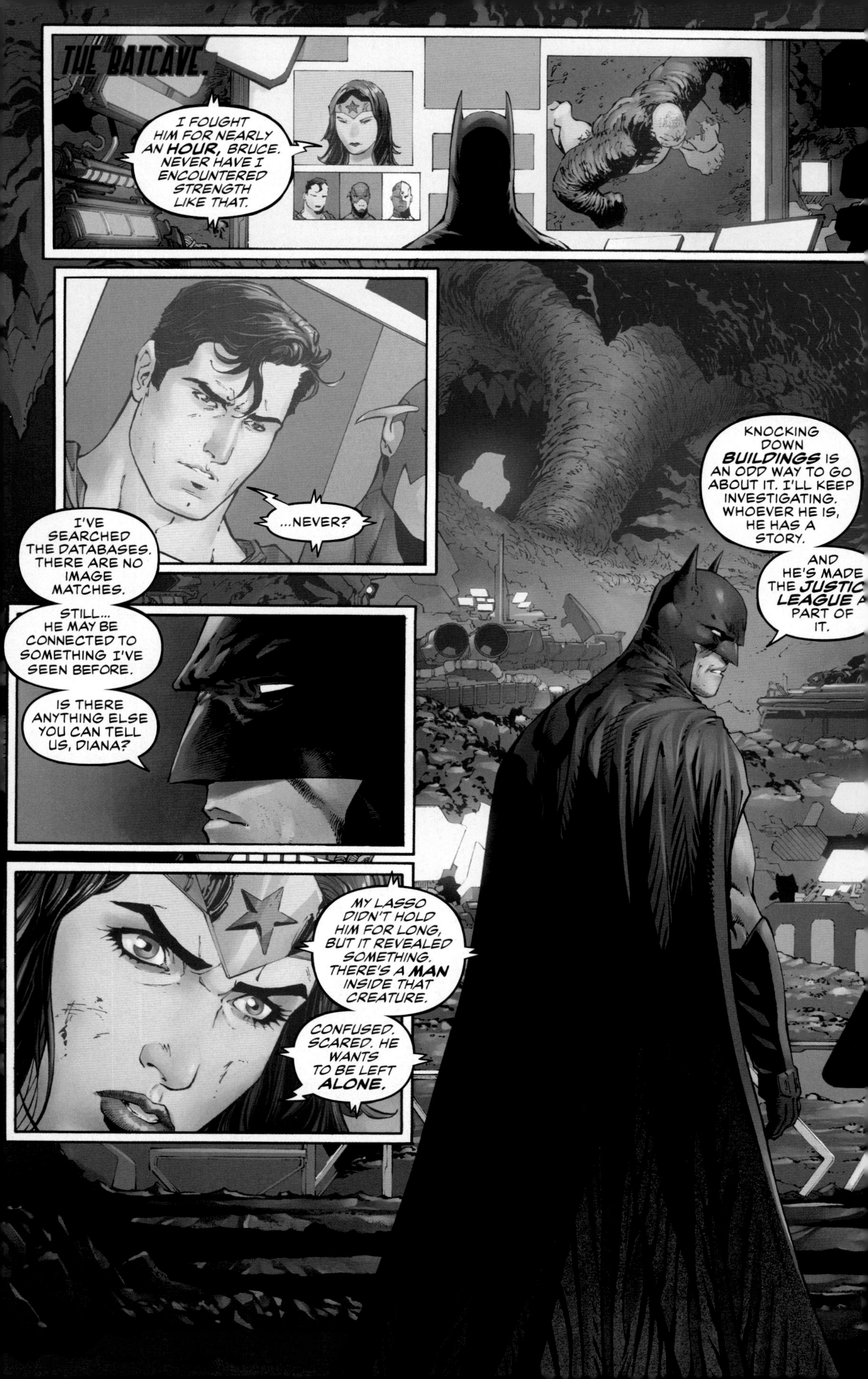
THE BATCAVE.
I FOUGHT HIM FOR NEARLY AN HOUR, BRUCE. NEVER HAVE I ENCOUNTERED STRENGTH LIKE THAT.
...NEVER?
I'VE SEARCHED THE DATABASES. THERE ARE NO IMAGE MATCHES.
STILL... HE MAY BE CONNECTED TO SOMETHING I'VE SEEN BEFORE.
IS THERE ANYTHING ELSE YOU CAN TELL US, DIANA?
MY LASSO DIDN'T HOLD HIM FOR LONG, BUT IT REVEALED SOMETHING. THERE'S A MAN INSIDE THAT CREATURE.
CONFUSED. SCARED. HE WANTS TO BE LEFT ALONE.
KNOCKING DOWN BUILDINGS IS AN ODD WAY TO GO ABOUT IT. I'LL KEEP INVESTIGATING. WHOEVER HE IS, HE HAS A STORY.

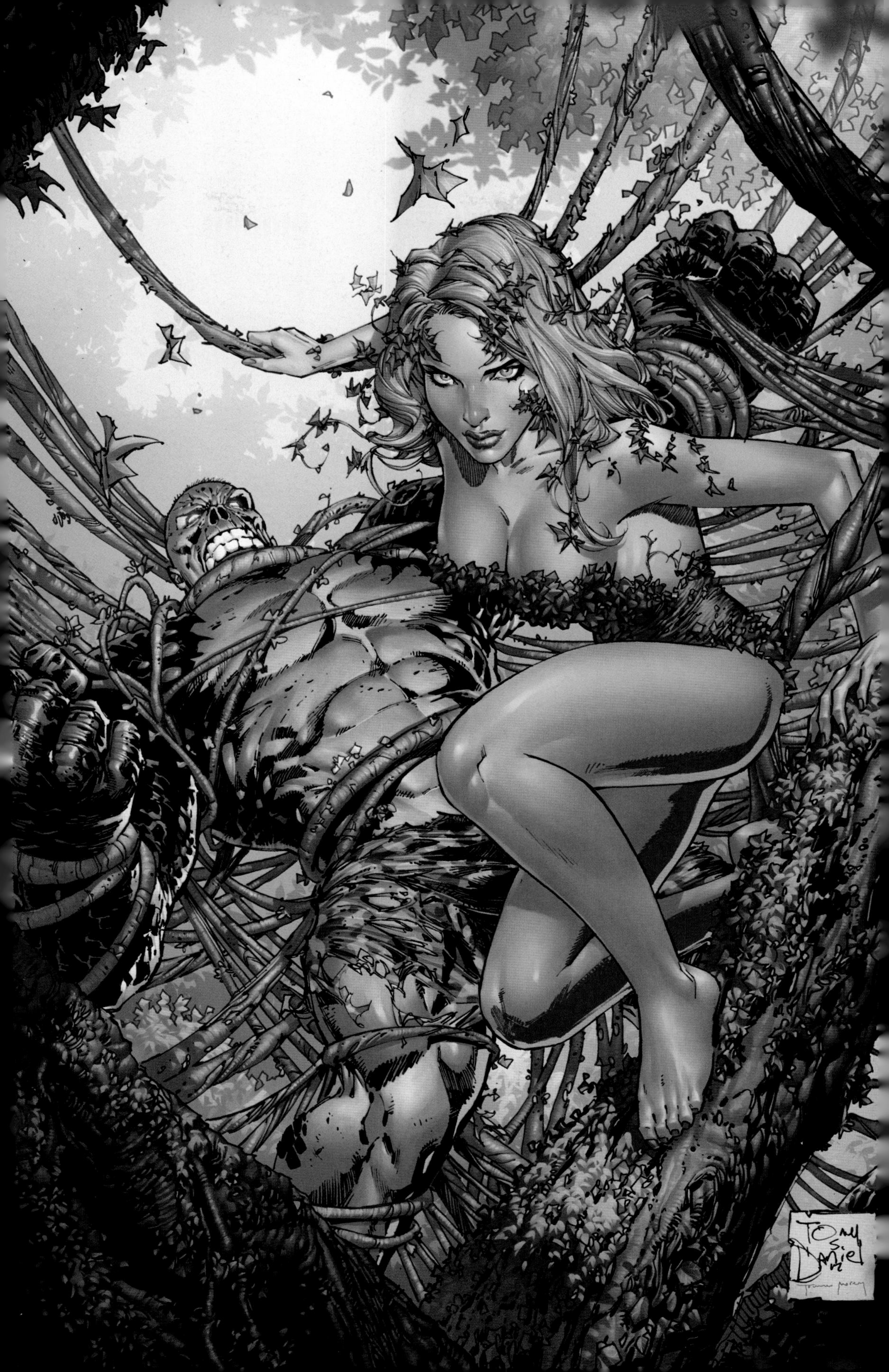

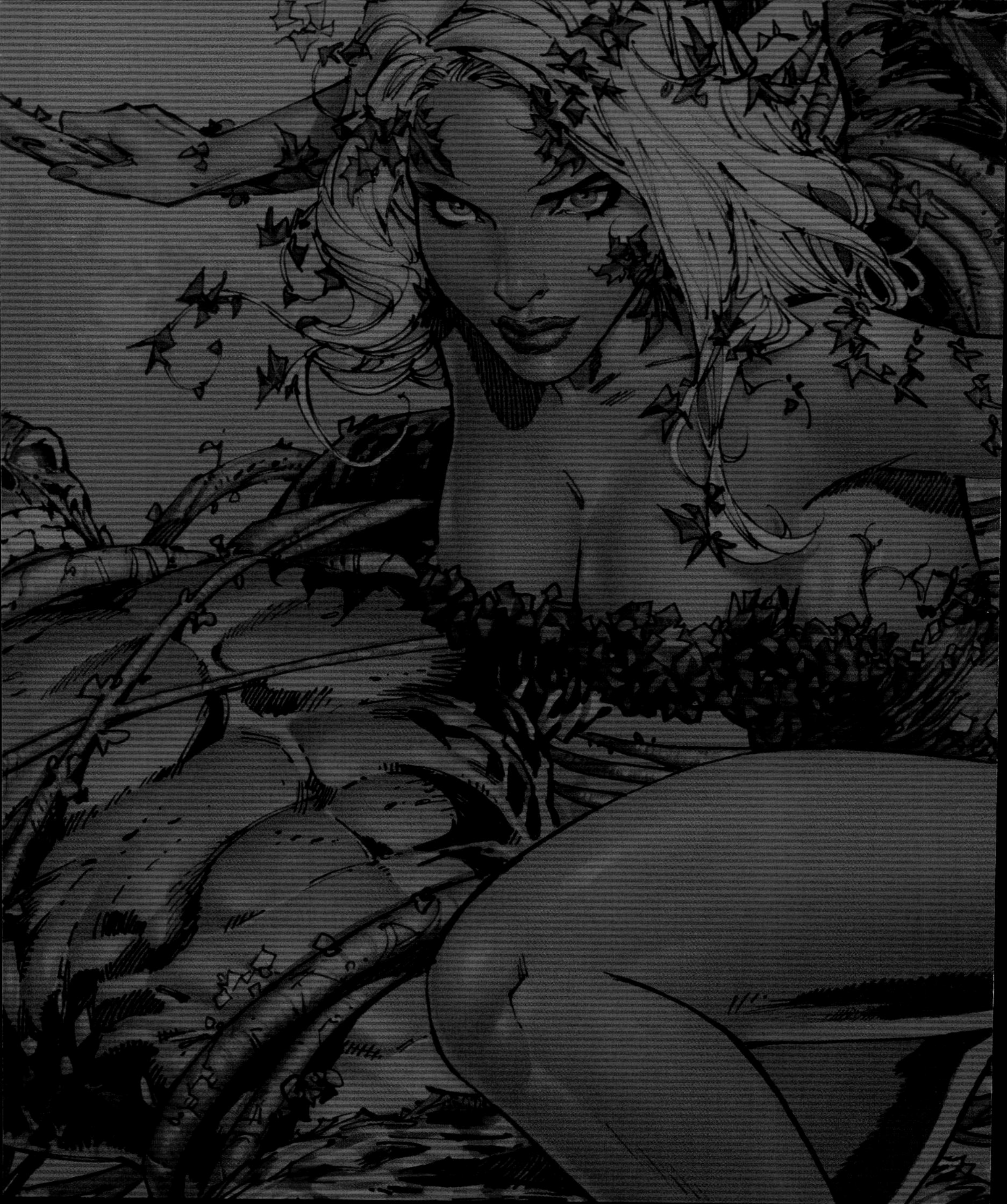

DAMAGE
#4

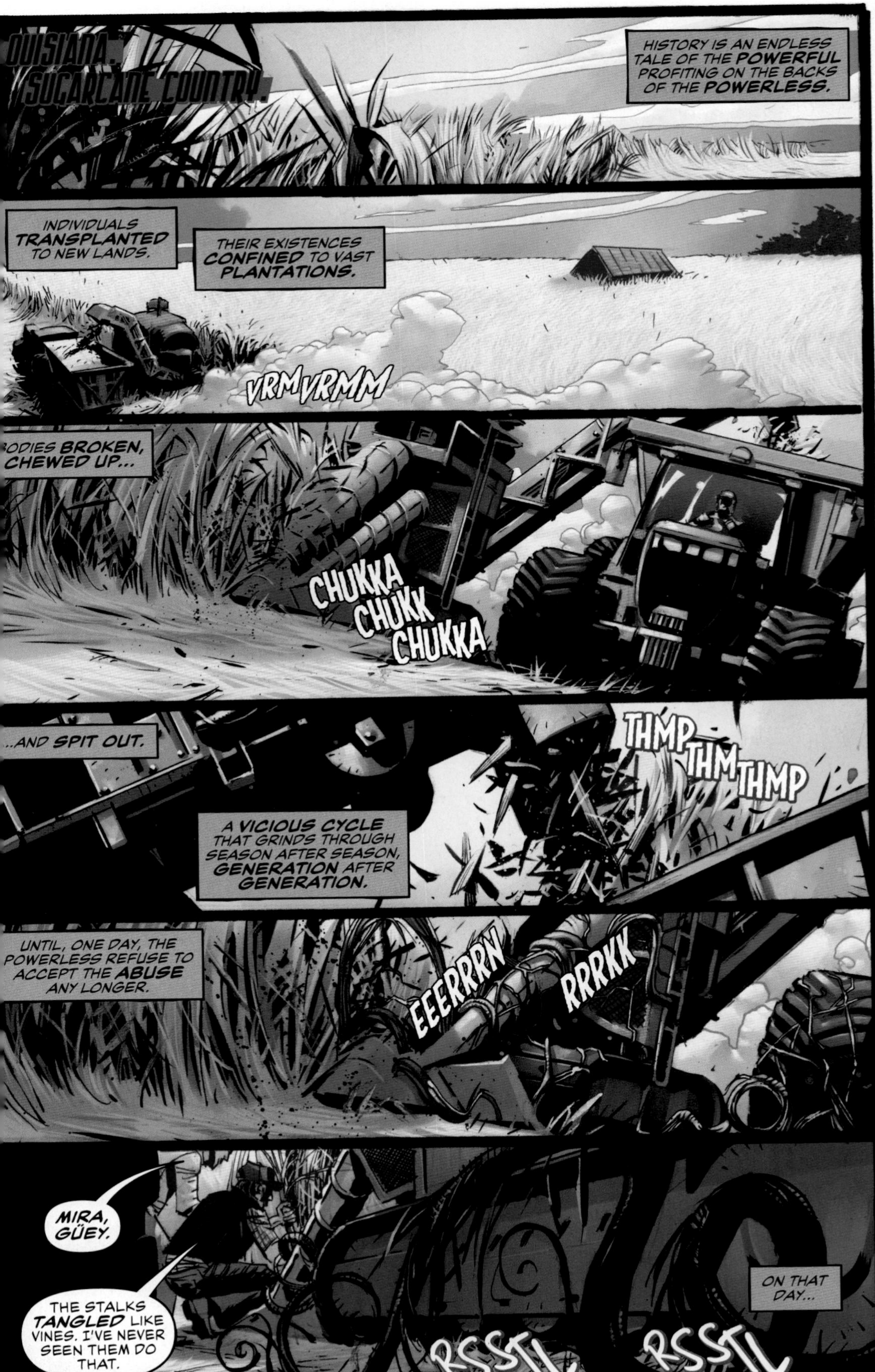

OUISIANA.
SUGARCANE COUNTRY.
HISTORY IS AN ENDLESS TALE OF THE POWERFUL PROFITING ON THE BACKS OF THE POWERLESS.
INDIVIDUALS TRANSPLANTED TO NEW LANDS.
THEIR EXISTENCES CONFINED TO VAST PLANTATIONS.
VRMVRMM
ODIES BROKEN, CHEWED UP...
CHUKKA CHUKK CHUKKA
...AND SPIT OUT.
THMP THM THMP
A VICIOUS CYCLE THAT GRINDS THROUGH SEASON AFTER SEASON, GENERATION AFTER GENERATION.
UNTIL, ONE DAY, THE POWERLESS REFUSE TO ACCEPT THE ABUSE ANY LONGER.
EEERRRN
RRRKK
MIRA, GÜEY.
THE STALKS TANGLED LIKE VINES. I'VE NEVER SEEN THEM DO THAT.
ON THAT DAY...
RSSTL
RSSTL

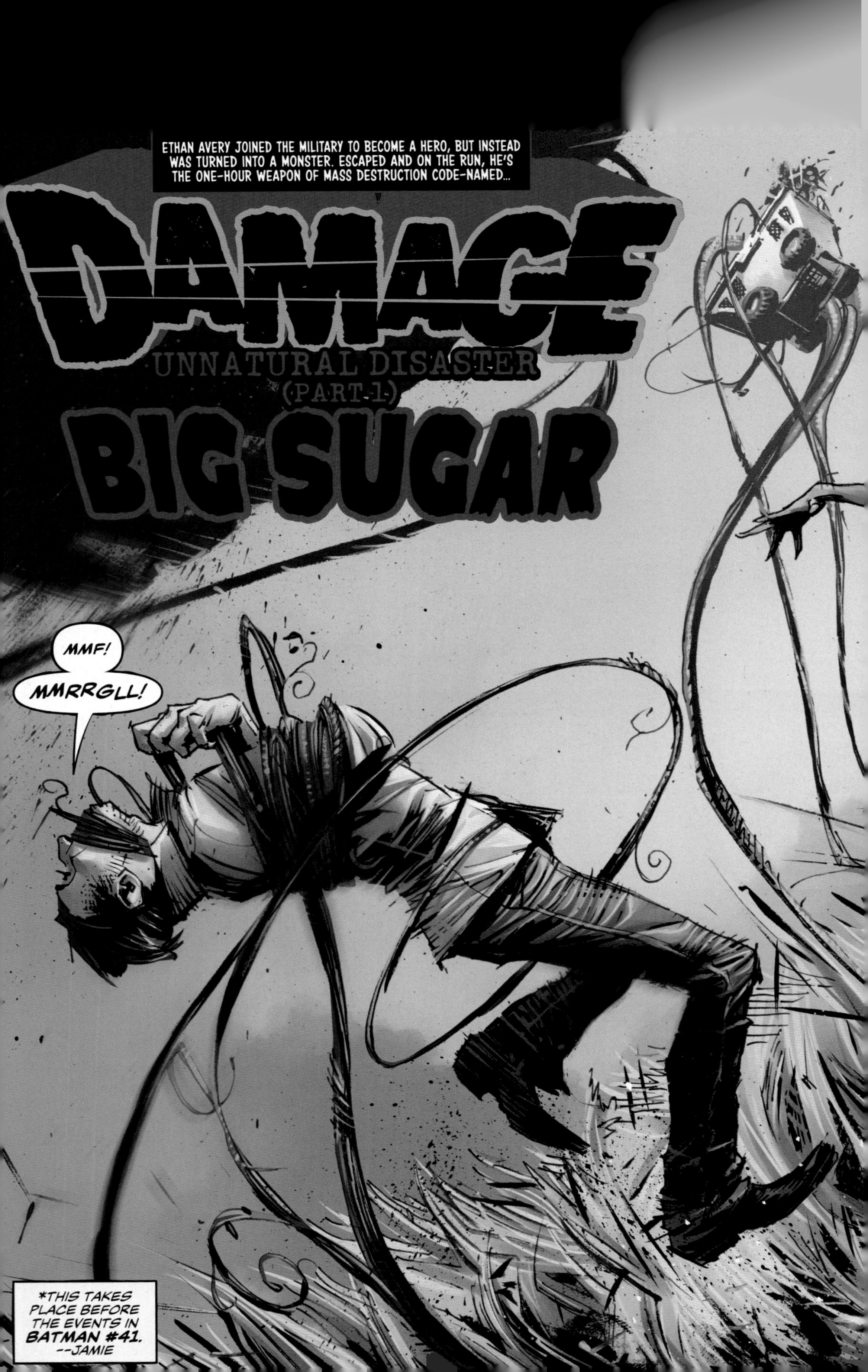
ETHAN AVERY JOINED THE MILITARY TO BECOME A HERO, BUT INSTEAD WAS TURNED INTO A MONSTER. ESCAPED AND ON THE RUN, HE'S THE ONE-HOUR WEAPON OF MASS DESTRUCTION CODE-NAMED...
DAMAGE
UNNATURAL DISASTER
(PART 1)
BIG SUGAR
MMF!
MMRRGLL!
*THIS TAKES PLACE BEFORE THE EVENTS IN BATMAN #41. --JAMIE

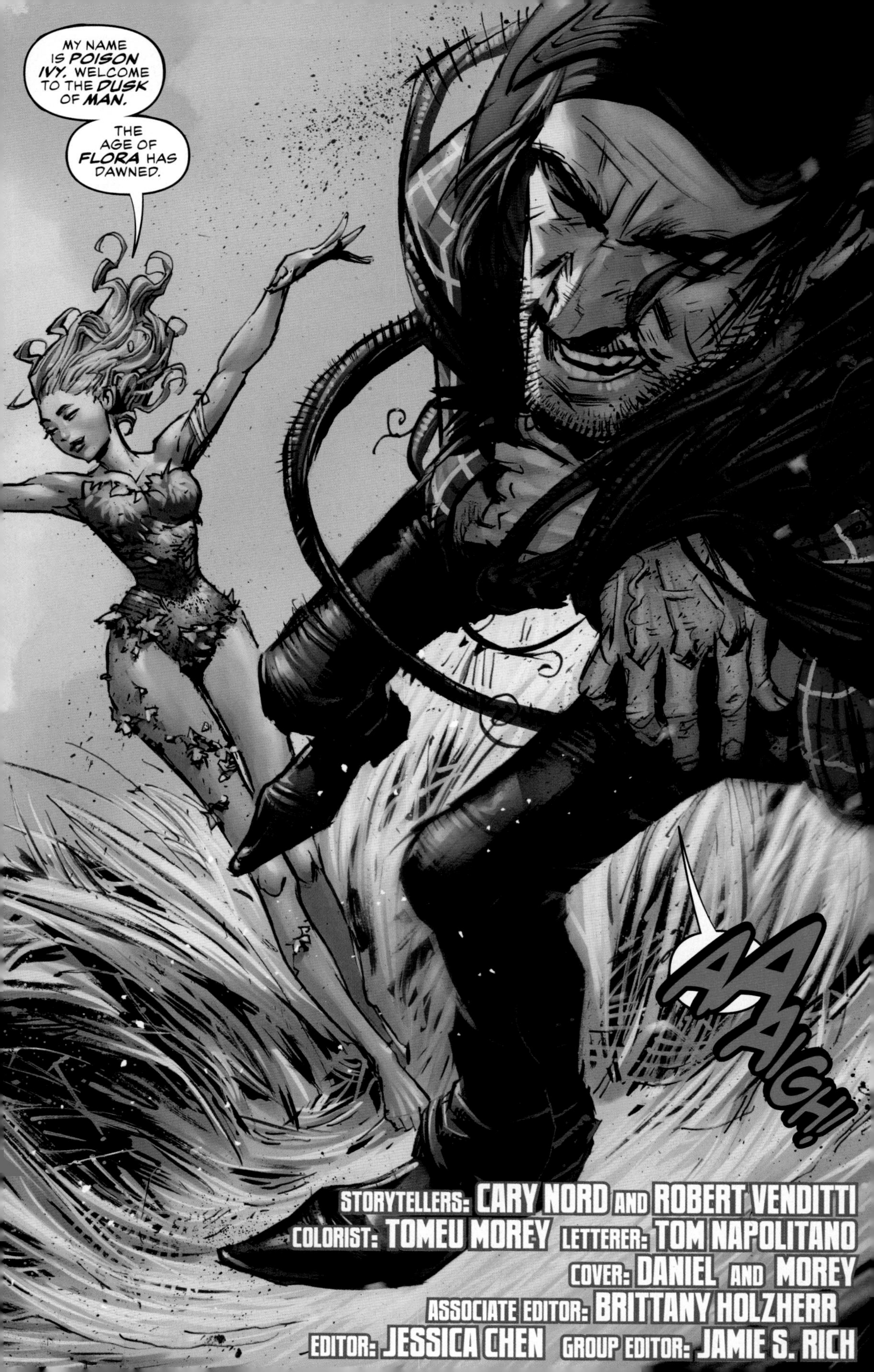
MY NAME IS POISON IVY. WELCOME TO THE DUSK OF MAN.
THE AGE OF FLORA HAS DAWNED.
AAAGH!
STORYTELLERS: CARY NORD AND ROBERT VENDITTI
COLORIST: TOMEU MOREY LETTERER: TOM NAPOLITANO
COVER: DANIEL AND MOREY
ASSOCIATE EDITOR: BRITTANY HOLZHERR
EDITOR: JESSICA CHEN GROUP EDITOR: JAMIE S. RICH

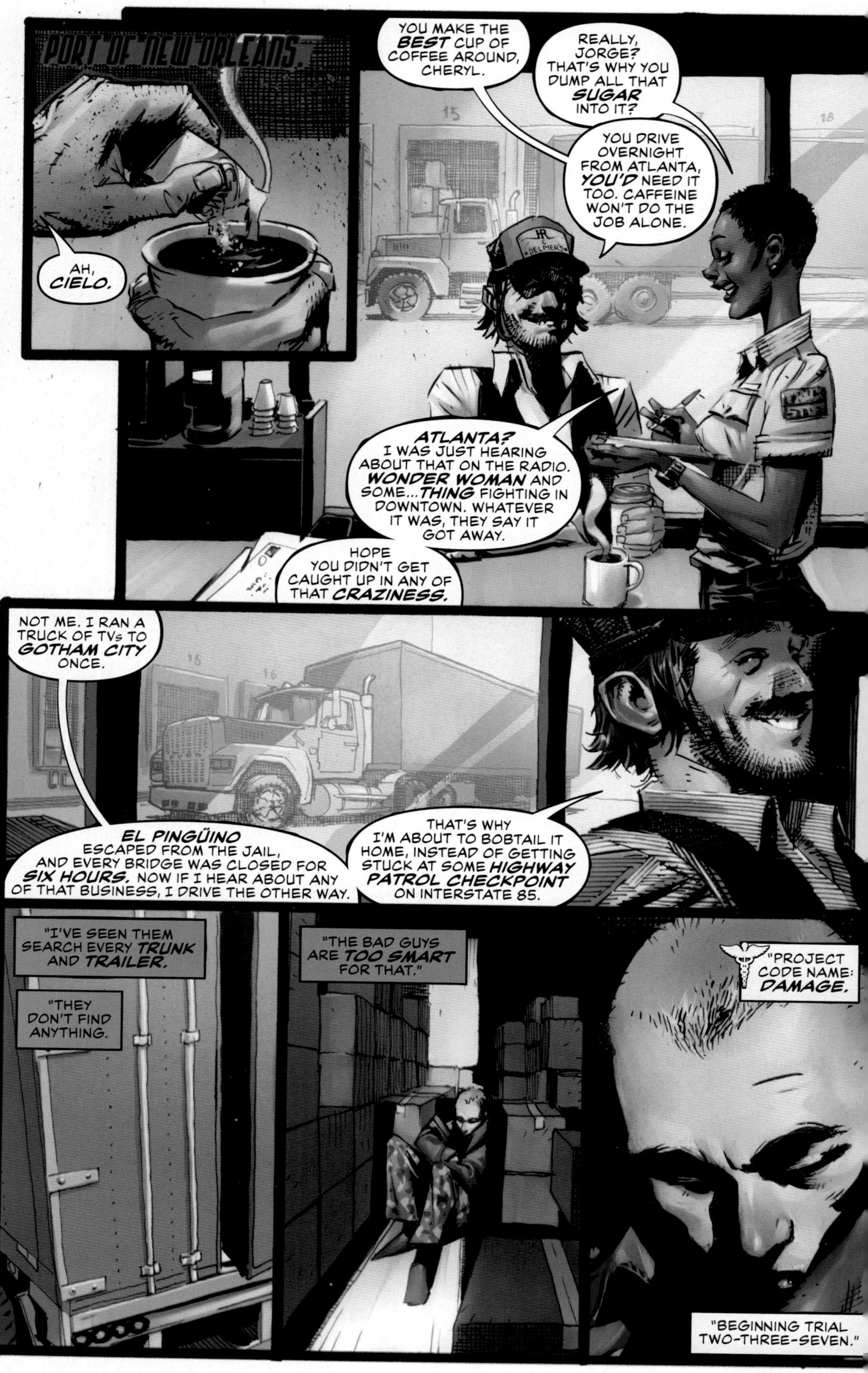
PORT OF NEW ORLEANS.
AH, CIELO.
YOU MAKE THE BEST CUP OF COFFEE AROUND, CHERYL.
REALLY, JORGE? THAT'S WHY YOU DUMP ALL THAT SUGAR INTO IT?
YOU DRIVE OVERNIGHT FROM ATLANTA, YOU'D NEED IT TOO. CAFFEINE WON'T DO THE JOB ALONE.
ATLANTA? I WAS JUST HEARING ABOUT THAT ON THE RADIO. WONDER WOMAN AND SOME...THING FIGHTING IN DOWNTOWN. WHATEVER IT WAS, THEY SAY IT GOT AWAY.
HOPE YOU DIDN'T GET CAUGHT UP IN ANY OF THAT CRAZINESS.
NOT ME. I RAN A TRUCK OF TVs TO GOTHAM CITY ONCE.
EL PINGÜINO ESCAPED FROM THE JAIL, AND EVERY BRIDGE WAS CLOSED FOR SIX HOURS. NOW IF I HEAR ABOUT ANY OF THAT BUSINESS, I DRIVE THE OTHER WAY.
THAT'S WHY I'M ABOUT TO BOBTAIL IT HOME, INSTEAD OF GETTING STUCK AT SOME HIGHWAY PATROL CHECKPOINT ON INTERSTATE 85.
"I'VE SEEN THEM SEARCH EVERY TRUNK AND TRAILER.
"THEY DON'T FIND ANYTHING.
"THE BAD GUYS ARE TOO SMART FOR THAT."
"PROJECT CODE NAME: DAMAGE.
"BEGINNING TRIAL TWO-THREE-SEVEN."

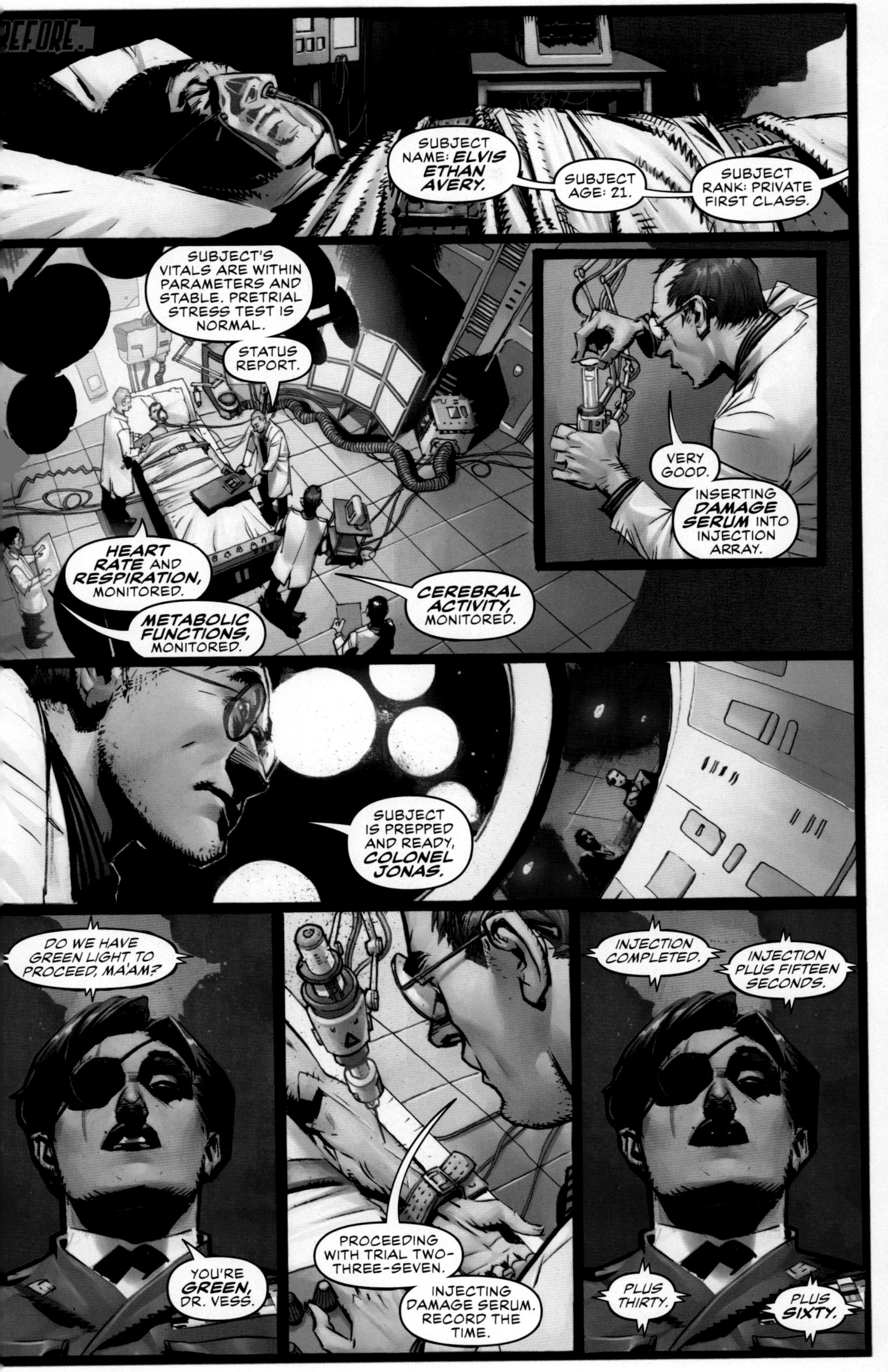

BEFORE.
SUBJECT NAME: *ELVIS ETHAN AVERY.*
SUBJECT AGE: 21.
SUBJECT RANK: PRIVATE FIRST CLASS.
STATUS REPORT.
SUBJECT'S VITALS ARE WITHIN PARAMETERS AND STABLE. PRETRIAL STRESS TEST IS NORMAL.
HEART RATE AND *RESPIRATION,* MONITORED.
METABOLIC FUNCTIONS, MONITORED.
CEREBRAL ACTIVITY, MONITORED.
VERY GOOD.
INSERTING *DAMAGE SERUM* INTO INJECTION ARRAY.
SUBJECT IS PREPPED AND READY, *COLONEL JONAS.*
DO WE HAVE GREEN LIGHT TO PROCEED, MA'AM?
YOU'RE *GREEN,* DR. VESS.
PROCEEDING WITH TRIAL TWO-THREE-SEVEN.
INJECTING DAMAGE SERUM. RECORD THE TIME.
INJECTION COMPLETED.
INJECTION PLUS FIFTEEN SECONDS.
PLUS THIRTY.
PLUS *SIXTY.*

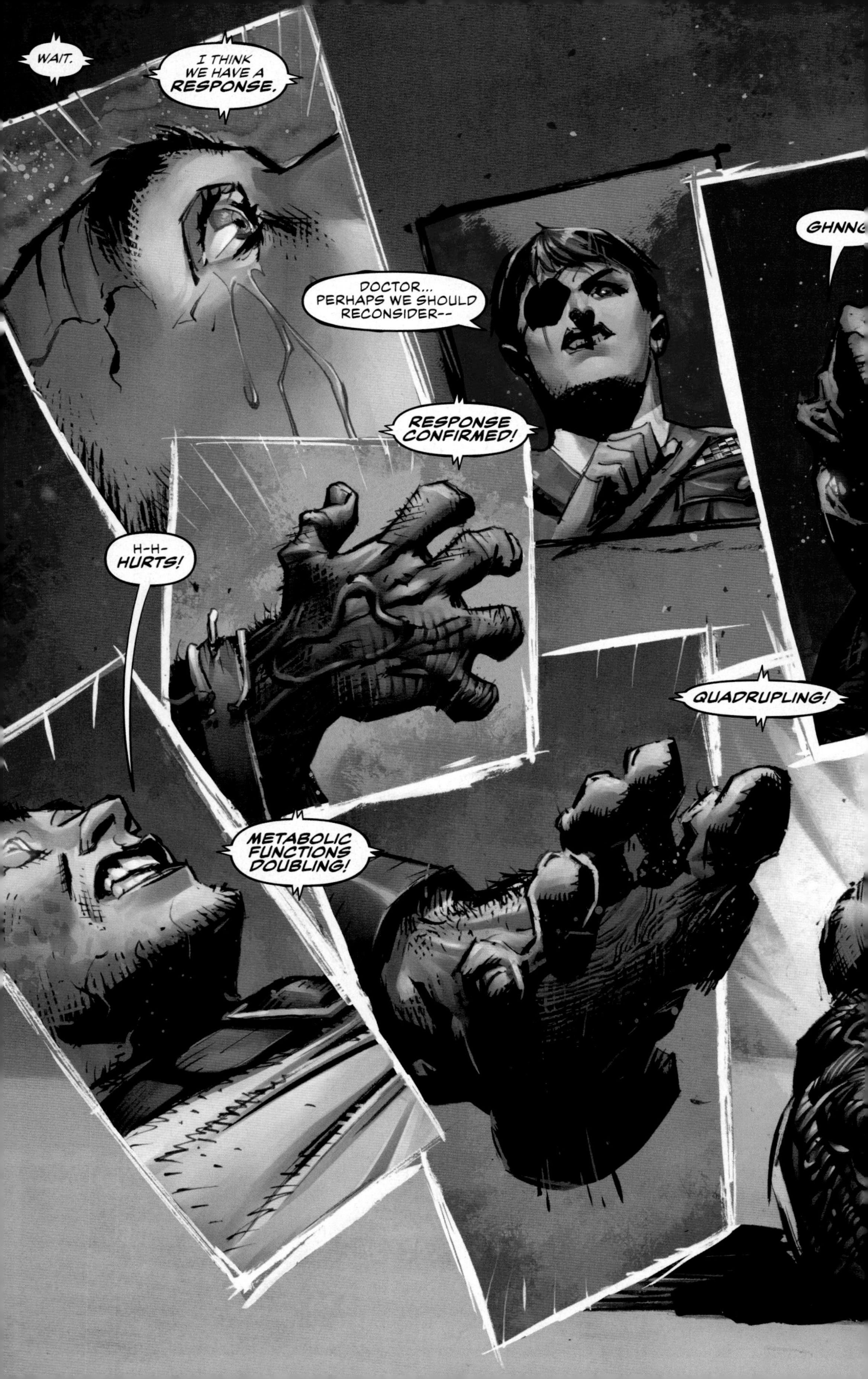
WAIT.
I THINK WE HAVE A RESPONSE.
DOCTOR... PERHAPS WE SHOULD RECONSIDER--
GHNNG
RESPONSE CONFIRMED!
H-H- HURTS!
QUADRUPLING!
METABOLIC FUNCTIONS DOUBLING!

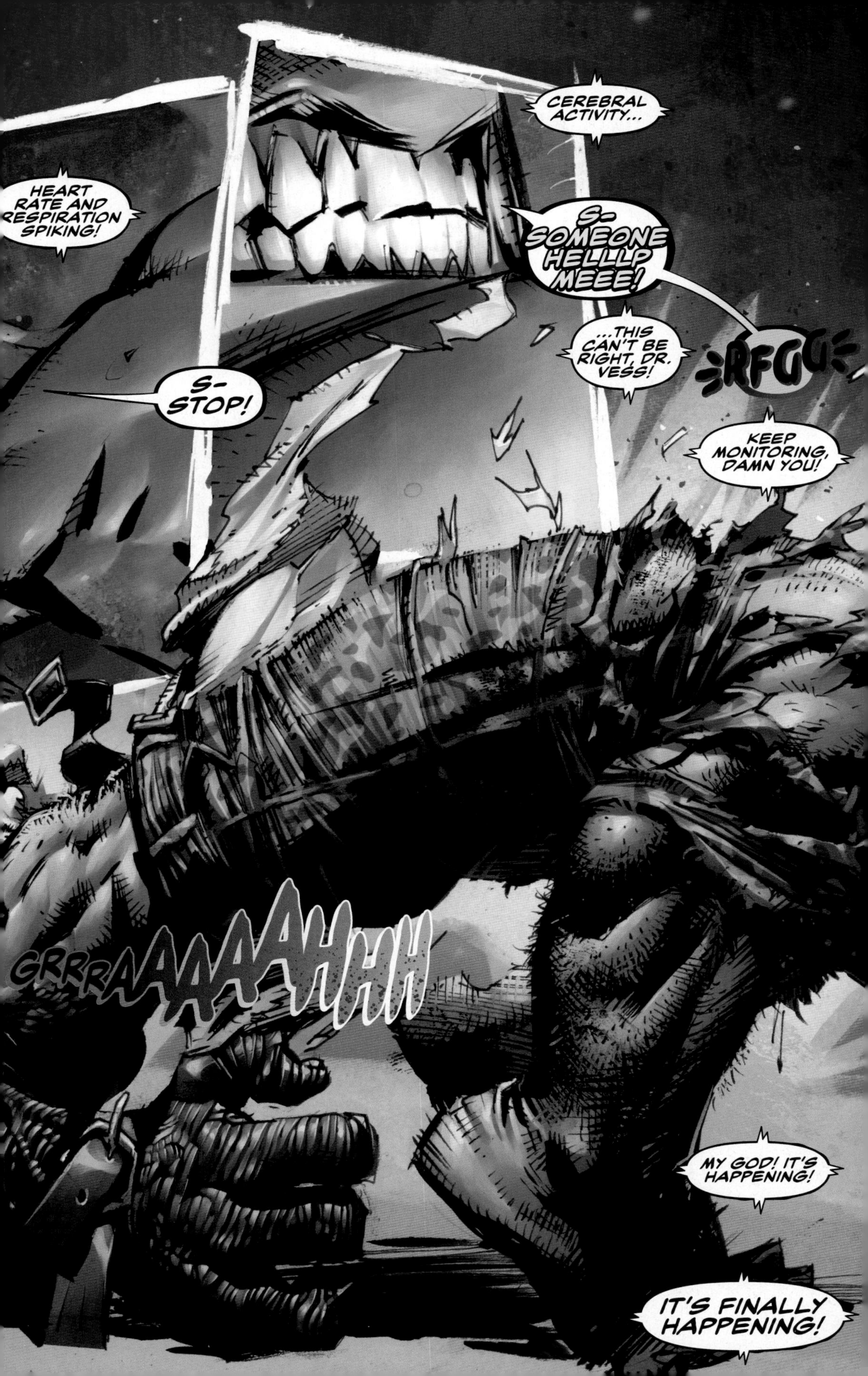
CEREBRAL ACTIVITY...
HEART RATE AND RESPIRATION SPIKING!
S- SOMEONE HELLLP MEEE!
...THIS CAN'T BE RIGHT, DR. VESS!
RFGG
S- STOP!
KEEP MONITORING, DAMN YOU!
GRRRAAAAAAHHH
MY GOD! IT'S HAPPENING!
IT'S FINALLY HAPPENING!

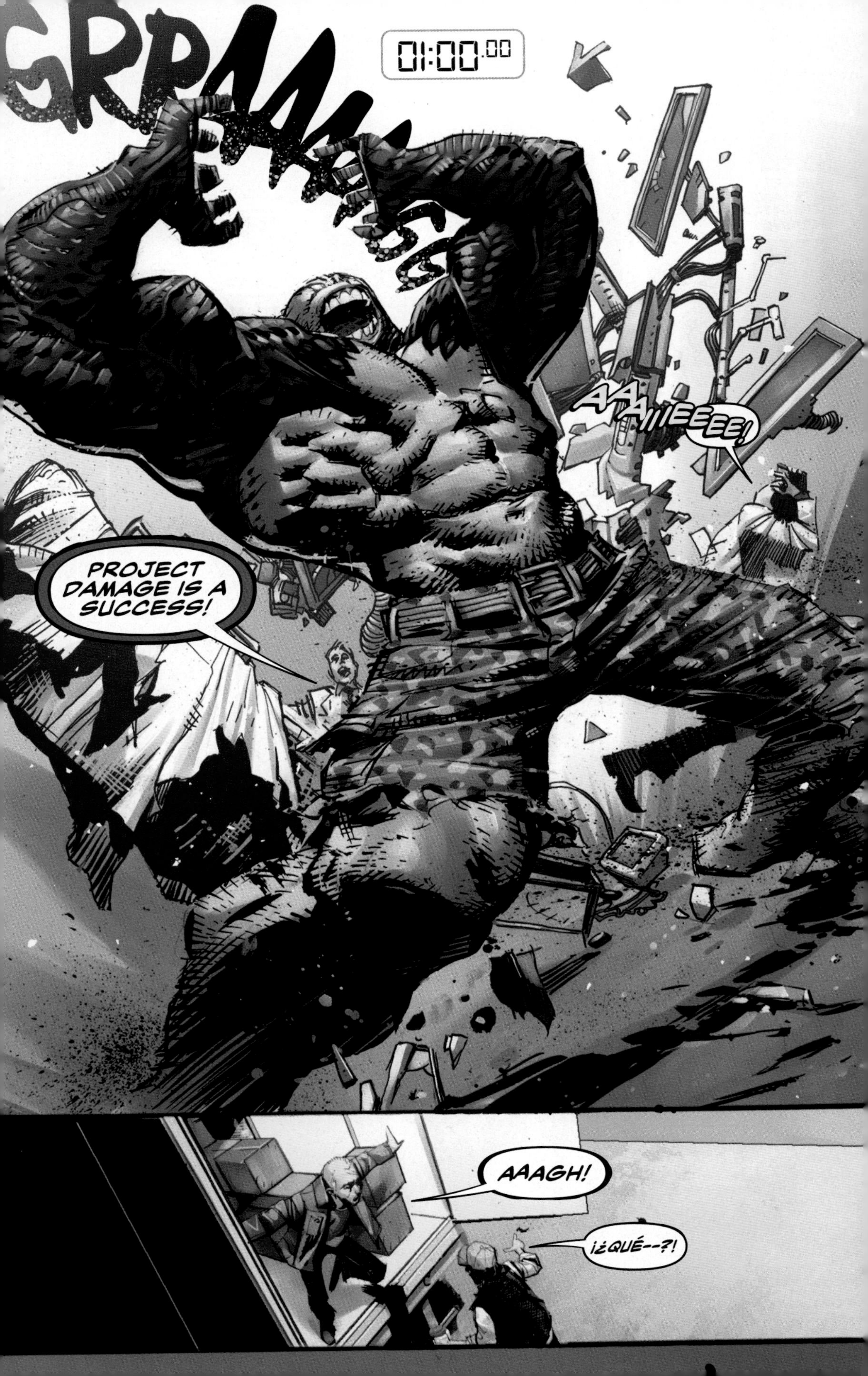
01:00.00
GRRAAAAAGG
AAAIIIEEEEEE!
PROJECT DAMAGE IS A SUCCESS!
AAAGH!
¡¿QUÉ--?!

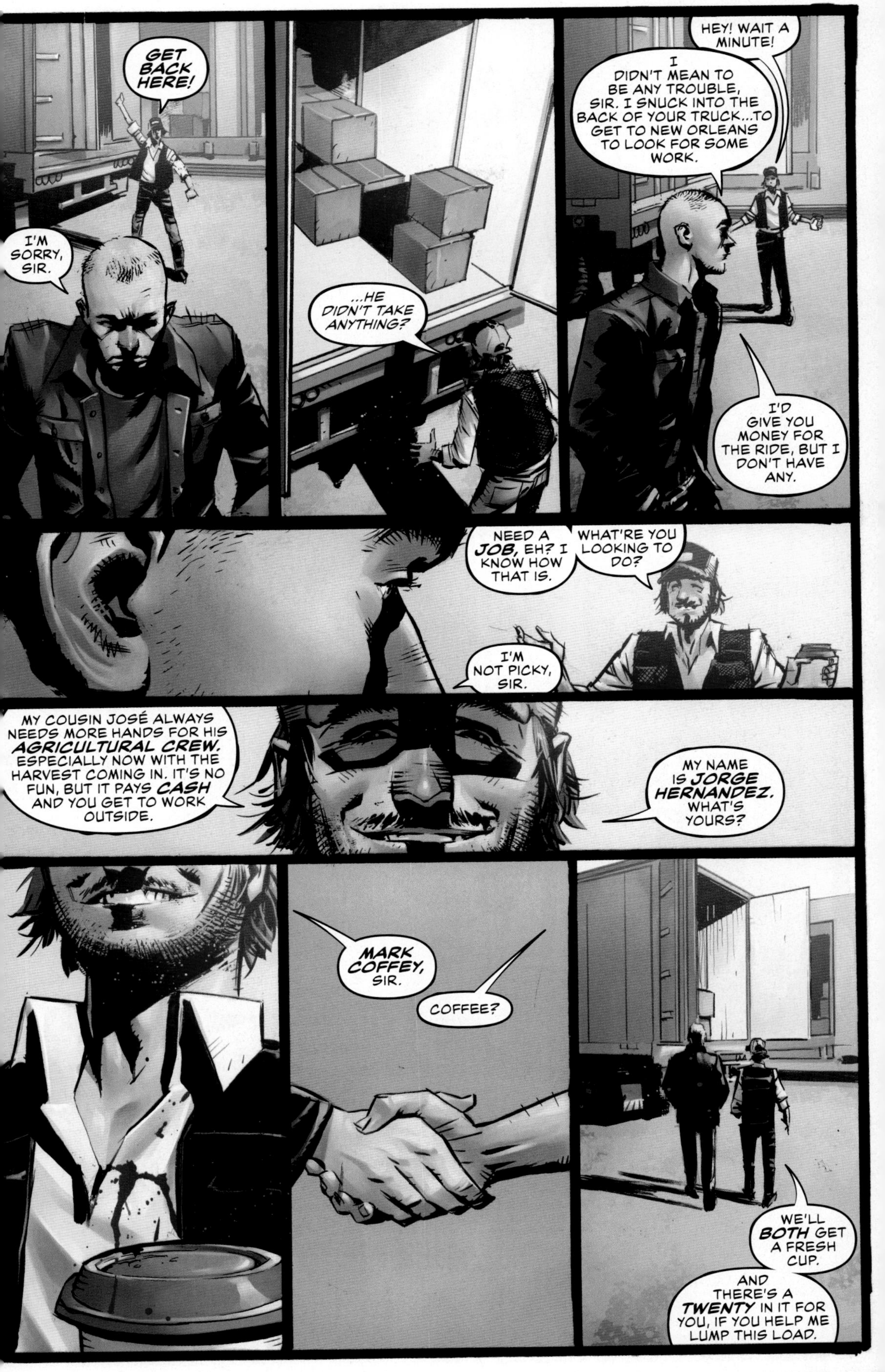
GET BACK HERE!
I'M SORRY, SIR.
...HE DIDN'T TAKE ANYTHING?
HEY! WAIT A MINUTE!
I DIDN'T MEAN TO BE ANY TROUBLE, SIR. I SNUCK INTO THE BACK OF YOUR TRUCK...TO GET TO NEW ORLEANS TO LOOK FOR SOME WORK.
I'D GIVE YOU MONEY FOR THE RIDE, BUT I DON'T HAVE ANY.
NEED A JOB, EH? I KNOW HOW THAT IS.
WHAT'RE YOU LOOKING TO DO?
I'M NOT PICKY, SIR.
MY COUSIN JOSÉ ALWAYS NEEDS MORE HANDS FOR HIS AGRICULTURAL CREW. ESPECIALLY NOW WITH THE HARVEST COMING IN. IT'S NO FUN, BUT IT PAYS CASH AND YOU GET TO WORK OUTSIDE.
MY NAME IS JORGE HERNANDEZ. WHAT'S YOURS?
MARK COFFEY, SIR.
COFFEE?
WE'LL BOTH GET A FRESH CUP.
AND THERE'S A TWENTY IN IT FOR YOU, IF YOU HELP ME LUMP THIS LOAD.

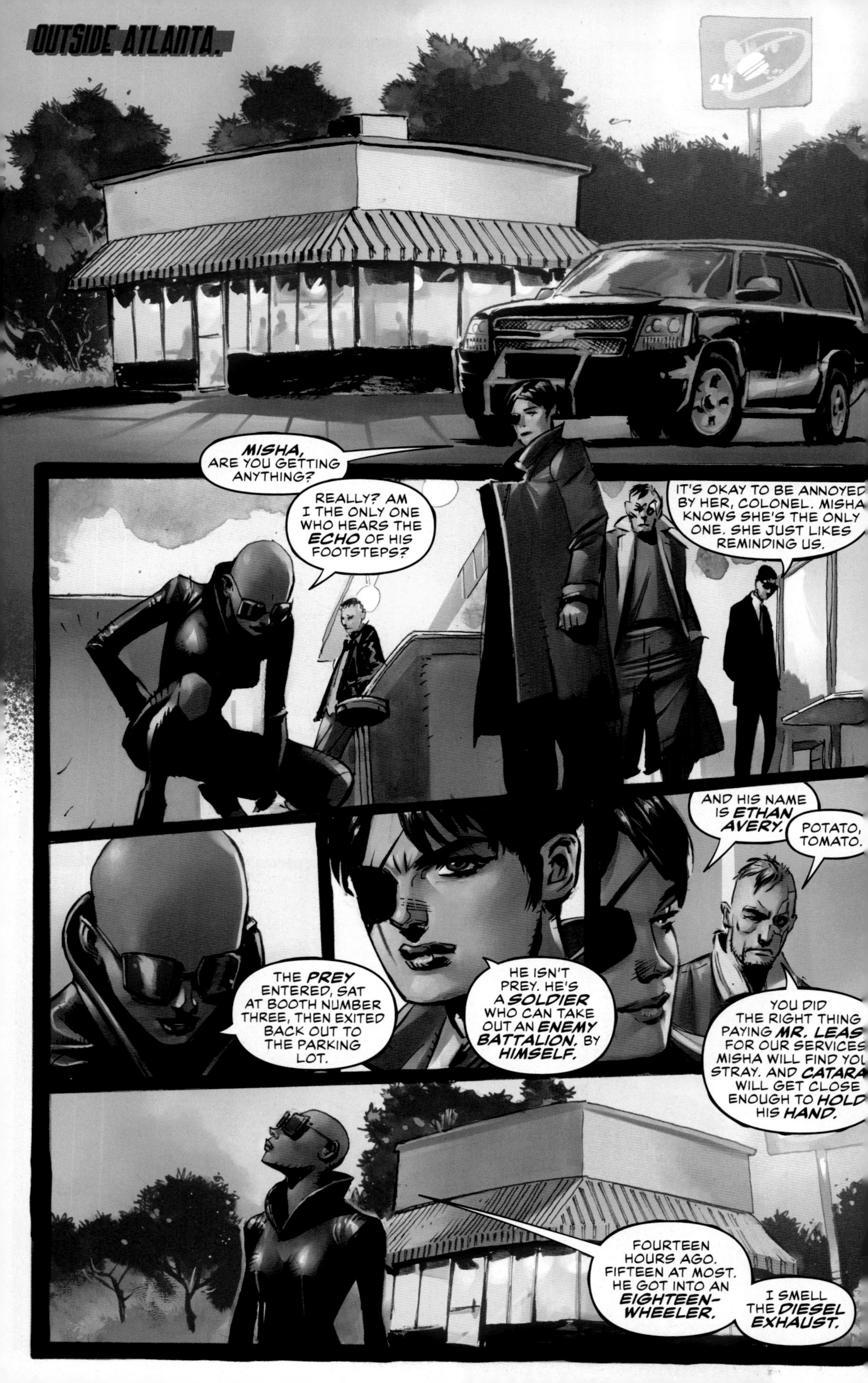
OUTSIDE ATLANTA.
MISHA, ARE YOU GETTING ANYTHING?
REALLY? AM I THE ONLY ONE WHO HEARS THE ECHO OF HIS FOOTSTEPS?
IT'S OKAY TO BE ANNOYED BY HER, COLONEL. MISHA KNOWS SHE'S THE ONLY ONE. SHE JUST LIKES REMINDING US.
THE PREY ENTERED, SAT AT BOOTH NUMBER THREE, THEN EXITED BACK OUT TO THE PARKING LOT.
HE ISN'T PREY. HE'S A SOLDIER WHO CAN TAKE OUT AN ENEMY BATTALION. BY HIMSELF.
AND HIS NAME IS ETHAN AVERY.
POTATO, TOMATO.
YOU DID THE RIGHT THING PAYING MR. LEAS FOR OUR SERVICES. MISHA WILL FIND YOU STRAY. AND CATARA WILL GET CLOSE ENOUGH TO HOLD HIS HAND.
FOURTEEN HOURS AGO. FIFTEEN AT MOST. HE GOT INTO AN EIGHTEEN-WHEELER.
I SMELL THE DIESEL EXHAUST.

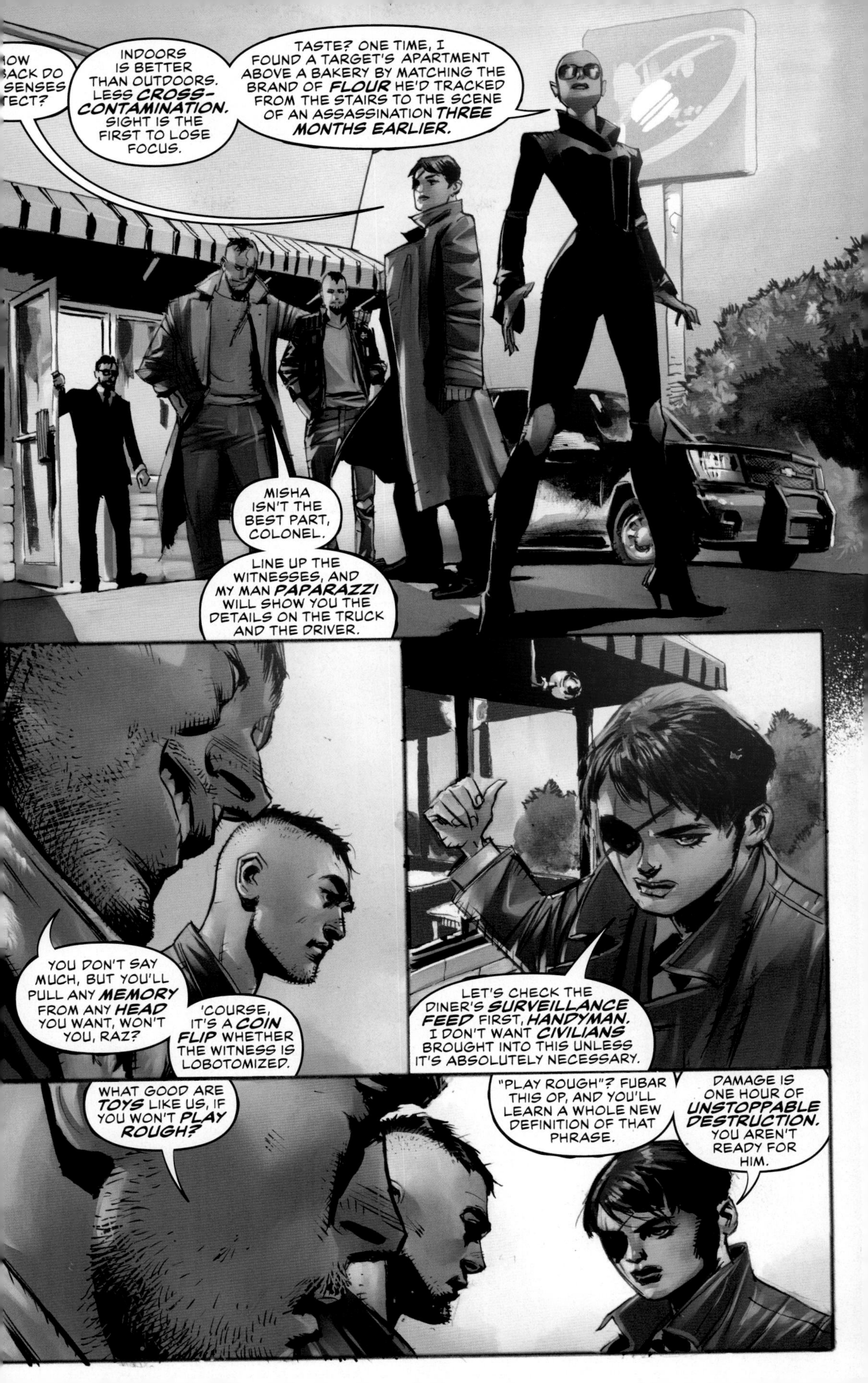

HOW BACK DO SENSES TECT?
INDOORS IS BETTER THAN OUTDOORS. LESS CROSS-CONTAMINATION. SIGHT IS THE FIRST TO LOSE FOCUS.
TASTE? ONE TIME, I FOUND A TARGET'S APARTMENT ABOVE A BAKERY BY MATCHING THE BRAND OF FLOUR HE'D TRACKED FROM THE STAIRS TO THE SCENE OF AN ASSASSINATION THREE MONTHS EARLIER.
MISHA ISN'T THE BEST PART, COLONEL.
LINE UP THE WITNESSES, AND MY MAN PAPARAZZI WILL SHOW YOU THE DETAILS ON THE TRUCK AND THE DRIVER.
YOU DON'T SAY MUCH, BUT YOU'LL PULL ANY MEMORY FROM ANY HEAD YOU WANT, WON'T YOU, RAZ?
'COURSE, IT'S A COIN FLIP WHETHER THE WITNESS IS LOBOTOMIZED.
LET'S CHECK THE DINER'S SURVEILLANCE FEED FIRST, HANDYMAN. I DON'T WANT CIVILIANS BROUGHT INTO THIS UNLESS IT'S ABSOLUTELY NECESSARY.
WHAT GOOD ARE TOYS LIKE US, IF YOU WON'T PLAY ROUGH?
"PLAY ROUGH"? FUBAR THIS OP, AND YOU'LL LEARN A WHOLE NEW DEFINITION OF THAT PHRASE.
DAMAGE IS ONE HOUR OF UNSTOPPABLE DESTRUCTION. YOU AREN'T READY FOR HIM.

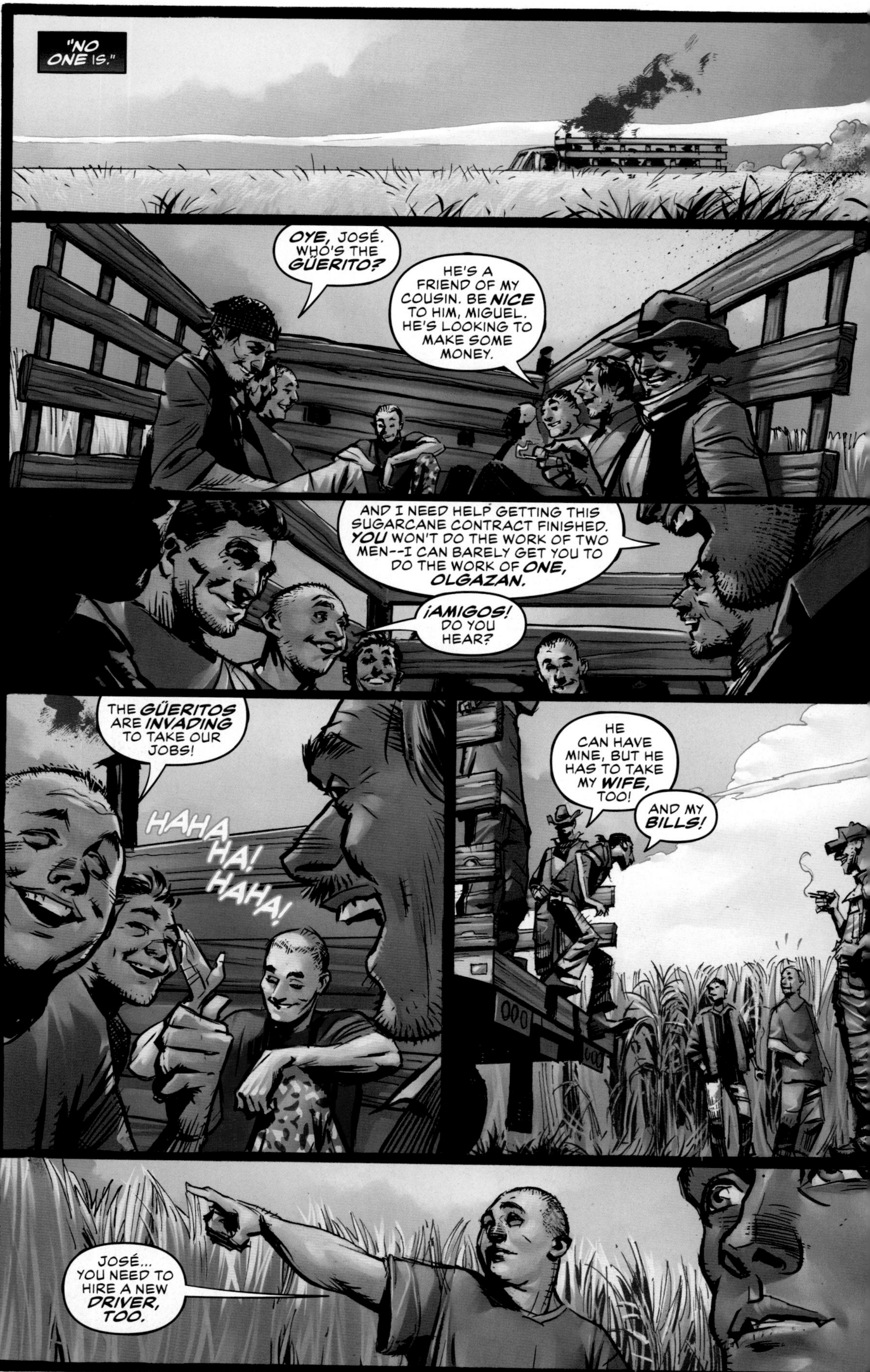
"NO ONE IS."
OYE, JOSÉ. WHO'S THE GÜERITO?
HE'S A FRIEND OF MY COUSIN. BE NICE TO HIM, MIGUEL. HE'S LOOKING TO MAKE SOME MONEY.
AND I NEED HELP GETTING THIS SUGARCANE CONTRACT FINISHED. YOU WON'T DO THE WORK OF TWO MEN--I CAN BARELY GET YOU TO DO THE WORK OF ONE, OLGAZAN.
¡AMIGOS! DO YOU HEAR?
THE GÜERITOS ARE INVADING TO TAKE OUR JOBS!
HAHAHA! HAHA!
HE CAN HAVE MINE, BUT HE HAS TO TAKE MY WIFE, TOO!
AND MY BILLS!
JOSÉ... YOU NEED TO HIRE A NEW DRIVER, TOO.

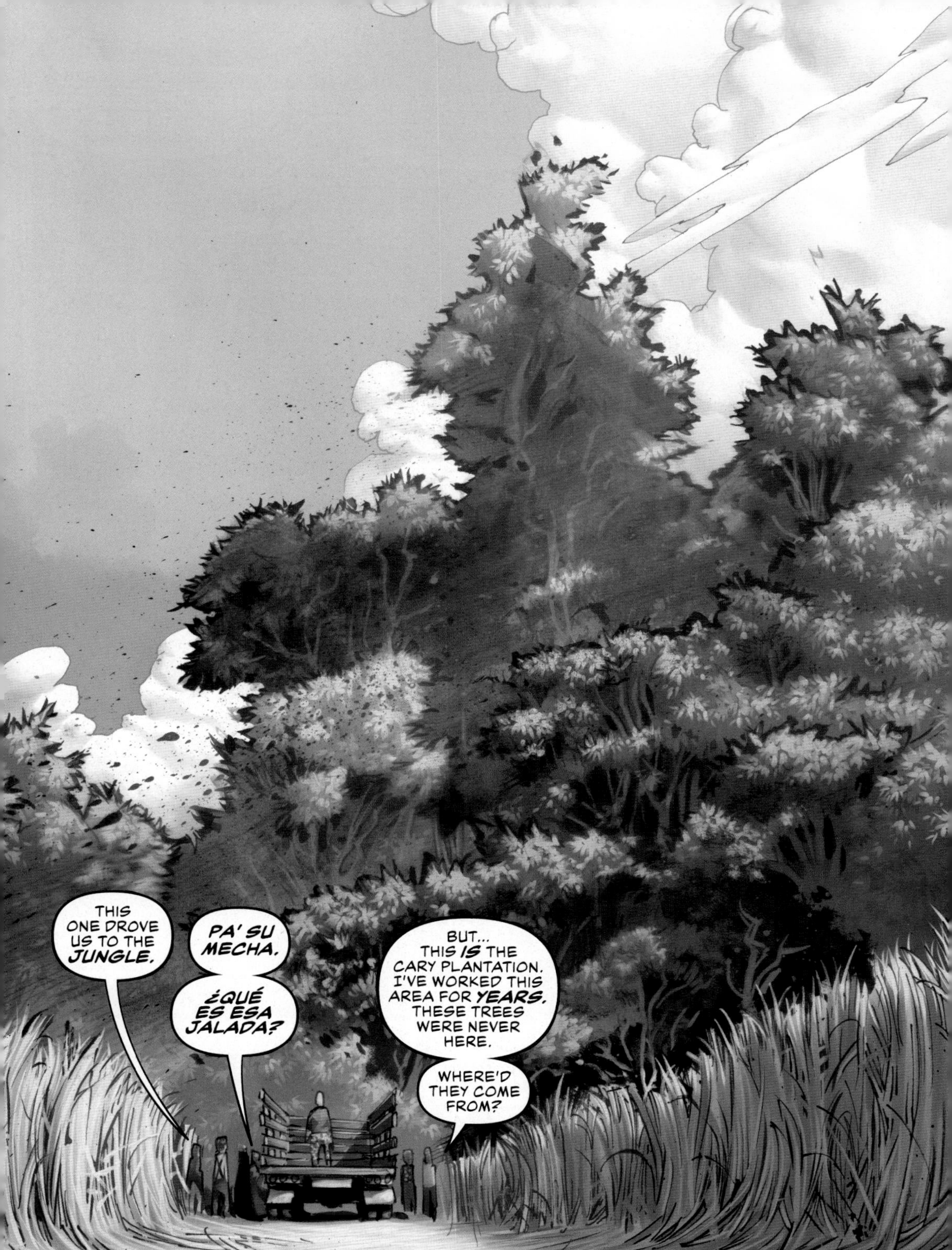
THIS ONE DROVE US TO THE JUNGLE.
PA' SU MECHA.
¿QUÉ ES ESA JALADA?
BUT... THIS IS THE CARY PLANTATION. I'VE WORKED THIS AREA FOR YEARS. THESE TREES WERE NEVER HERE.
WHERE'D THEY COME FROM?

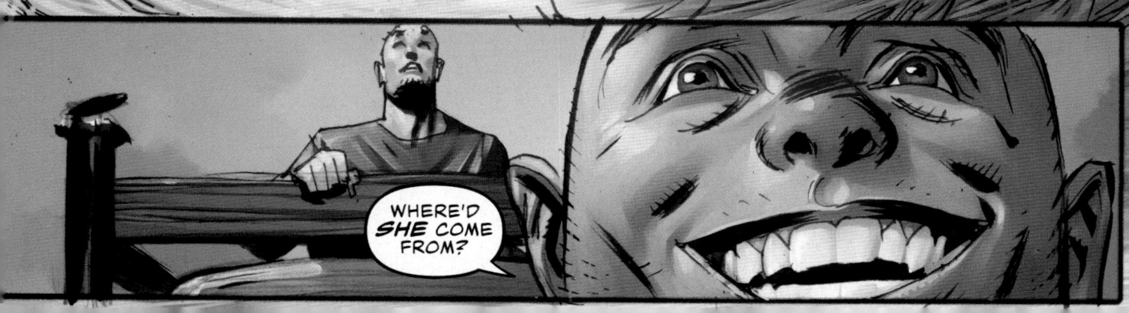
WHERE'D SHE COME FROM?

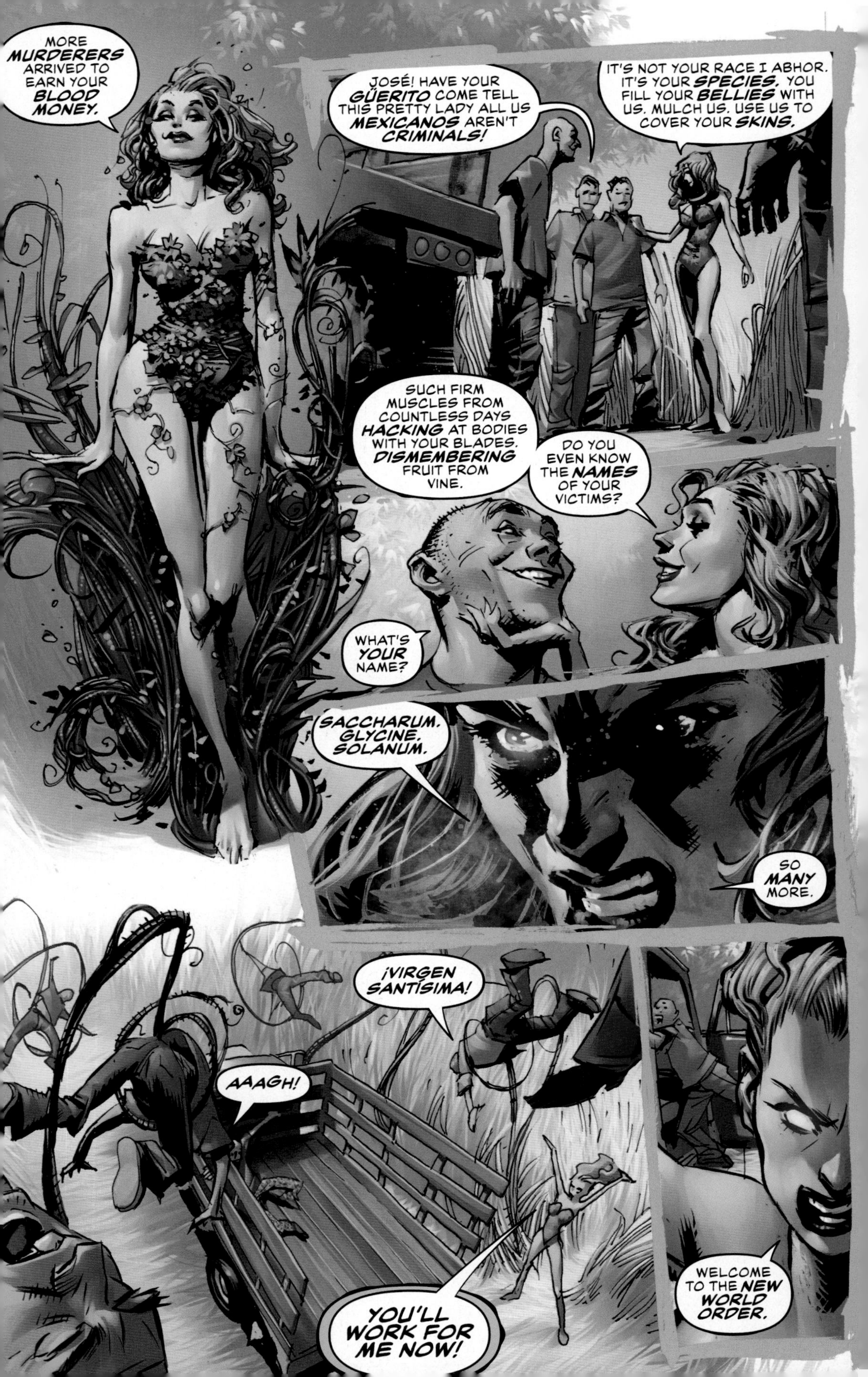

MORE MURDERERS ARRIVED TO EARN YOUR BLOOD MONEY.
JOSÉ! HAVE YOUR GÜERITO COME TELL THIS PRETTY LADY ALL US MEXICANOS AREN'T CRIMINALS!
IT'S NOT YOUR RACE I ABHOR. IT'S YOUR SPECIES. YOU FILL YOUR BELLIES WITH US. MULCH US. USE US TO COVER YOUR SKINS.
SUCH FIRM MUSCLES FROM COUNTLESS DAYS HACKING AT BODIES WITH YOUR BLADES. DISMEMBERING FRUIT FROM VINE.
DO YOU EVEN KNOW THE NAMES OF YOUR VICTIMS?
WHAT'S YOUR NAME?
SACCHARUM. GLYCINE. SOLANUM.
SO MANY MORE.
¡VIRGEN SANTÍSIMA!
AAAGH!
YOU'LL WORK FOR ME NOW!
WELCOME TO THE NEW WORLD ORDER.

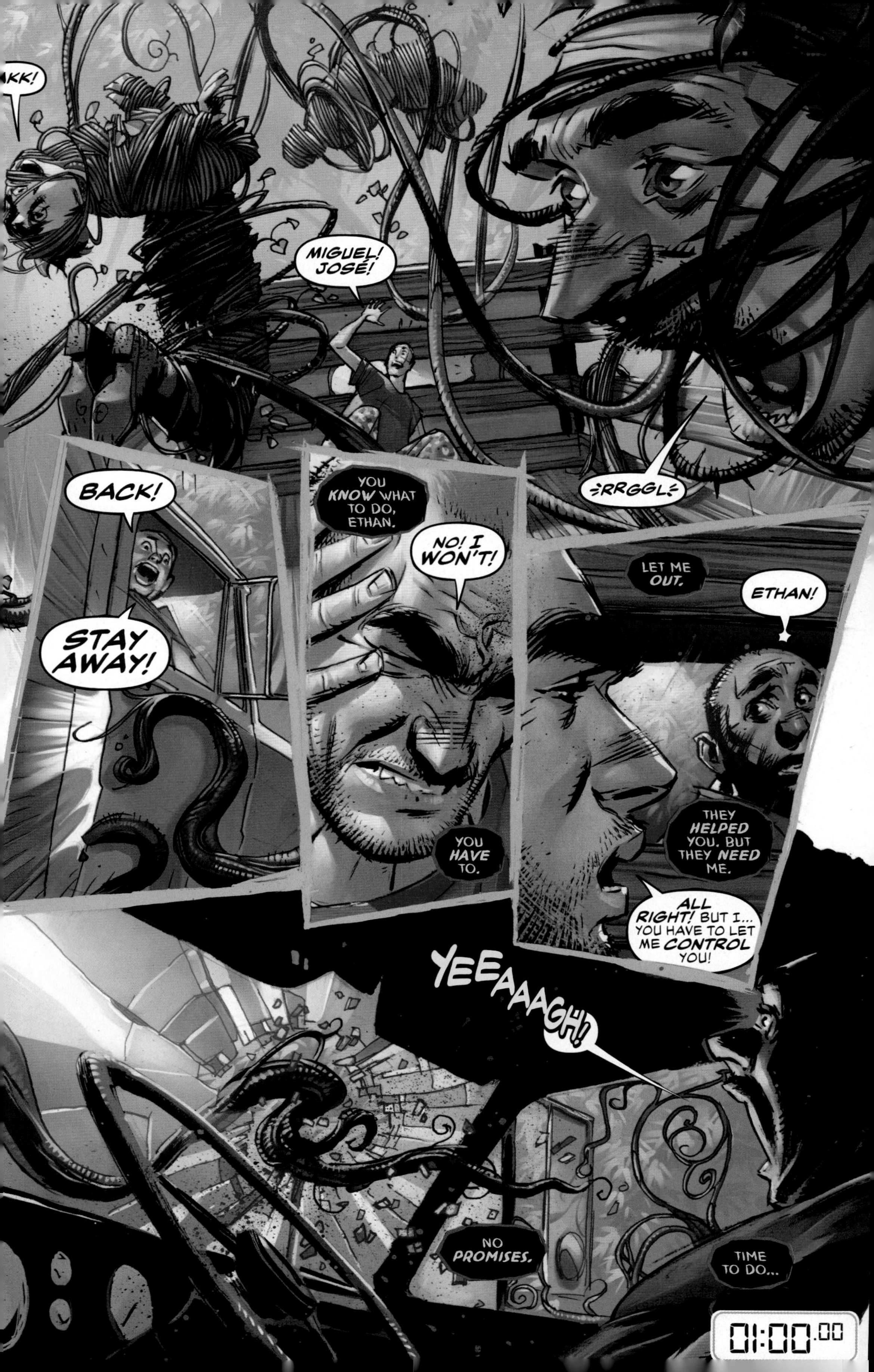
AKK!
MIGUEL! JOSÉ!
RRGGL
BACK!
STAY AWAY!
YOU KNOW WHAT TO DO, ETHAN.
NO! I WON'T!
YOU HAVE TO.
LET ME OUT.
ETHAN!
THEY HELPED YOU. BUT THEY NEED ME.
ALL RIGHT! BUT I... YOU HAVE TO LET ME CONTROL YOU!
YEEAAAAGH!
NO PROMISES.
TIME TO DO...
01:00.00

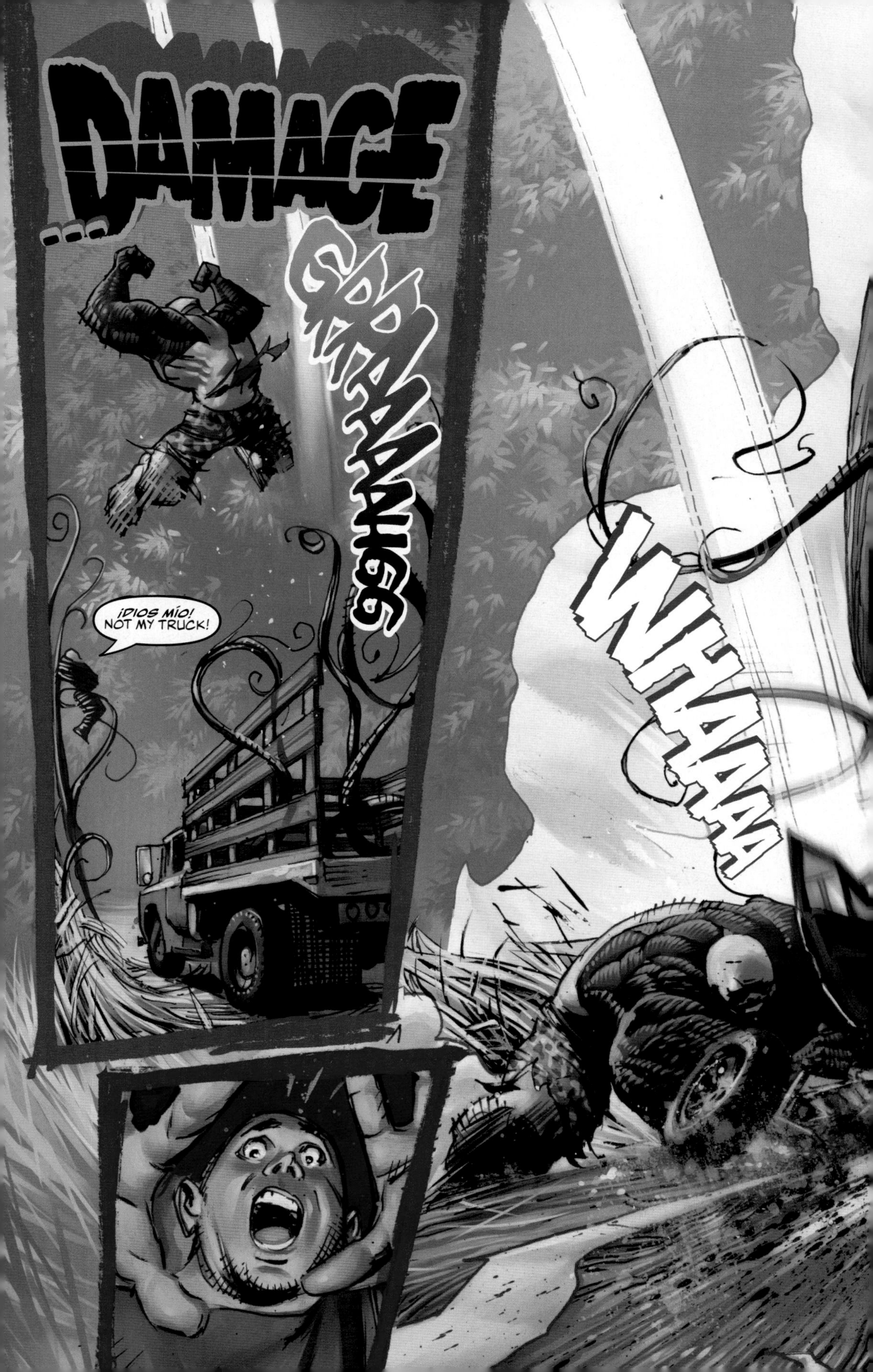
DAMAGE...
GRRAAAAHHGG
¡DIOS MÍO! NOT MY TRUCK!
WHAAAA

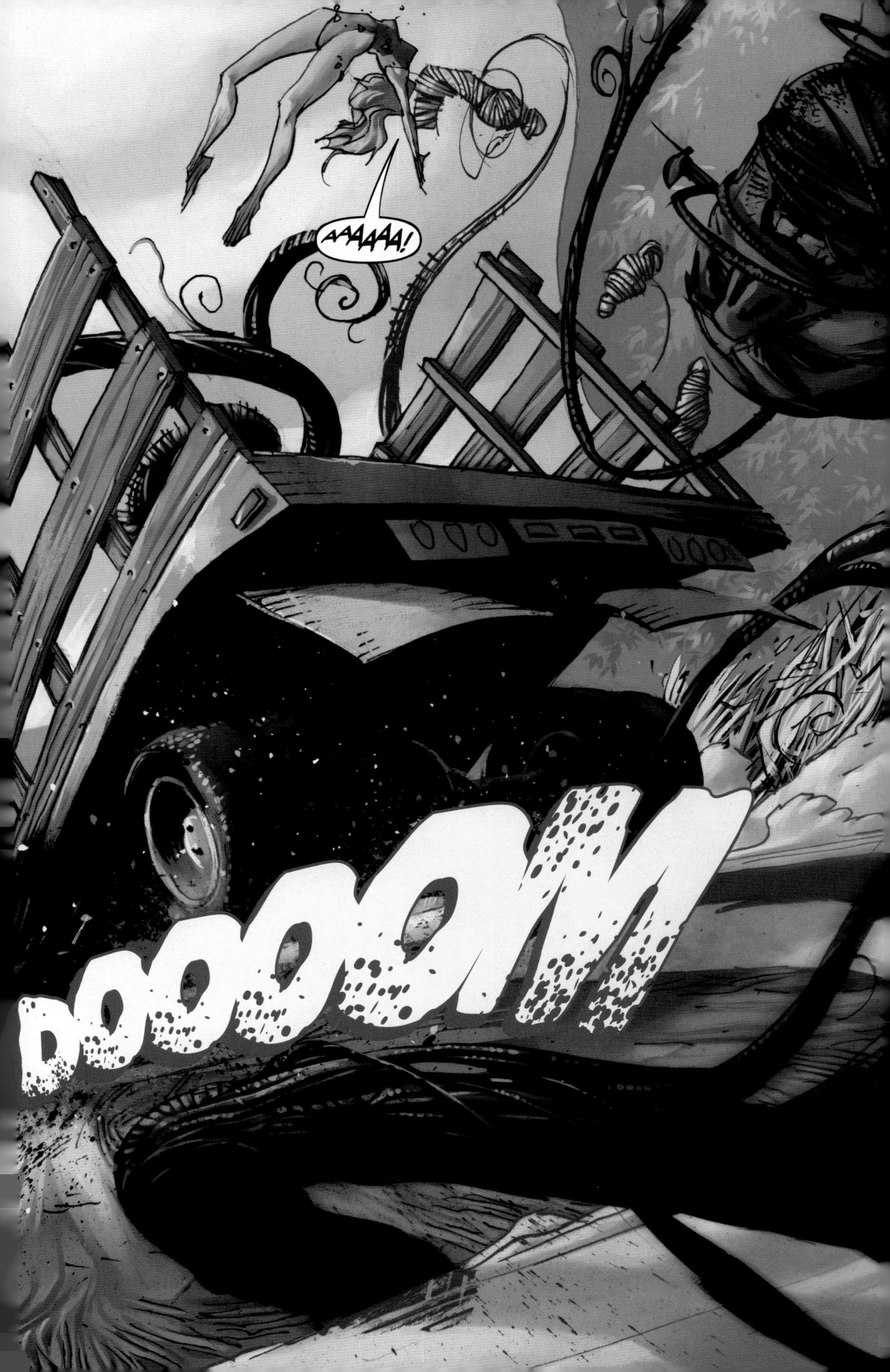
AAAAAA!
DOOOOM

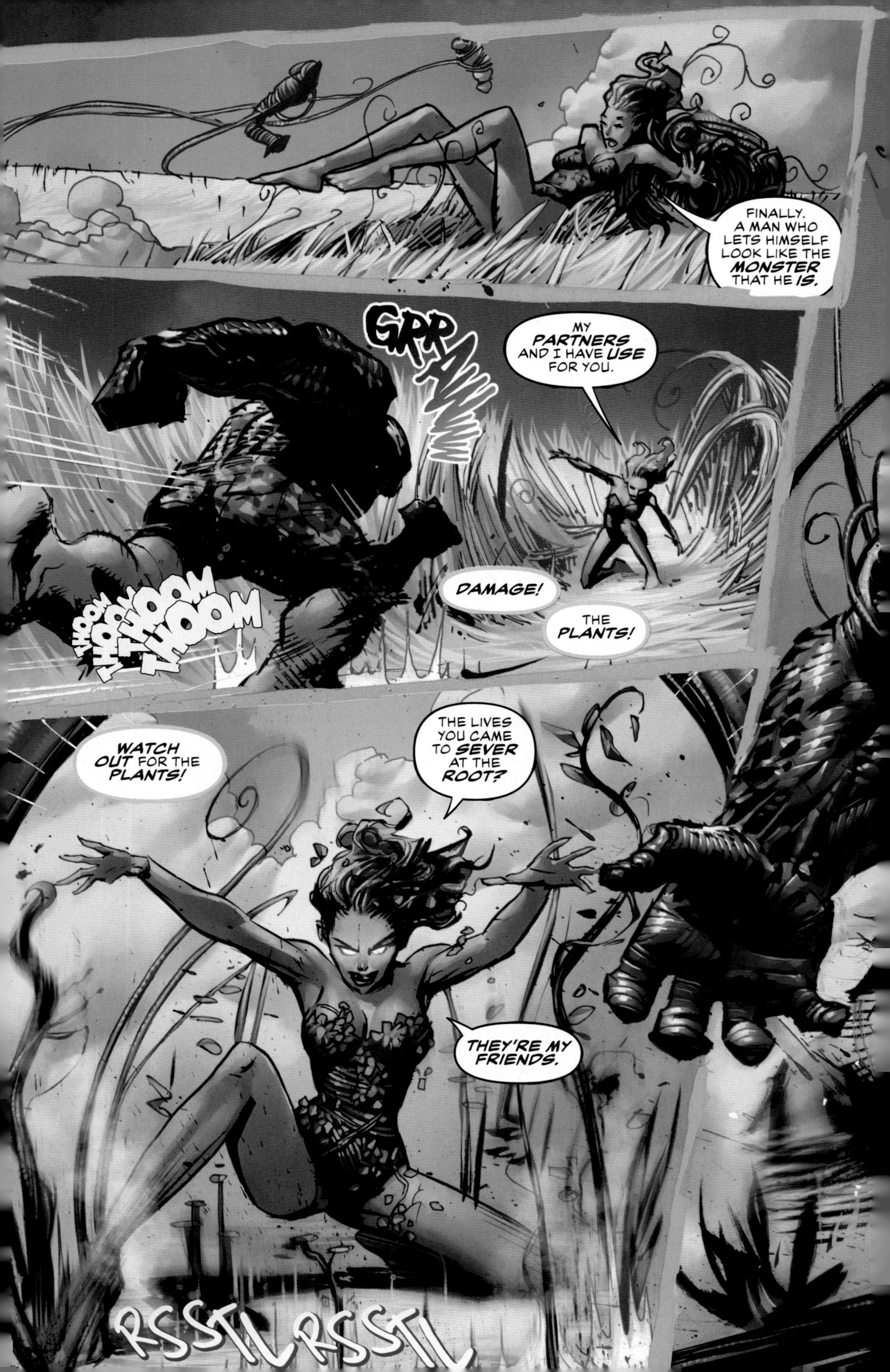
FINALLY. A MAN WHO LETS HIMSELF LOOK LIKE THE MONSTER THAT HE IS.
GRRAWWW
MY PARTNERS AND I HAVE USE FOR YOU.
THOOM THOOM THOOM THOOM
DAMAGE!
THE PLANTS!
WATCH OUT FOR THE PLANTS!
THE LIVES YOU CAME TO SEVER AT THE ROOT?
THEY'RE MY FRIENDS.
RSSTL RSSTL

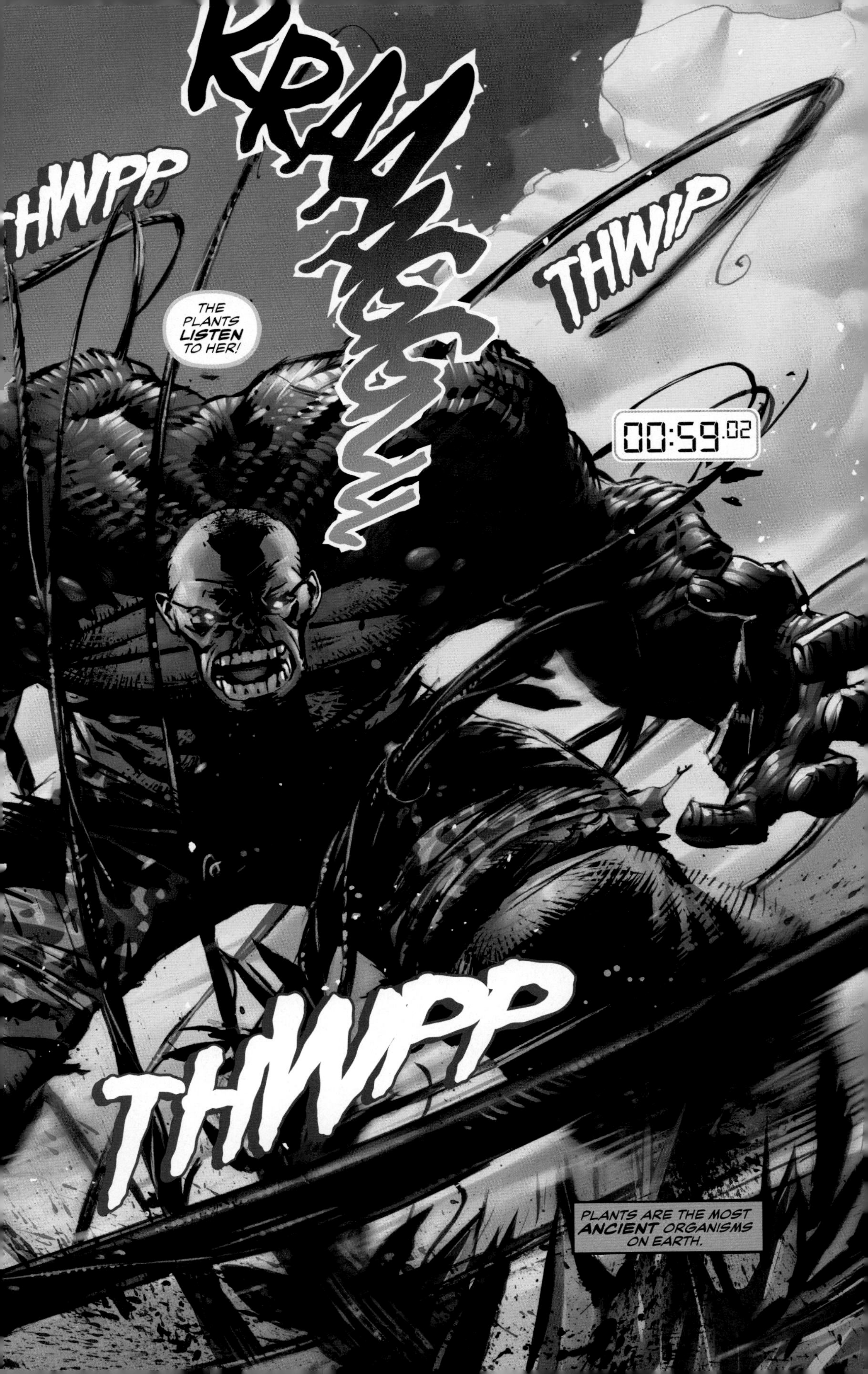
KRAAKOOM
THWPP
THE PLANTS LISTEN TO HER!
THWIP
00:59.02
THWPP
PLANTS ARE THE MOST ANCIENT ORGANISMS ON EARTH.

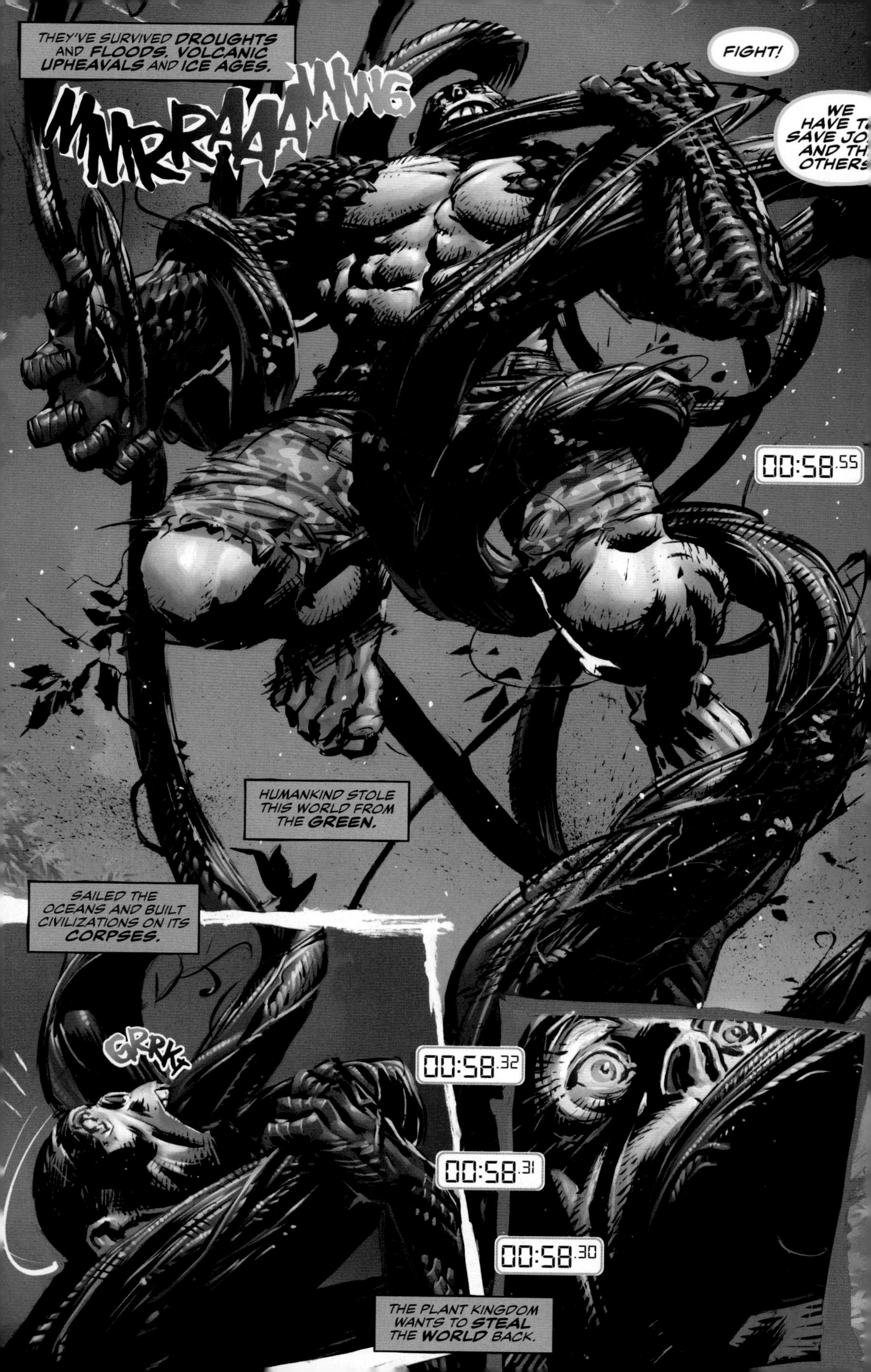
THEY'VE SURVIVED DROUGHTS AND FLOODS, VOLCANIC UPHEAVALS AND ICE AGES.
MMRRAAAAWWG
FIGHT!
WE HAVE TO SAVE JO... AND THE OTHERS
00:58.55
HUMANKIND STOLE THIS WORLD FROM THE GREEN.
SAILED THE OCEANS AND BUILT CIVILIZATIONS ON ITS CORPSES.
GRRK
00:58.32
00:58.31
00:58.30
THE PLANT KINGDOM WANTS TO STEAL THE WORLD BACK.

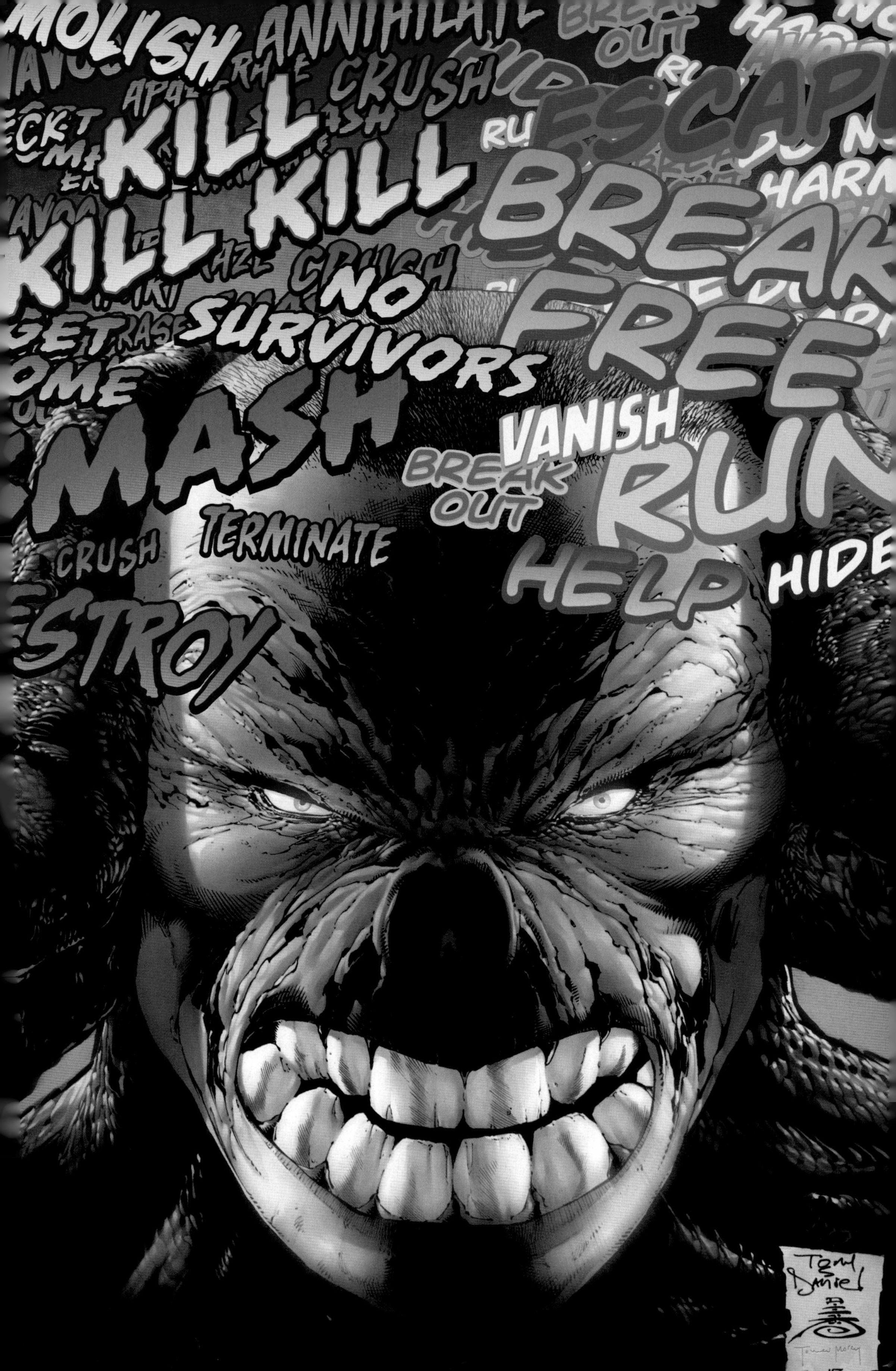
MOLISH
ANNIHILATE
KILL
KILL
KILL
CRUSH
ESCAP
BREAK
NO SURVIVORS
FREE
MASH
VANISH
BREAK OUT
RUN
CRUSH
TERMINATE
HELP
HIDE
STROY
Tony Daniel

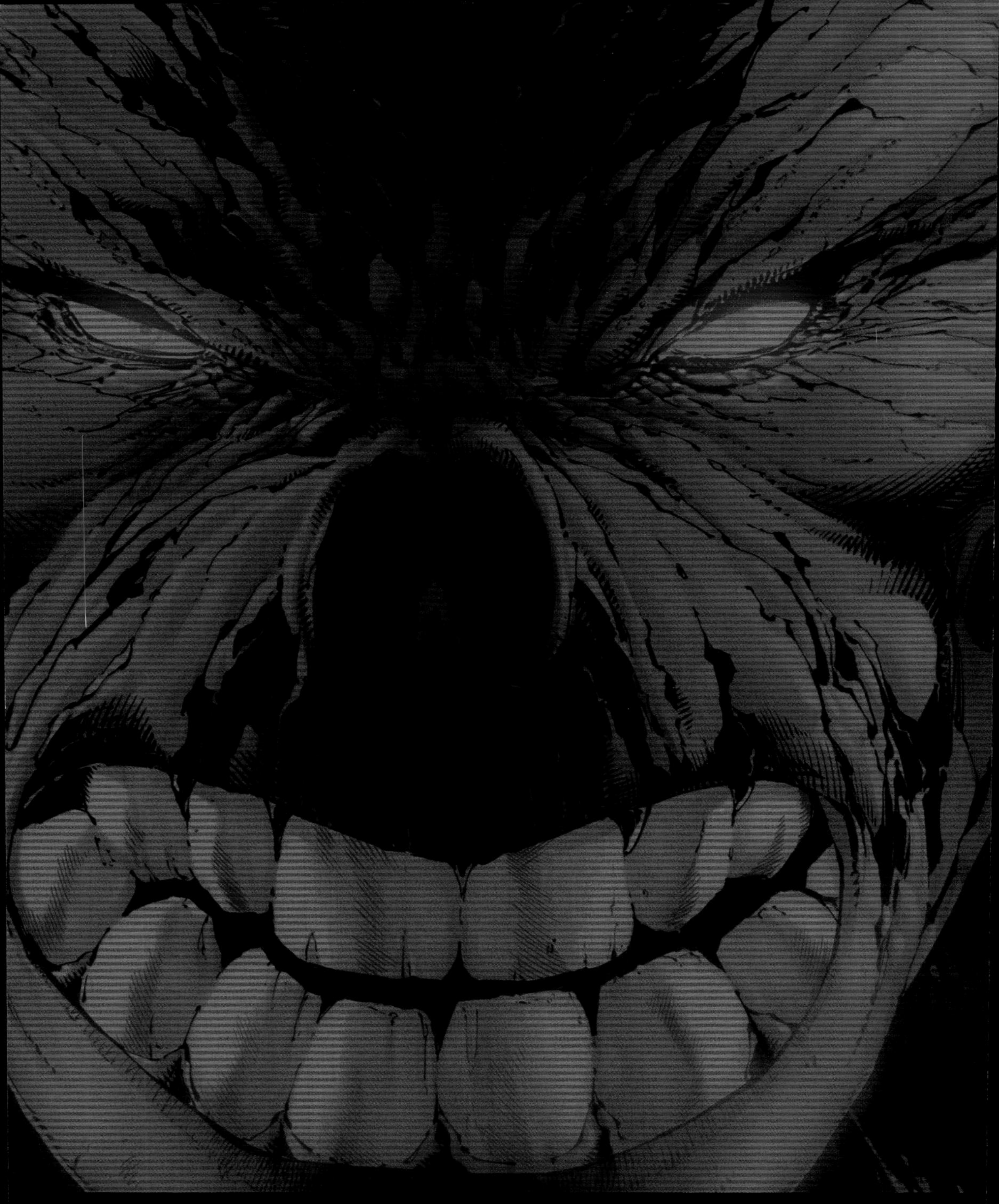

DAMAGE
#5

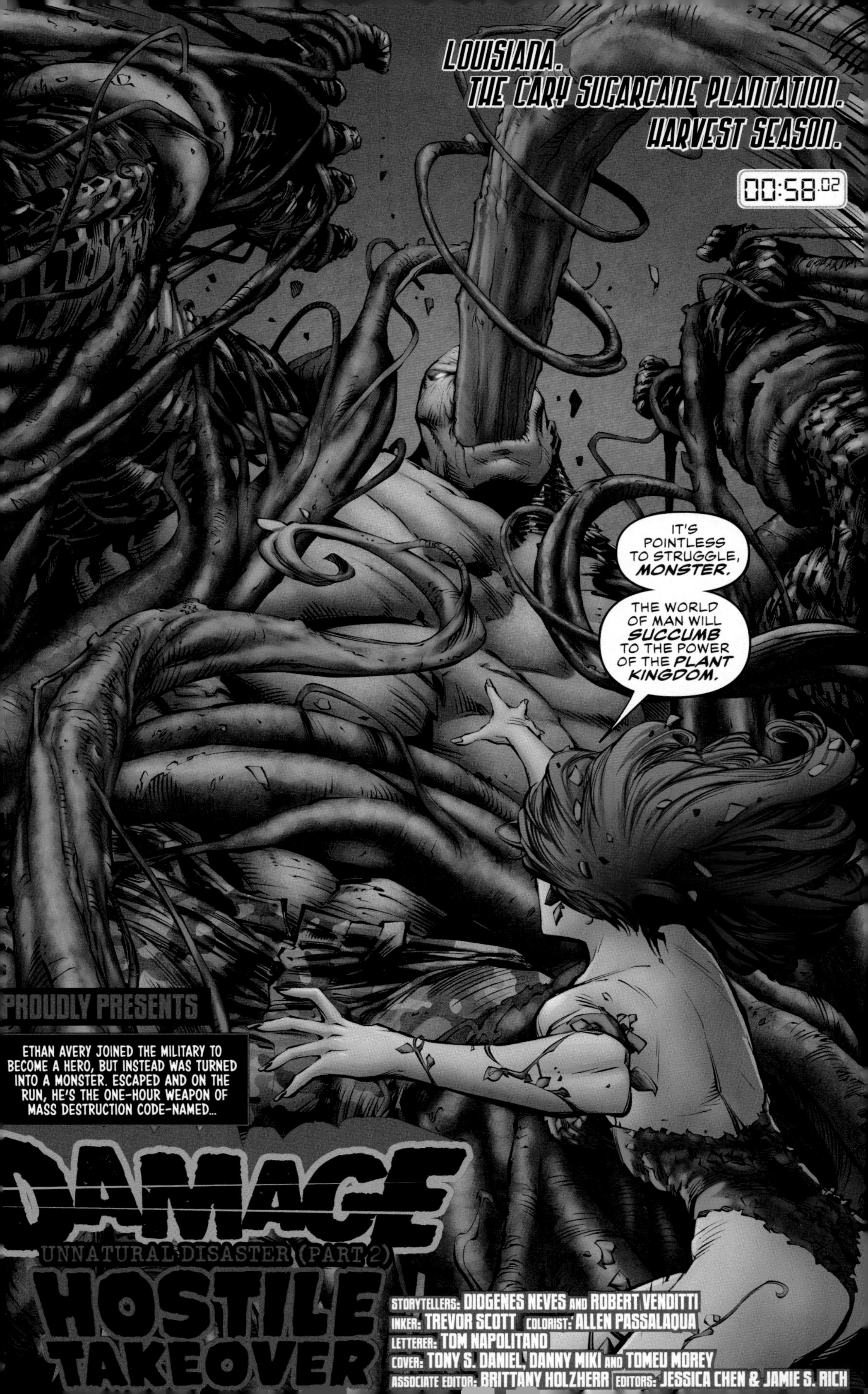
LOUISIANA.
THE CARY SUGARCANE PLANTATION.
HARVEST SEASON.
00:58.02
IT'S POINTLESS TO STRUGGLE, MONSTER.
THE WORLD OF MAN WILL SUCCUMB TO THE POWER OF THE PLANT KINGDOM.
PROUDLY PRESENTS
ETHAN AVERY JOINED THE MILITARY TO BECOME A HERO, BUT INSTEAD WAS TURNED INTO A MONSTER. ESCAPED AND ON THE RUN, HE'S THE ONE-HOUR WEAPON OF MASS DESTRUCTION CODE-NAMED...
DAMAGE
UNNATURAL DISASTER (PART 2)
HOSTILE TAKEOVER
STORYTELLERS: DIOGENES NEVES AND ROBERT VENDITTI
INKER: TREVOR SCOTT COLORIST: ALLEN PASSALAQUA
LETTERER: TOM NAPOLITANO
COVER: TONY S. DANIEL, DANNY MIKI AND TOMEU MOREY
ASSOCIATE EDITOR: BRITTANY HOLZHERR EDITORS: JESSICA CHEN & JAMIE S. RICH

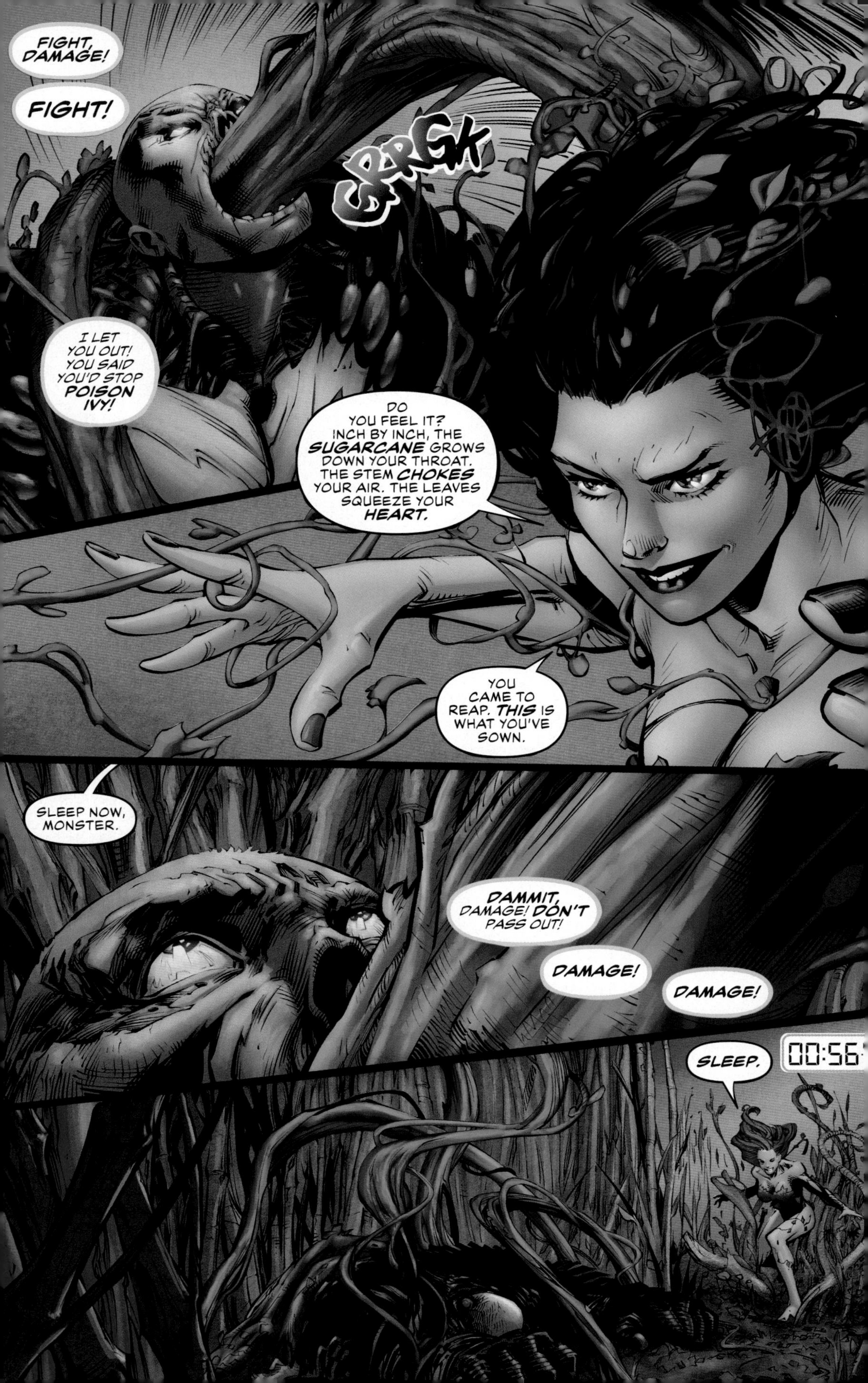
FIGHT, DAMAGE!
FIGHT!
GRRGK
I LET YOU OUT! YOU SAID YOU'D STOP POISON IVY!
DO YOU FEEL IT? INCH BY INCH, THE SUGARCANE GROWS DOWN YOUR THROAT. THE STEM CHOKES YOUR AIR. THE LEAVES SQUEEZE YOUR HEART.
YOU CAME TO REAP. THIS IS WHAT YOU'VE SOWN.
SLEEP NOW, MONSTER.
DAMMIT, DAMAGE! DON'T PASS OUT!
DAMAGE!
DAMAGE!
00:56
SLEEP.

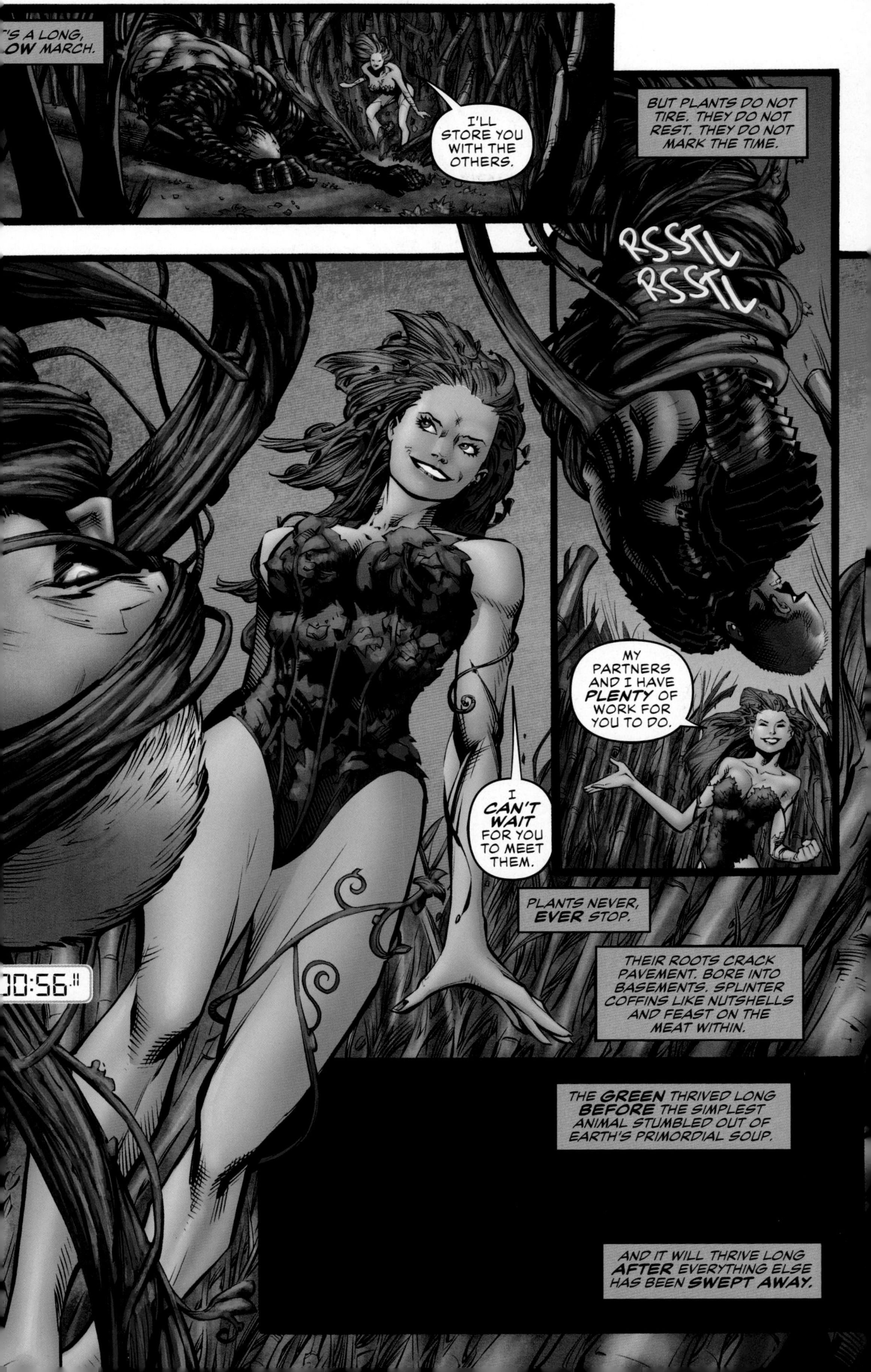
'S A LONG,
OW MARCH.
I'LL STORE YOU WITH THE OTHERS.
BUT PLANTS DO NOT TIRE. THEY DO NOT REST. THEY DO NOT MARK THE TIME.
RSSTL RSSTL
MY PARTNERS AND I HAVE PLENTY OF WORK FOR YOU TO DO.
I CAN'T WAIT FOR YOU TO MEET THEM.
PLANTS NEVER, EVER STOP.
00:56"
THEIR ROOTS CRACK PAVEMENT. BORE INTO BASEMENTS. SPLINTER COFFINS LIKE NUTSHELLS AND FEAST ON THE MEAT WITHIN.
THE GREEN THRIVED LONG BEFORE THE SIMPLEST ANIMAL STUMBLED OUT OF EARTH'S PRIMORDIAL SOUP.
AND IT WILL THRIVE LONG AFTER EVERYTHING ELSE HAS BEEN SWEPT AWAY.

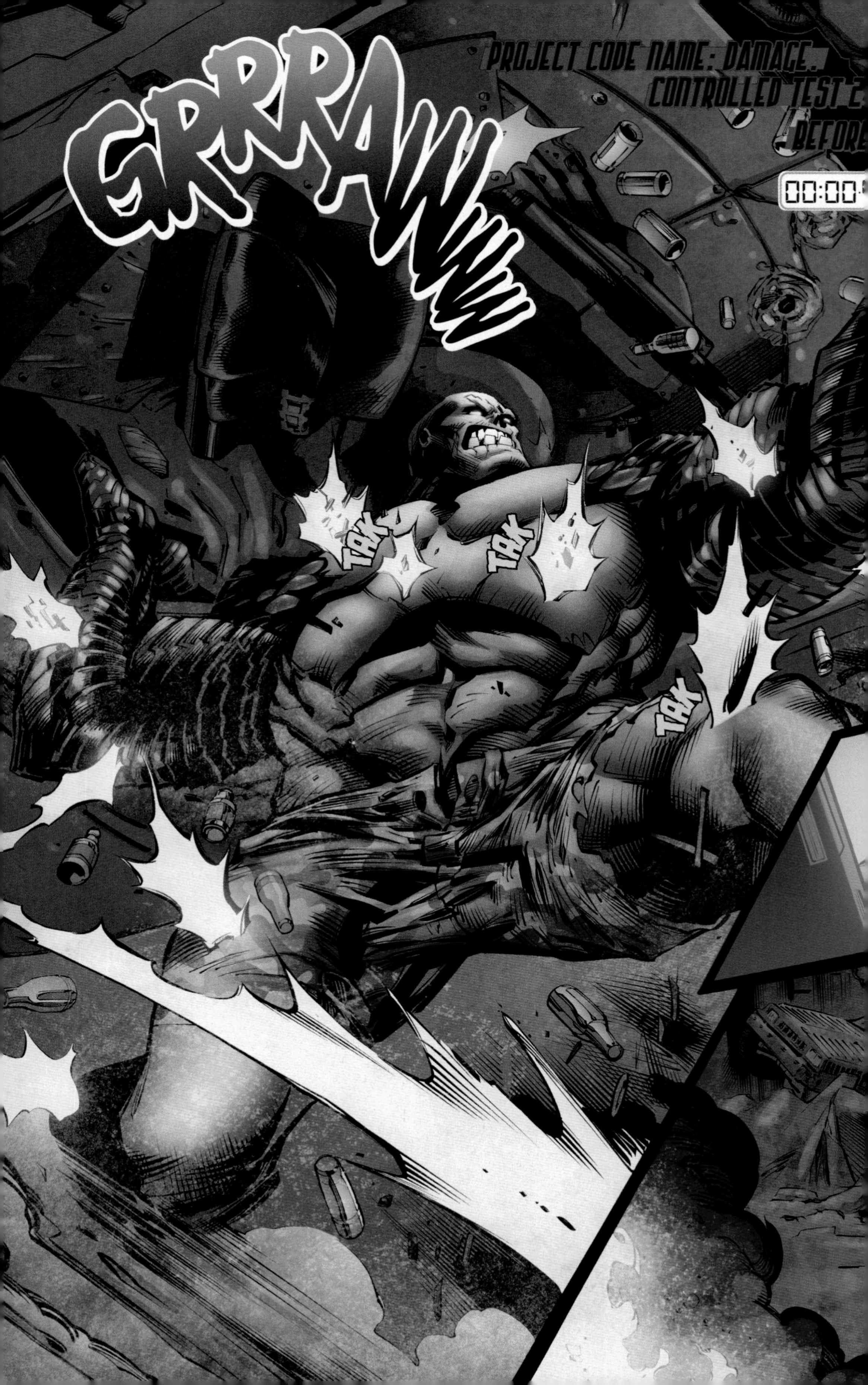
PROJECT CODE NAME: DAMAGE.
CONTROLLED TEST 2
BEFORE
GRRRAWWW
TAK
TAK
TAK

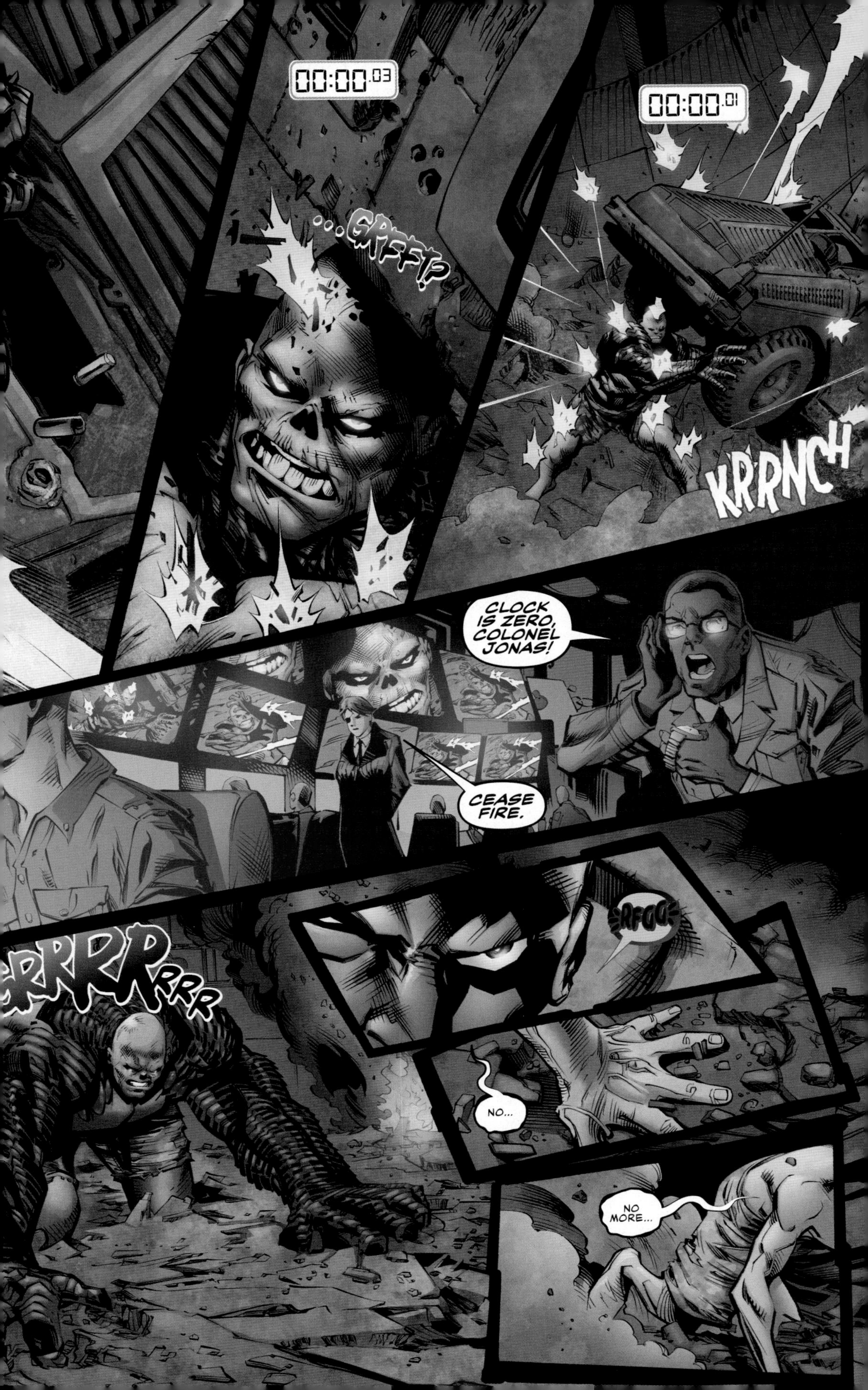
00:00.03
...GRFFT!?
00:00.01
KRRNCH
CLOCK IS ZERO, COLONEL JONAS!
CEASE FIRE.
RRRRrrr
RFGG
NO...
NO MORE...

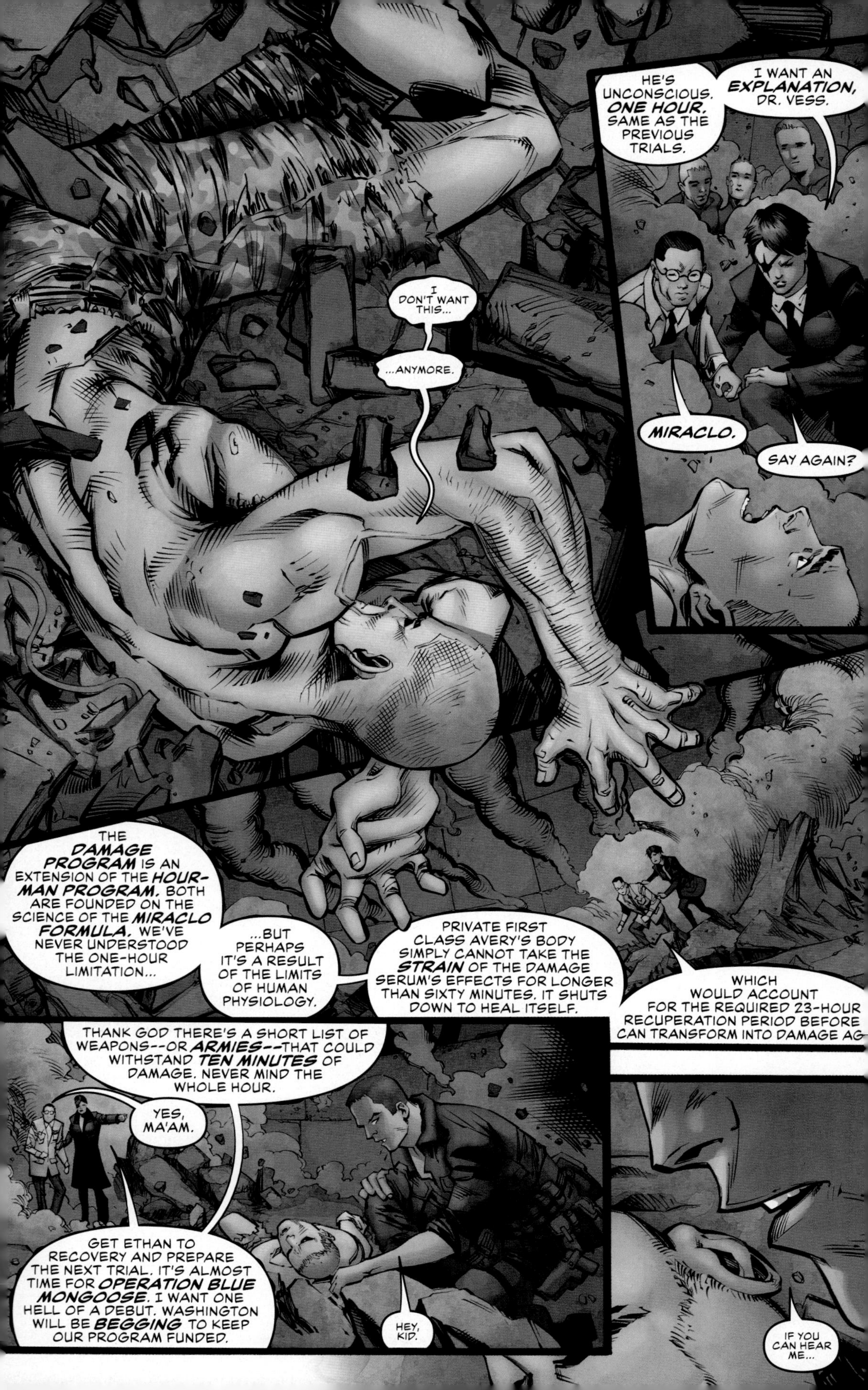
I DON'T WANT THIS...
...ANYMORE.
HE'S UNCONSCIOUS. ONE HOUR. SAME AS THE PREVIOUS TRIALS.
I WANT AN EXPLANATION, DR. VESS.
MIRACLO.
SAY AGAIN?
THE DAMAGE PROGRAM IS AN EXTENSION OF THE HOURMAN PROGRAM. BOTH ARE FOUNDED ON THE SCIENCE OF THE MIRACLO FORMULA. WE'VE NEVER UNDERSTOOD THE ONE-HOUR LIMITATION...
...BUT PERHAPS IT'S A RESULT OF THE LIMITS OF HUMAN PHYSIOLOGY.
PRIVATE FIRST CLASS AVERY'S BODY SIMPLY CANNOT TAKE THE STRAIN OF THE DAMAGE SERUM'S EFFECTS FOR LONGER THAN SIXTY MINUTES. IT SHUTS DOWN TO HEAL ITSELF.
WHICH WOULD ACCOUNT FOR THE REQUIRED 23-HOUR RECUPERATION PERIOD BEFORE CAN TRANSFORM INTO DAMAGE AG
THANK GOD THERE'S A SHORT LIST OF WEAPONS--OR ARMIES--THAT COULD WITHSTAND TEN MINUTES OF DAMAGE. NEVER MIND THE WHOLE HOUR.
YES, MA'AM.
GET ETHAN TO RECOVERY AND PREPARE THE NEXT TRIAL. IT'S ALMOST TIME FOR OPERATION BLUE MONGOOSE. I WANT ONE HELL OF A DEBUT. WASHINGTON WILL BE BEGGING TO KEEP OUR PROGRAM FUNDED.
HEY, KID.
IF YOU CAN HEAR ME...

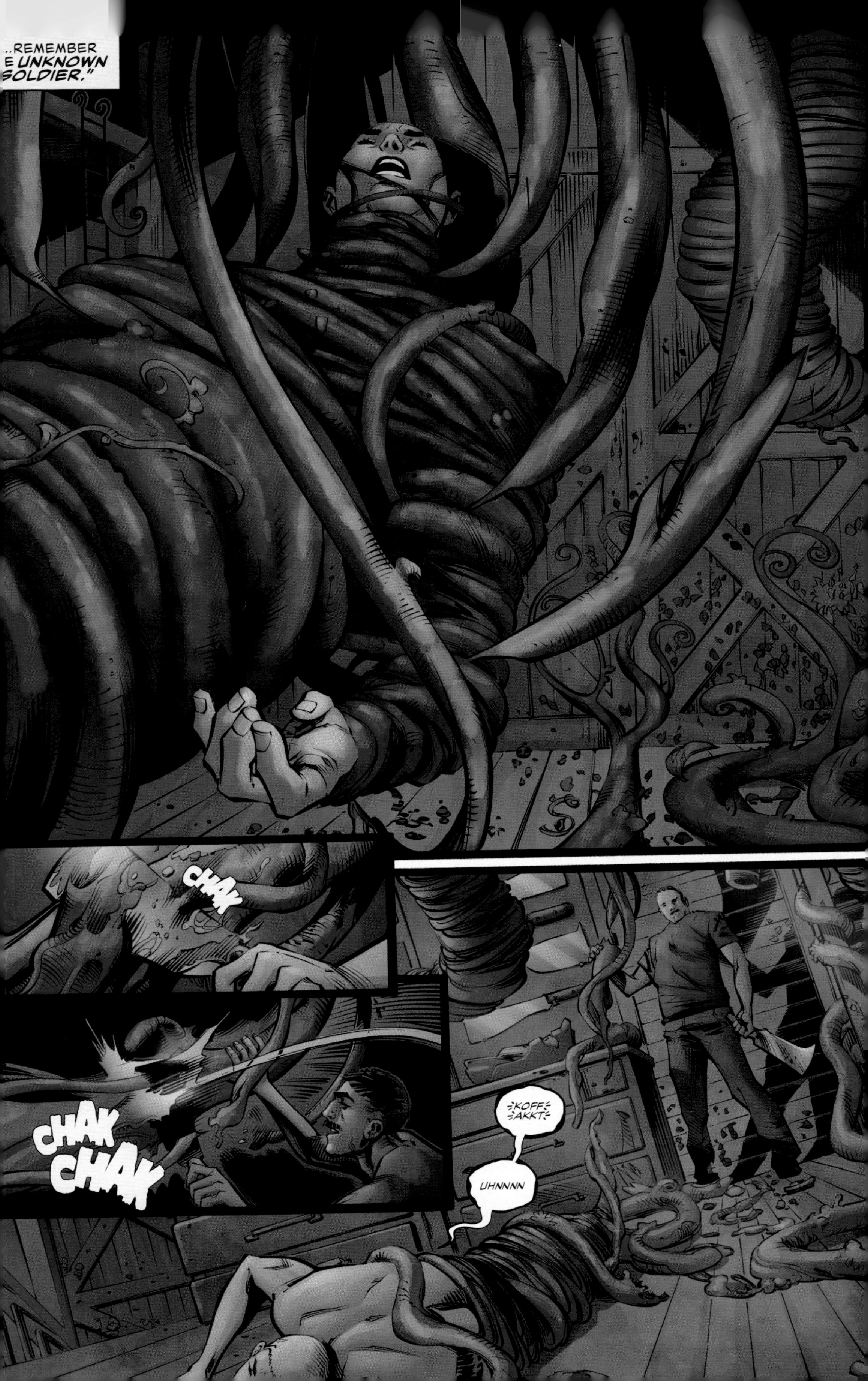
..REMEMBER E UNKNOWN SOLDIER."
CHAK
CHAK CHAK
KOFF AKKT
UHNNNN

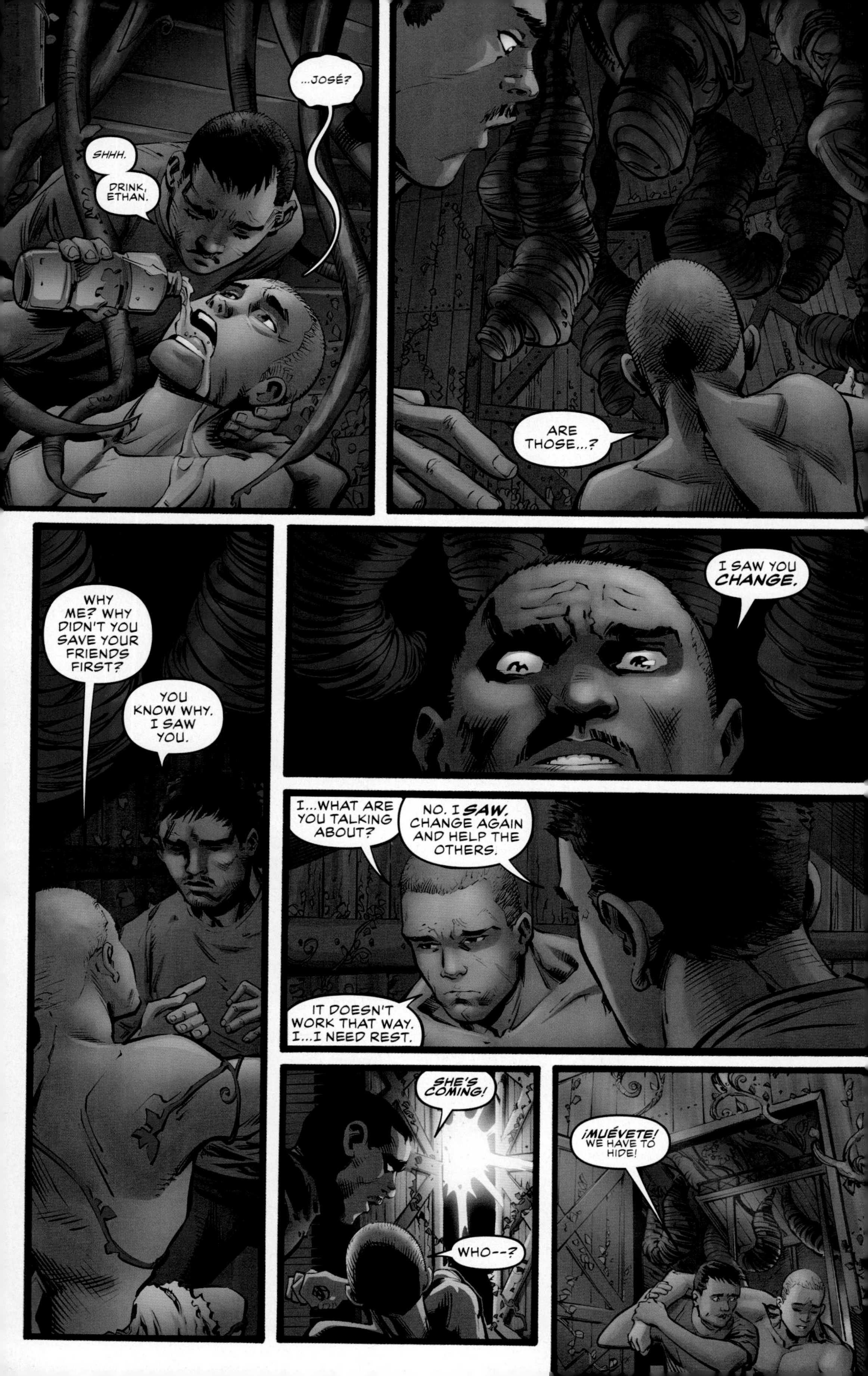
...JOSÉ?
SHHH.
DRINK, ETHAN.
ARE THOSE...?
WHY ME? WHY DIDN'T YOU SAVE YOUR FRIENDS FIRST?
YOU KNOW WHY. I SAW YOU.
I SAW YOU CHANGE.
I...WHAT ARE YOU TALKING ABOUT?
NO. I SAW. CHANGE AGAIN AND HELP THE OTHERS.
IT DOESN'T WORK THAT WAY. I...I NEED REST.
SHE'S COMING!
WHO--?
¡MUÉVETE! WE HAVE TO HIDE!

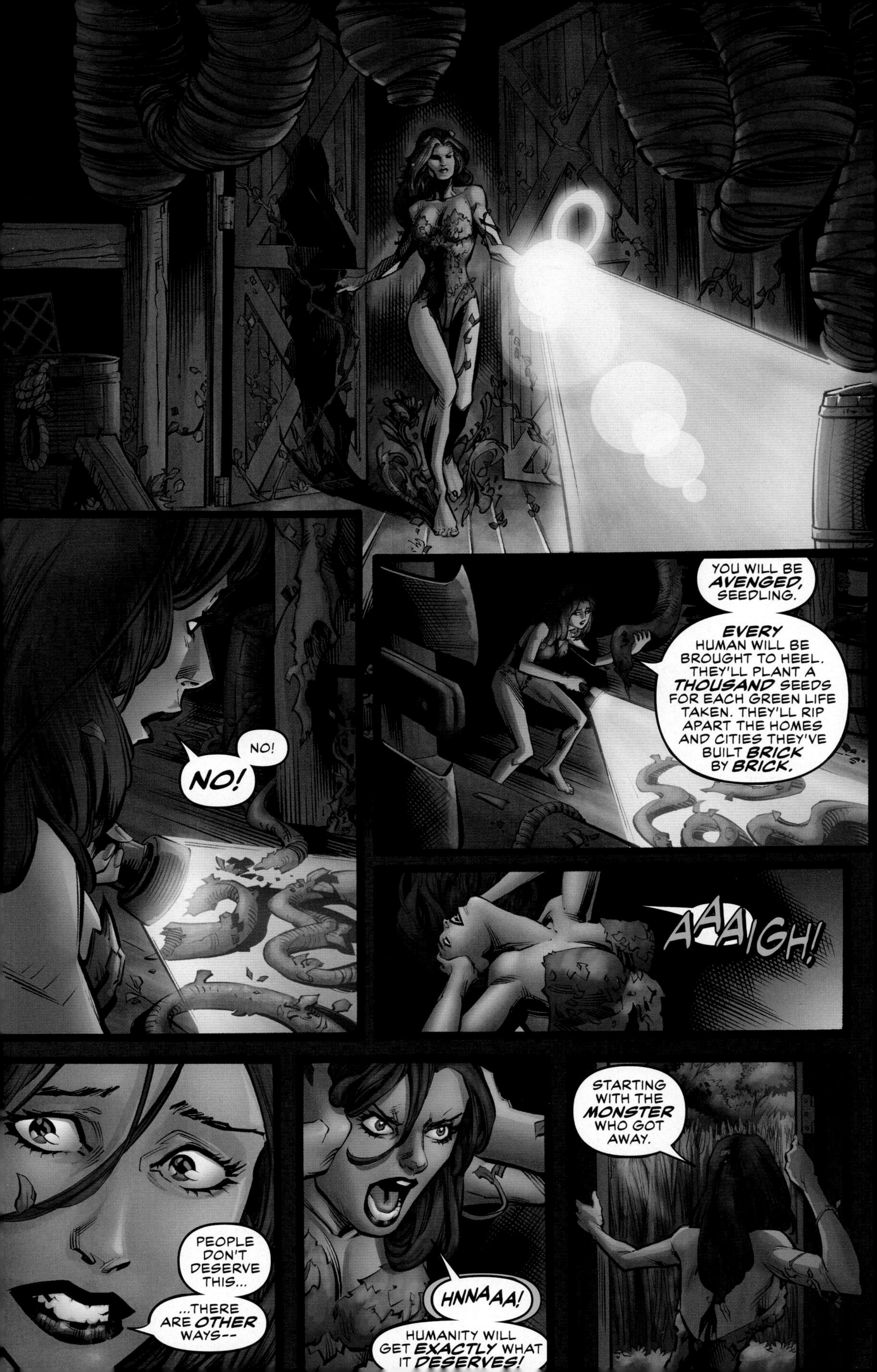
NO!
NO!
YOU WILL BE AVENGED, SEEDLING.
EVERY HUMAN WILL BE BROUGHT TO HEEL. THEY'LL PLANT A THOUSAND SEEDS FOR EACH GREEN LIFE TAKEN. THEY'LL RIP APART THE HOMES AND CITIES THEY'VE BUILT BRICK BY BRICK.
AAAIGH!
PEOPLE DON'T DESERVE THIS...
...THERE ARE OTHER WAYS--
HNNAAA!
HUMANITY WILL GET EXACTLY WHAT IT DESERVES!
STARTING WITH THE MONSTER WHO GOT AWAY.

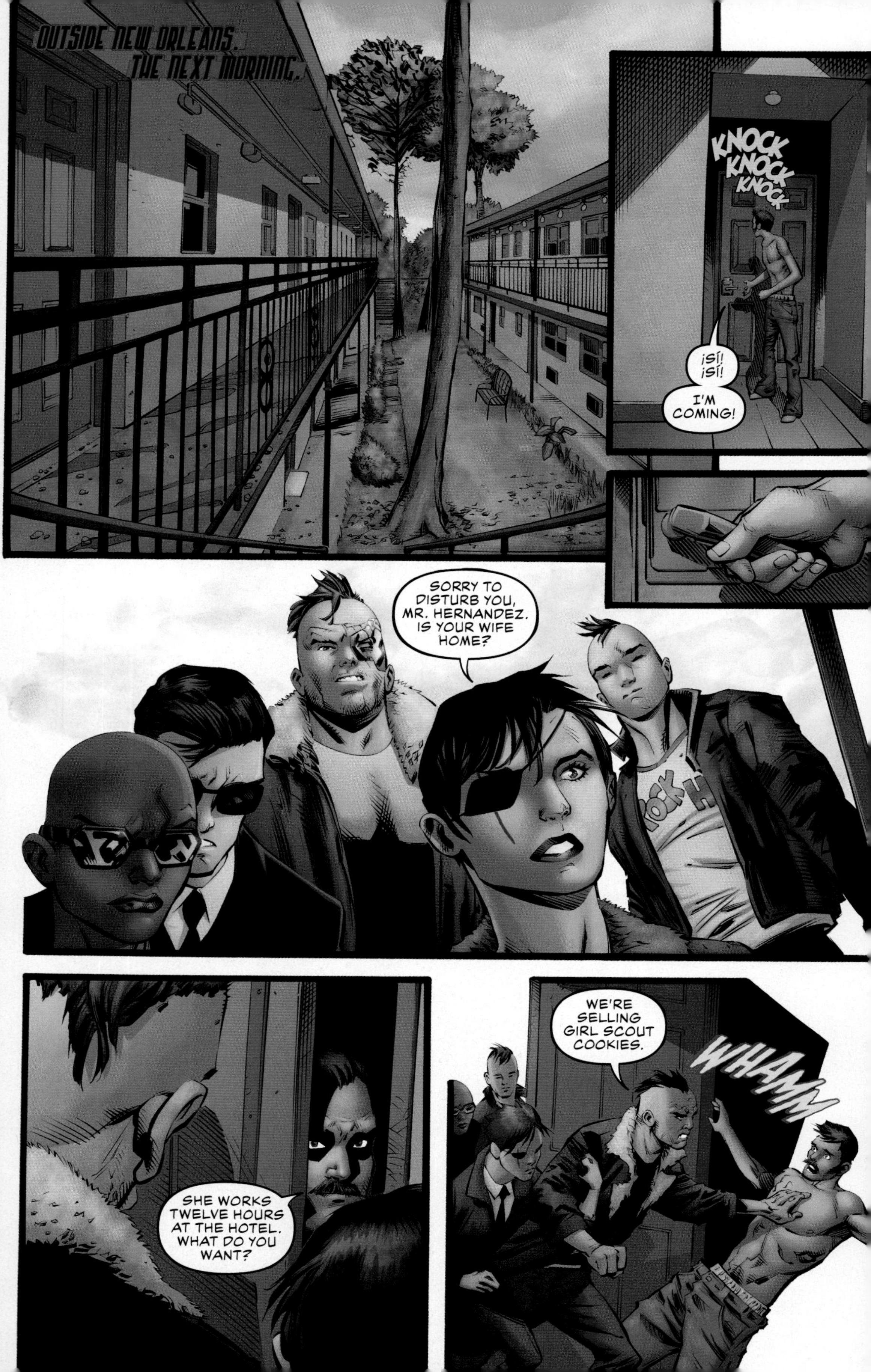
OUTSIDE NEW ORLEANS.
THE NEXT MORNING.
KNOCK
KNOCK
KNOCK
¡SÍ! ¡SÍ!
I'M COMING!
SORRY TO DISTURB YOU, MR. HERNANDEZ. IS YOUR WIFE HOME?
SHE WORKS TWELVE HOURS AT THE HOTEL. WHAT DO YOU WANT?
WE'RE SELLING GIRL SCOUT COOKIES.
WHAMM

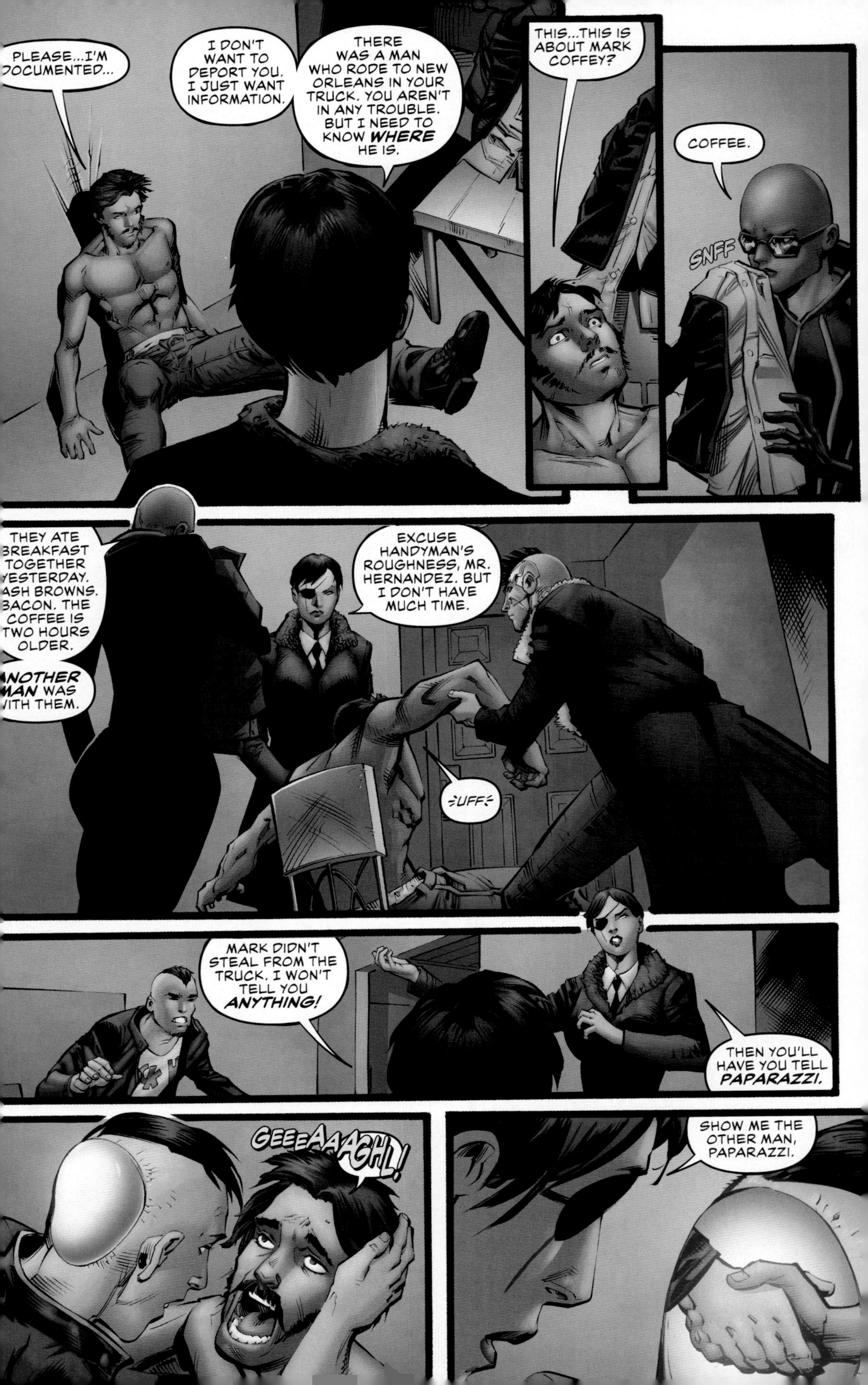
PLEASE...I'M OCUMENTED...
I DON'T WANT TO DEPORT YOU. I JUST WANT INFORMATION.
THERE WAS A MAN WHO RODE TO NEW ORLEANS IN YOUR TRUCK. YOU AREN'T IN ANY TROUBLE. BUT I NEED TO KNOW WHERE HE IS.
THIS...THIS IS ABOUT MARK COFFEY?
COFFEE.
SNFF
THEY ATE REAKFAST TOGETHER ESTERDAY. ASH BROWNS. ACON. THE COFFEE IS TWO HOURS OLDER.
NOTHER MAN WAS ITH THEM.
EXCUSE HANDYMAN'S ROUGHNESS, MR. HERNANDEZ. BUT I DON'T HAVE MUCH TIME.
UFF
MARK DIDN'T STEAL FROM THE TRUCK. I WON'T TELL YOU ANYTHING!
THEN YOU'LL HAVE YOU TELL PAPARAZZI.
GEEEAAAGHL!
SHOW ME THE OTHER MAN, PAPARAZZI.

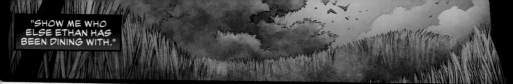

"SHOW ME WHO ELSE ETHAN HAS BEEN DINING WITH."

HOW LONG WAS I ASLEEP?

IT'S ALMOST NOON.

EAT. THE SUGAR WILL GIVE YOU ENERGY.

WHERE ARE WE?

STILL AT THE PLANTATION. BUT A PLACE THE PLANTS CAN'T SEE US. I DON'T TRUST THEM. THE WOMAN...I THINK THE PLANTS TALK TO HER.

LIKE THE JUNGLE OUTSIDE. HOW CAN THERE BE JUNGLE HERE? HOW DOES IT GROW SO FAST?

THAT...BIG MAN INSIDE YOU.

ON THE NEWS, THEY CALLED IT A MONSTER. THEY SAID IT ATTACKED ATLANTA.

BUT YOU ONLY CHANGED BECAUSE THE WOMAN ATTACKED US.

I THINK SOMEONE ATTACKED YOU IN ATLANTA, TOO.

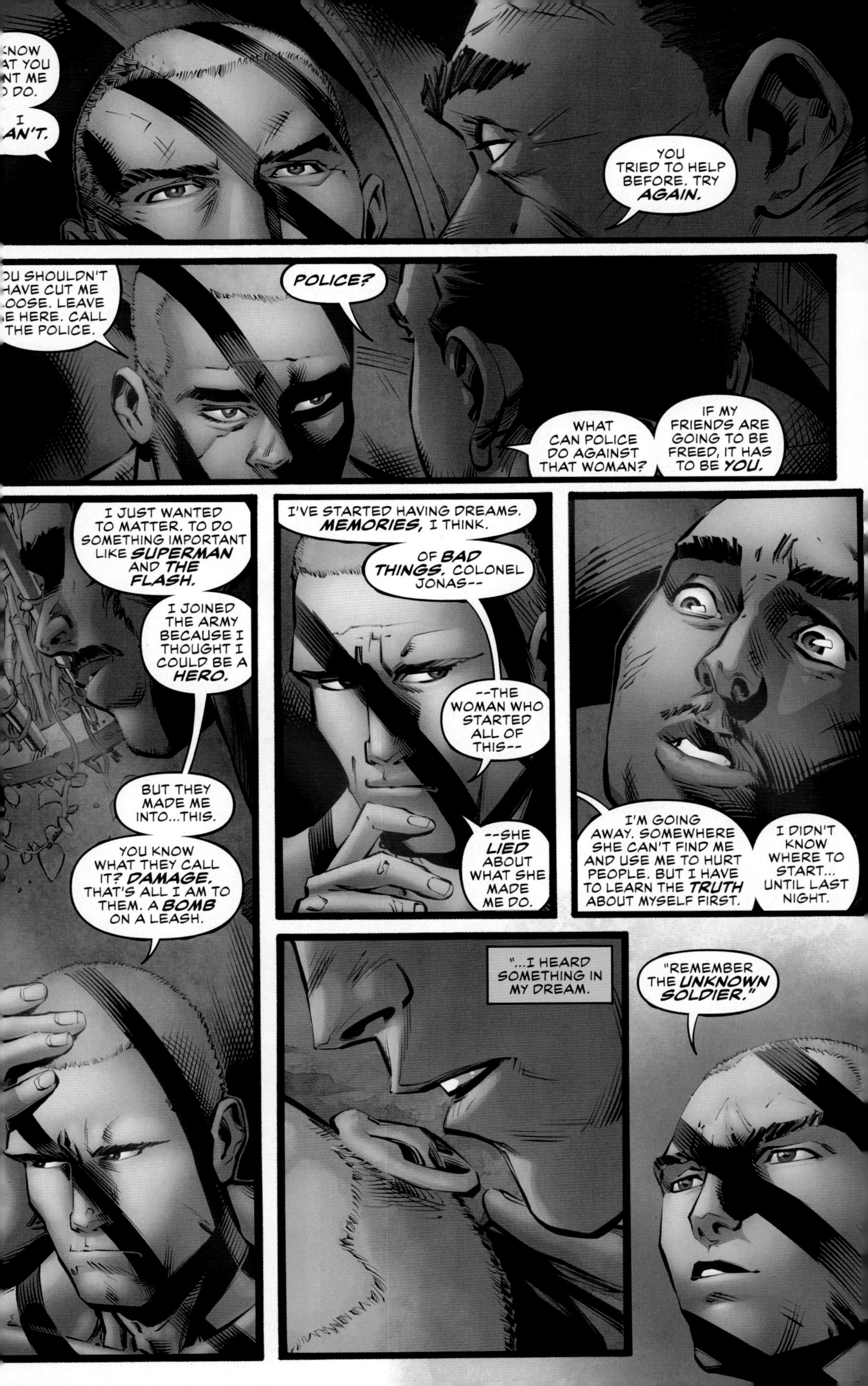

KNOW
AT YOU
NT ME
O DO.
I
AN'T.
YOU TRIED TO HELP BEFORE. TRY AGAIN.
OU SHOULDN'T HAVE CUT ME LOOSE. LEAVE E HERE. CALL THE POLICE.
POLICE?
WHAT CAN POLICE DO AGAINST THAT WOMAN?
IF MY FRIENDS ARE GOING TO BE FREED, IT HAS TO BE YOU.
I JUST WANTED TO MATTER. TO DO SOMETHING IMPORTANT LIKE SUPERMAN AND THE FLASH.
I JOINED THE ARMY BECAUSE I THOUGHT I COULD BE A HERO.
BUT THEY MADE ME INTO...THIS.
YOU KNOW WHAT THEY CALL IT? DAMAGE. THAT'S ALL I AM TO THEM. A BOMB ON A LEASH.
I'VE STARTED HAVING DREAMS. MEMORIES, I THINK.
OF BAD THINGS. COLONEL JONAS--
--THE WOMAN WHO STARTED ALL OF THIS--
--SHE LIED ABOUT WHAT SHE MADE ME DO.
I'M GOING AWAY. SOMEWHERE SHE CAN'T FIND ME AND USE ME TO HURT PEOPLE. BUT I HAVE TO LEARN THE TRUTH ABOUT MYSELF FIRST.
I DIDN'T KNOW WHERE TO START... UNTIL LAST NIGHT.
"...I HEARD SOMETHING IN MY DREAM.
"REMEMBER THE UNKNOWN SOLDIER."

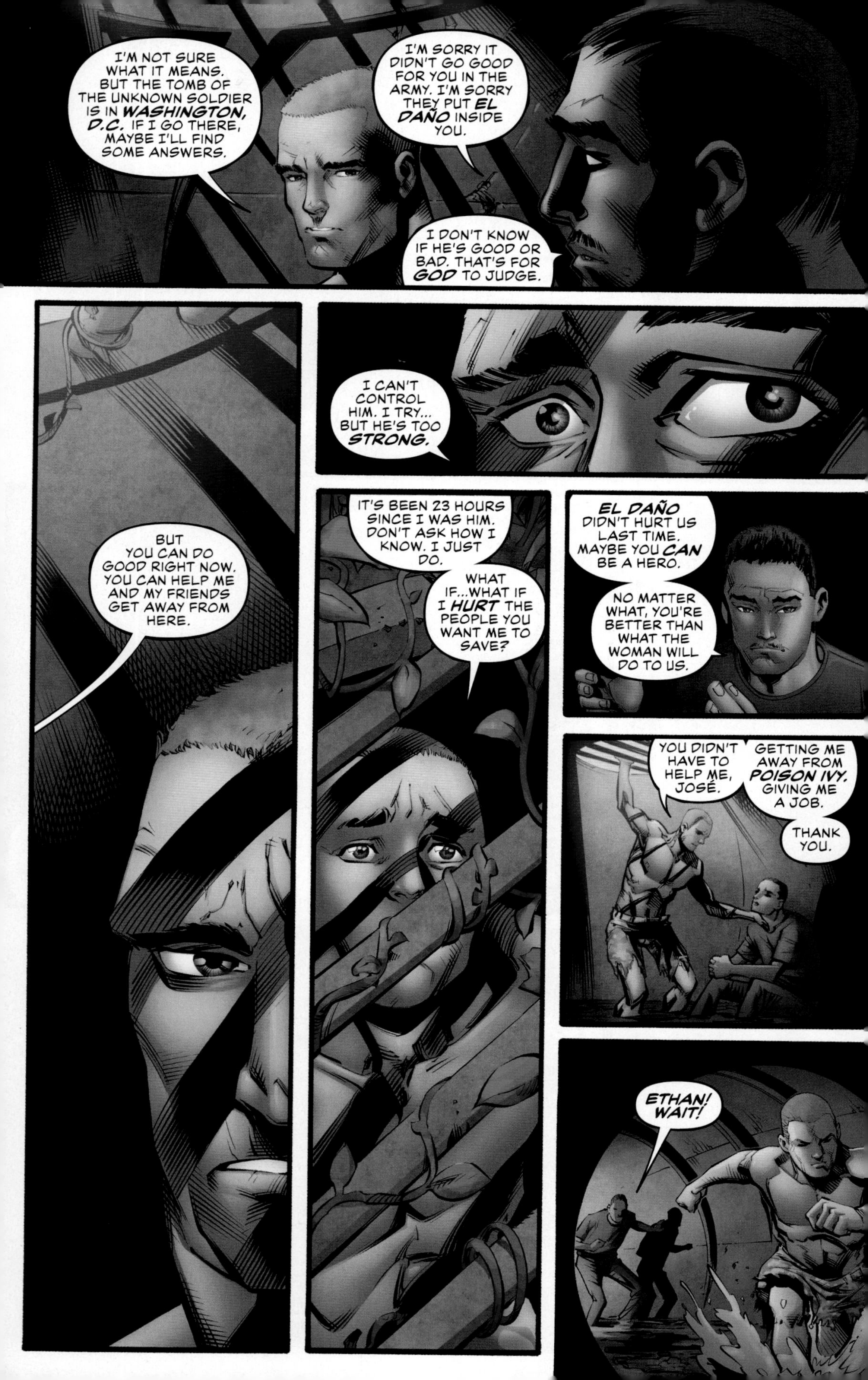
I'M NOT SURE WHAT IT MEANS. BUT THE TOMB OF THE UNKNOWN SOLDIER IS IN WASHINGTON, D.C. IF I GO THERE, MAYBE I'LL FIND SOME ANSWERS.
I'M SORRY IT DIDN'T GO GOOD FOR YOU IN THE ARMY. I'M SORRY THEY PUT EL DAÑO INSIDE YOU.
I DON'T KNOW IF HE'S GOOD OR BAD. THAT'S FOR GOD TO JUDGE.
I CAN'T CONTROL HIM. I TRY... BUT HE'S TOO STRONG.
BUT YOU CAN DO GOOD RIGHT NOW. YOU CAN HELP ME AND MY FRIENDS GET AWAY FROM HERE.
IT'S BEEN 23 HOURS SINCE I WAS HIM. DON'T ASK HOW I KNOW. I JUST DO.
WHAT IF...WHAT IF I HURT THE PEOPLE YOU WANT ME TO SAVE?
EL DAÑO DIDN'T HURT US LAST TIME. MAYBE YOU CAN BE A HERO.
NO MATTER WHAT, YOU'RE BETTER THAN WHAT THE WOMAN WILL DO TO US.
YOU DIDN'T HAVE TO HELP ME, JOSÉ.
GETTING ME AWAY FROM POISON IVY. GIVING ME A JOB.
THANK YOU.
ETHAN! WAIT!

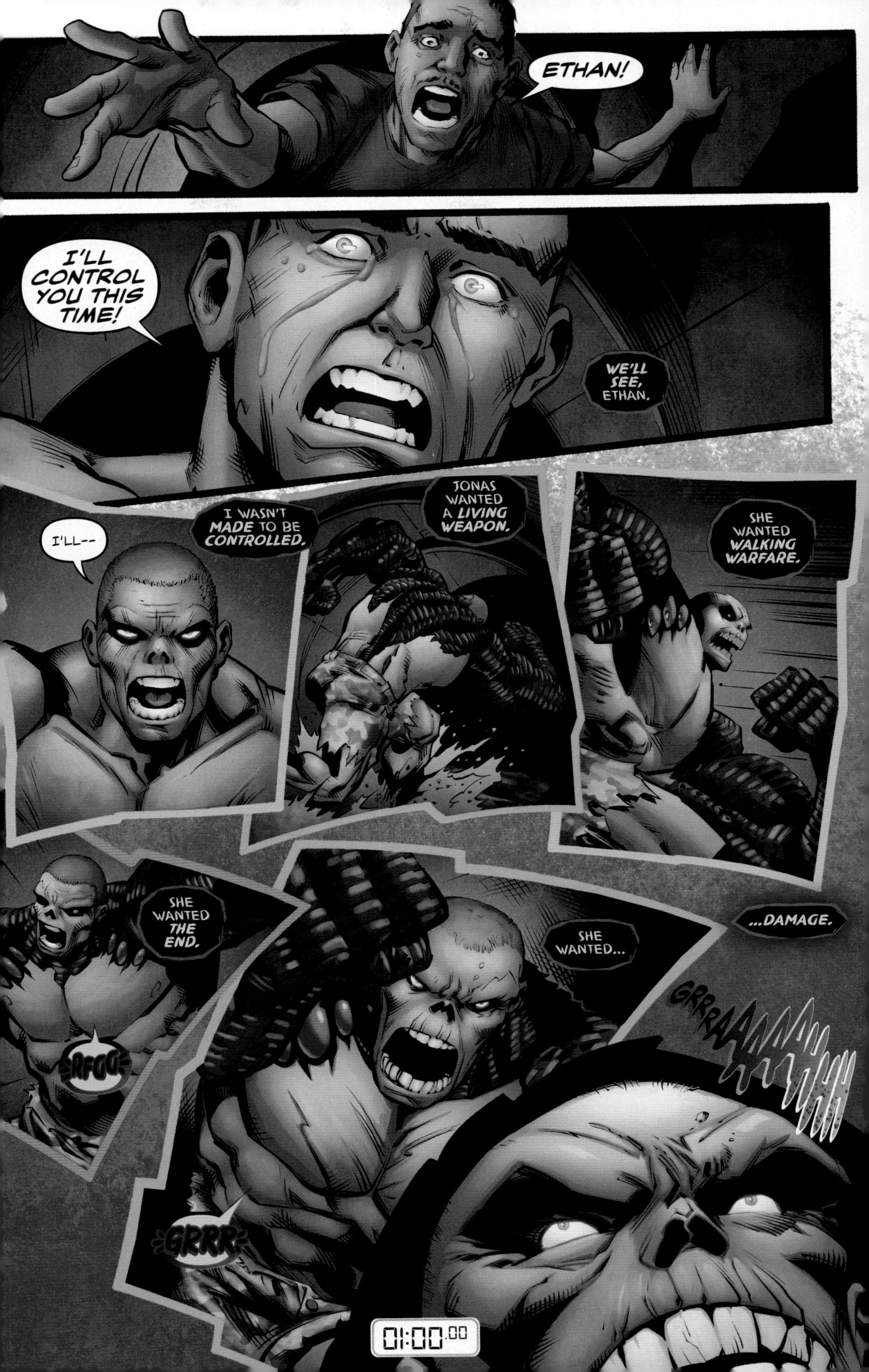
ETHAN!
I'LL CONTROL YOU THIS TIME!
WE'LL SEE, ETHAN.
I'LL--
I WASN'T MADE TO BE CONTROLLED.
JONAS WANTED A LIVING WEAPON.
SHE WANTED WALKING WARFARE.
SHE WANTED THE END.
RFGG
SHE WANTED...
...DAMAGE.
GRRRAAAAAAAHHH
GRRR
01:00.00

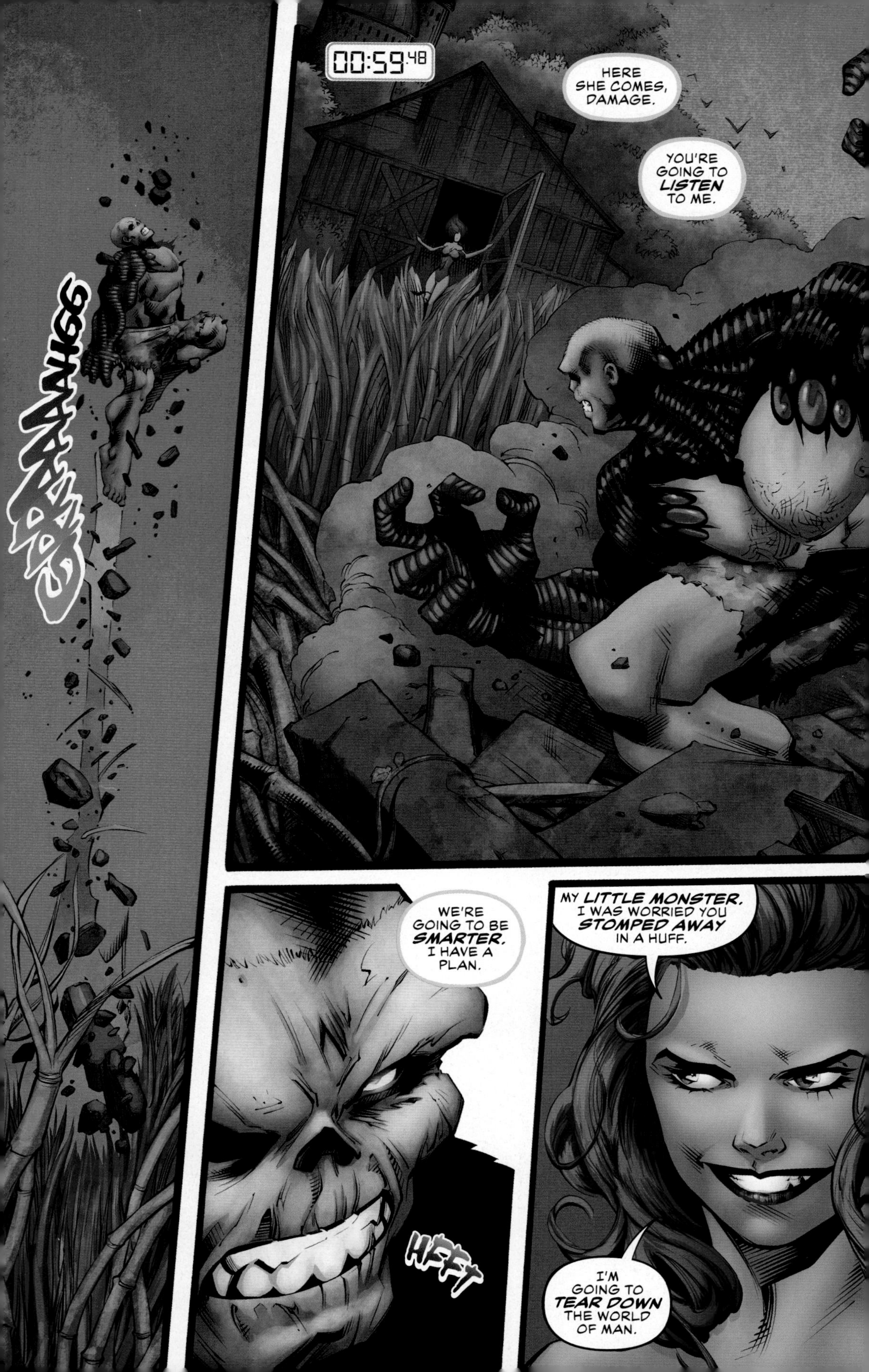
00:59.48
HERE SHE COMES, DAMAGE.
YOU'RE GOING TO LISTEN TO ME.
WE'RE GOING TO BE SMARTER. I HAVE A PLAN.
HEFT
MY LITTLE MONSTER. I WAS WORRIED YOU STOMPED AWAY IN A HUFF.
I'M GOING TO TEAR DOWN THE WORLD OF MAN.

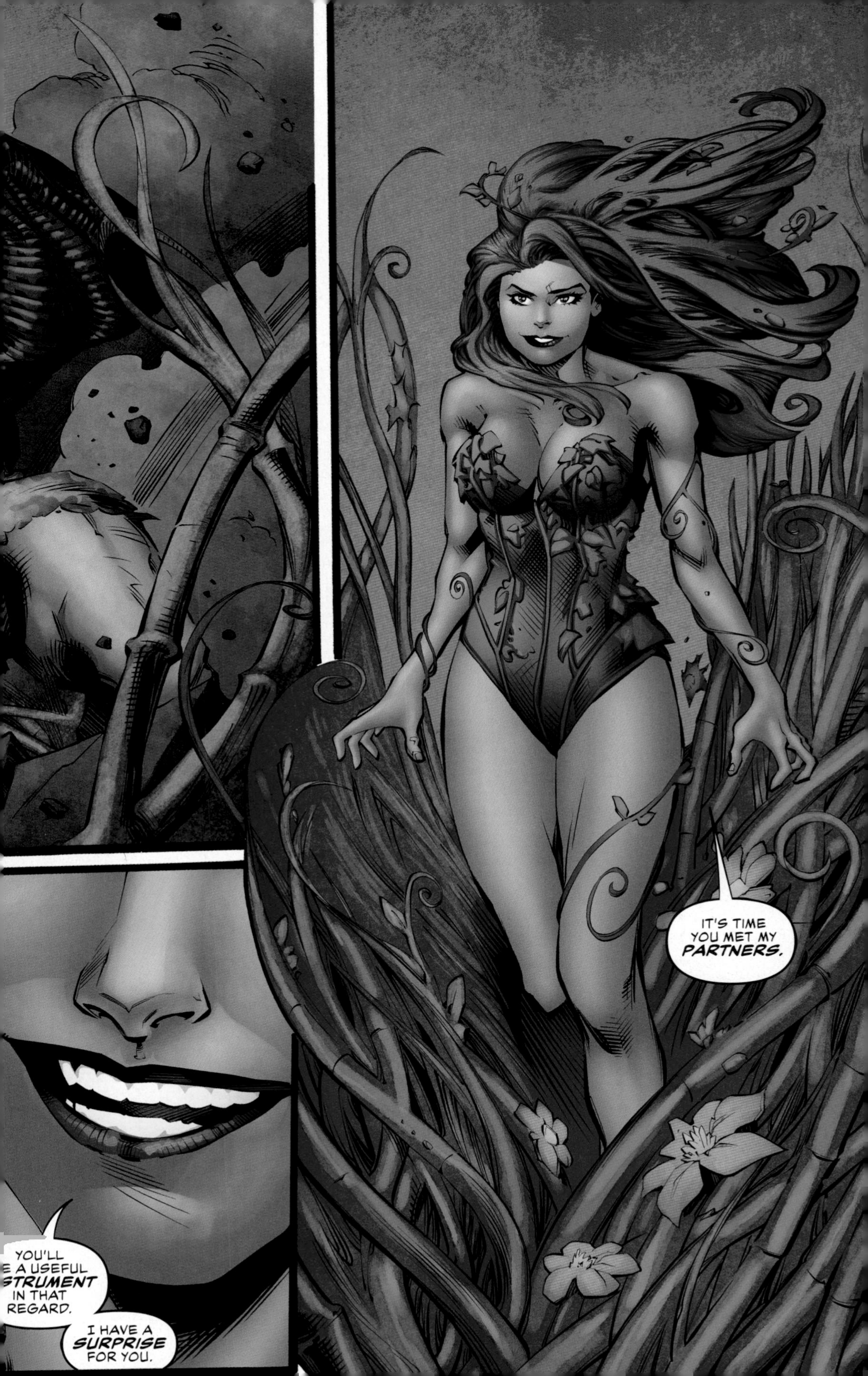
IT'S TIME YOU MET MY PARTNERS.
YOU'LL E A USEFUL STRUMENT IN THAT REGARD.
I HAVE A SURPRISE FOR YOU.

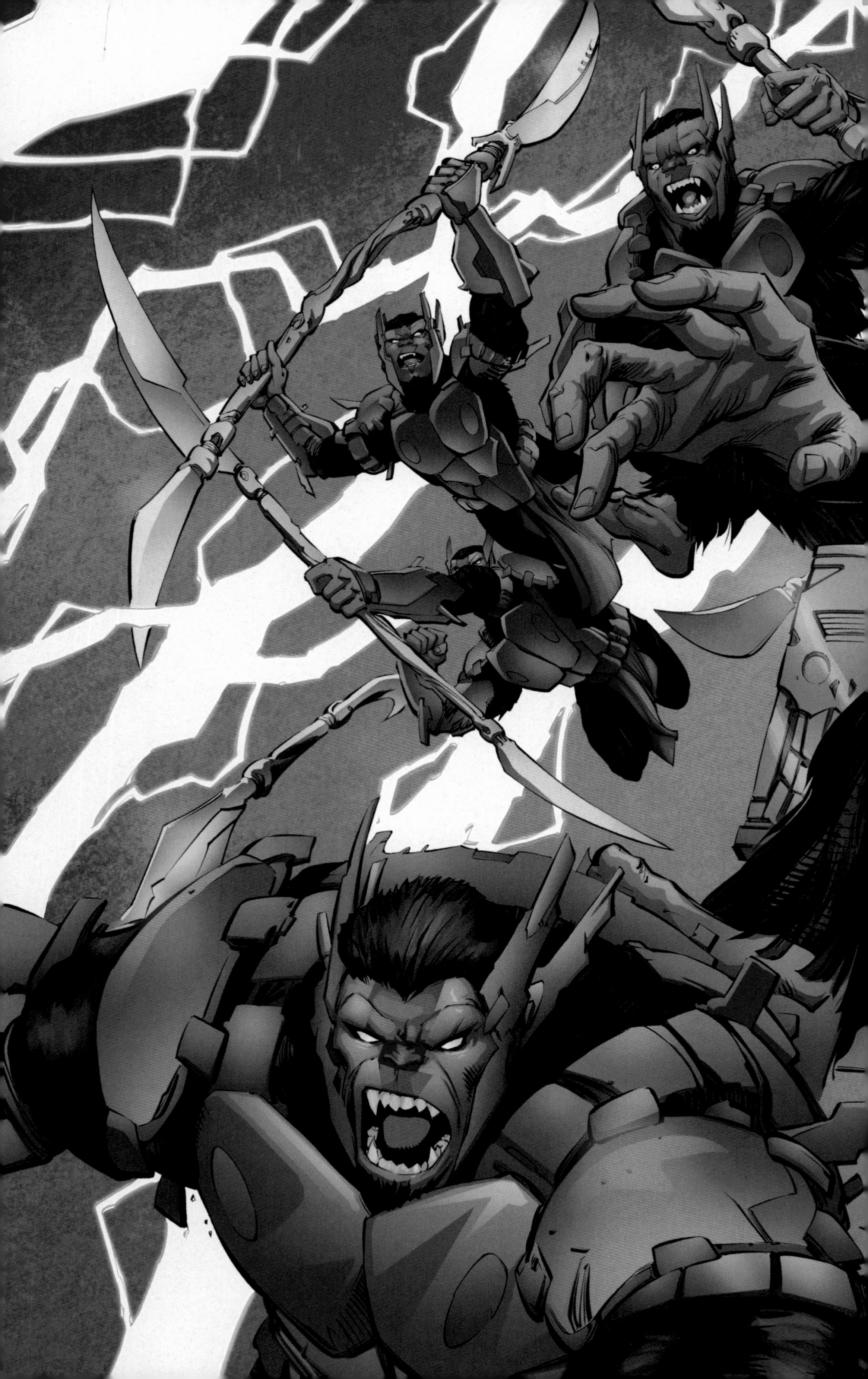

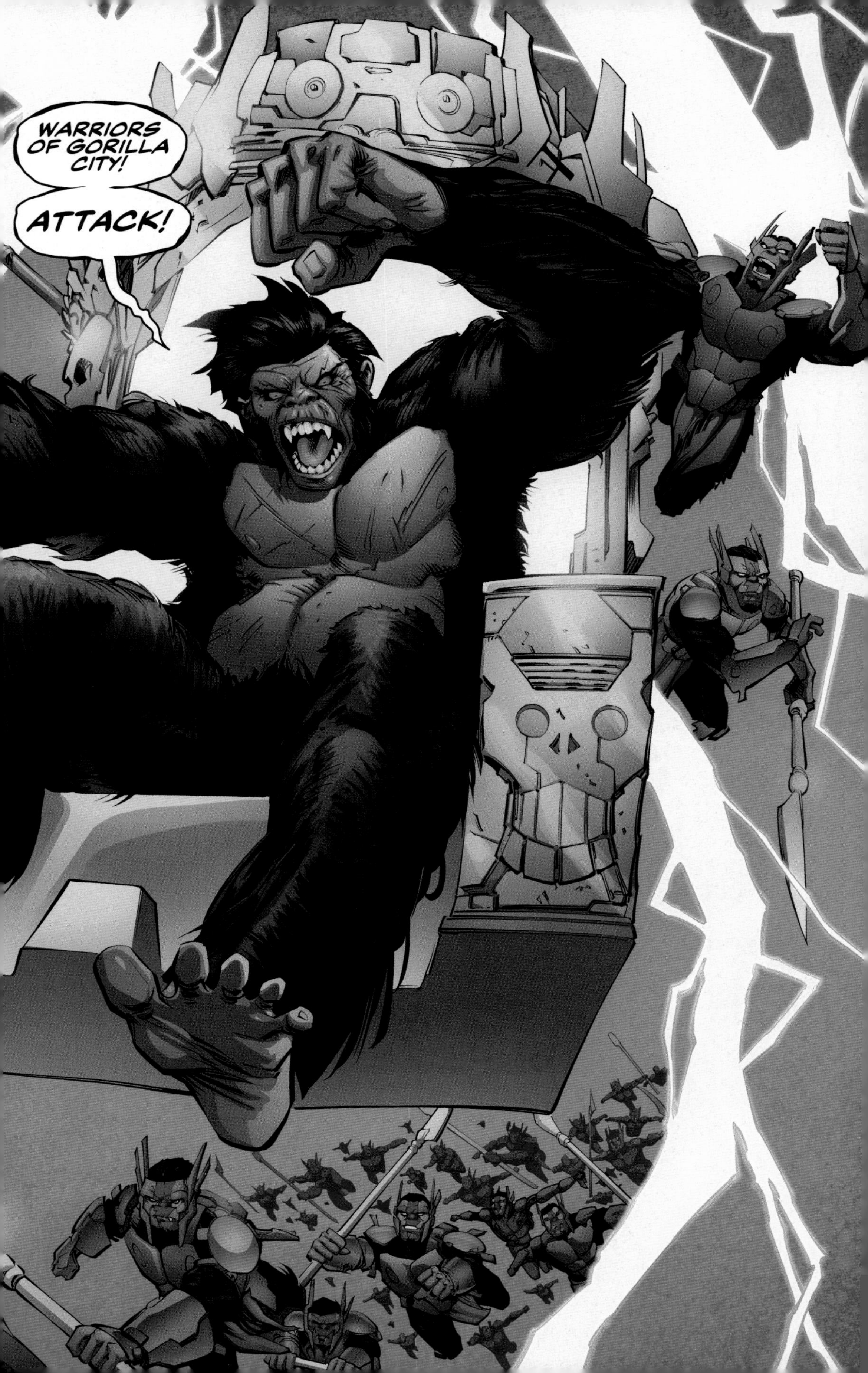
WARRIORS OF GORILLA CITY!
ATTACK!

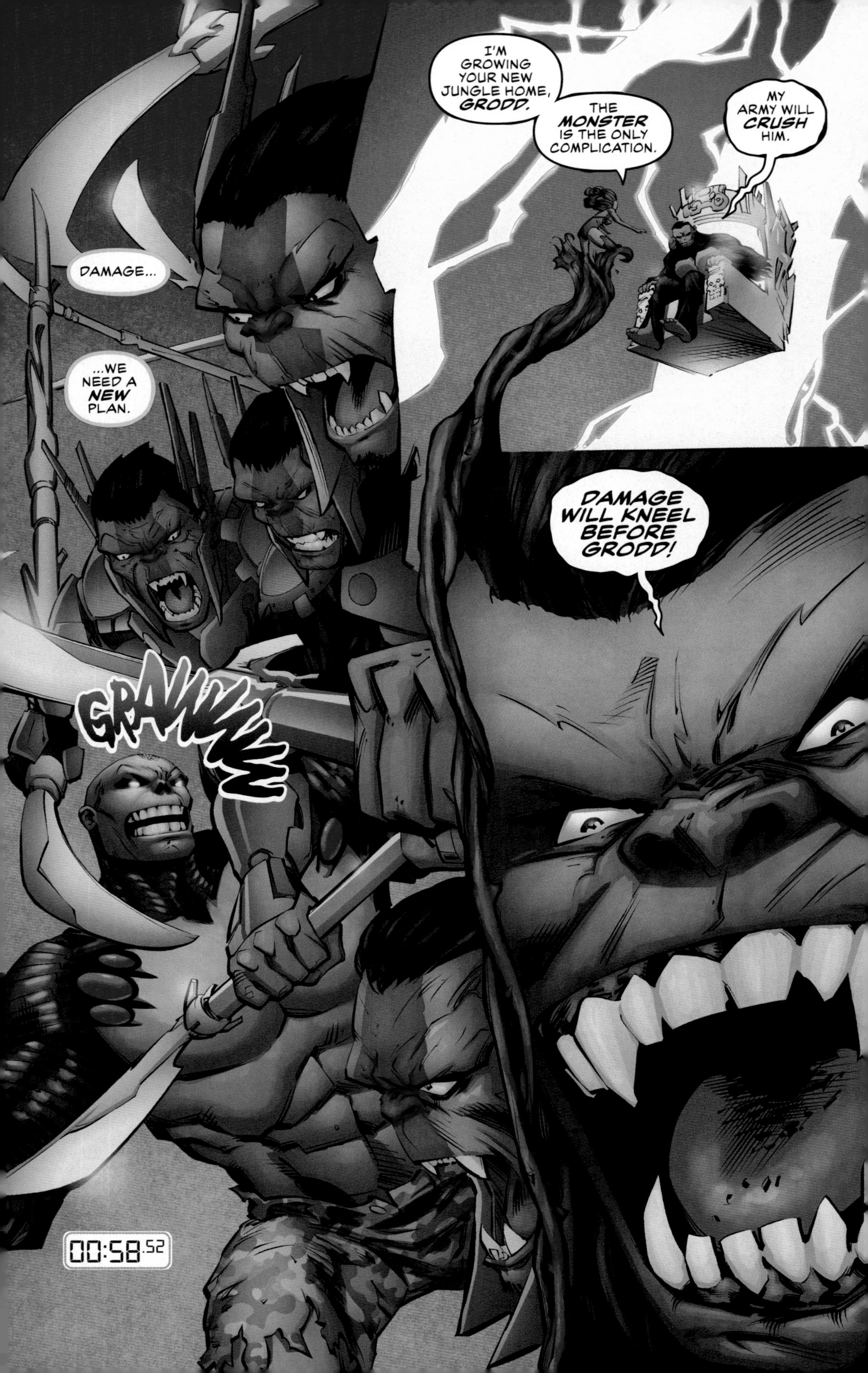
I'M GROWING YOUR NEW JUNGLE HOME, GRODD.
THE MONSTER IS THE ONLY COMPLICATION.
MY ARMY WILL CRUSH HIM.
DAMAGE...
...WE NEED A NEW PLAN.
DAMAGE WILL KNEEL BEFORE GRODD!
GRAWWW
00:58.52

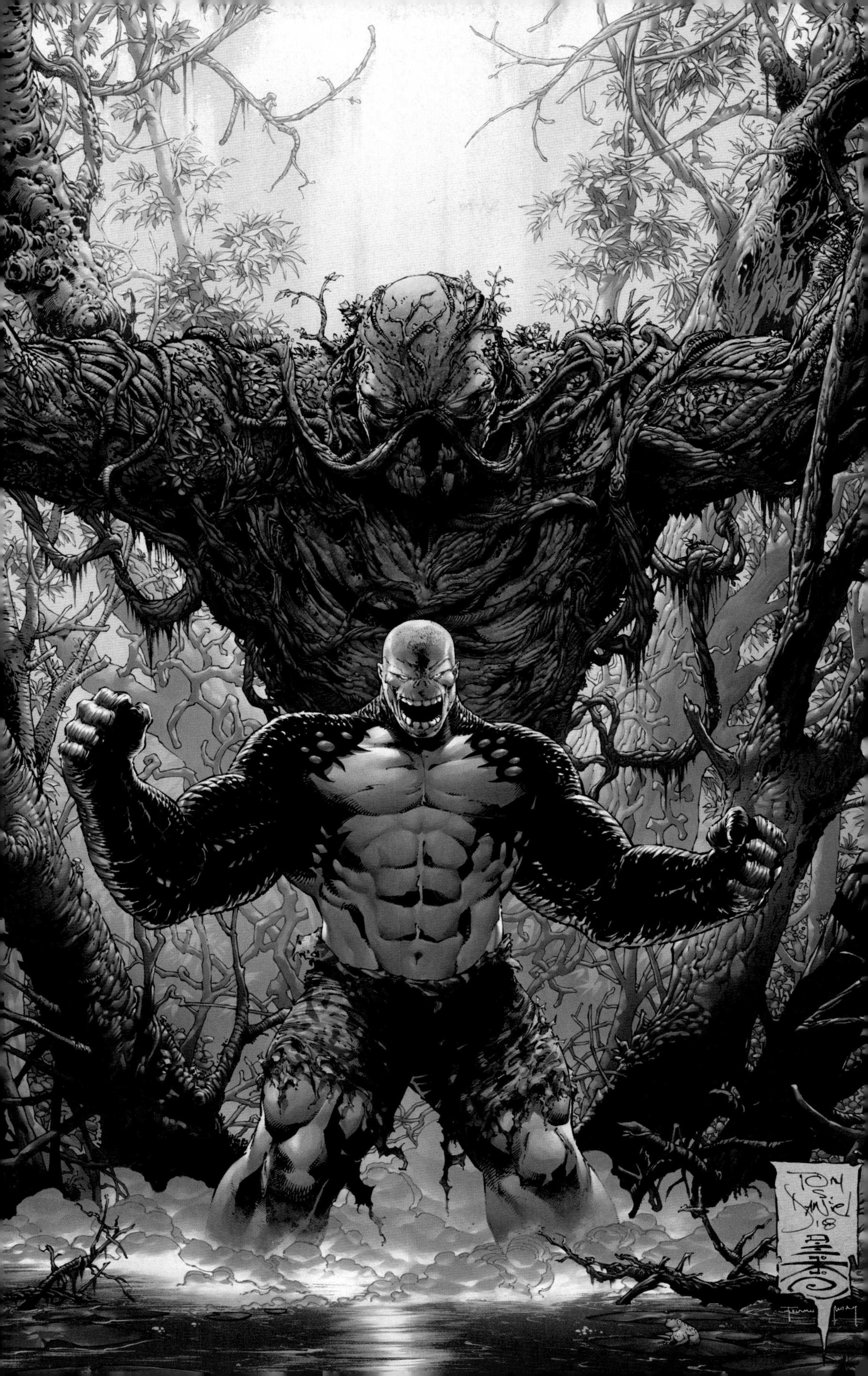

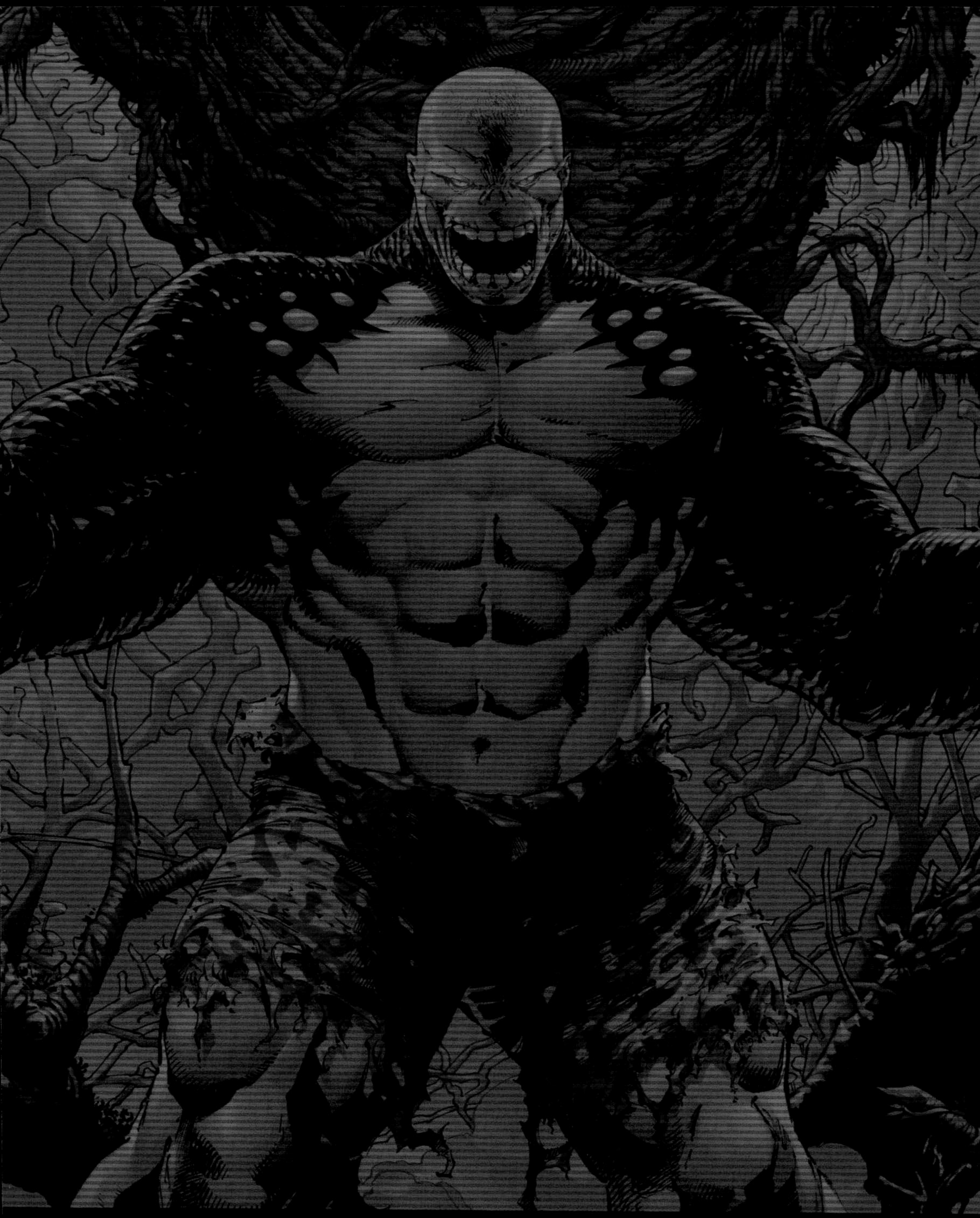

DAMAGE
#6

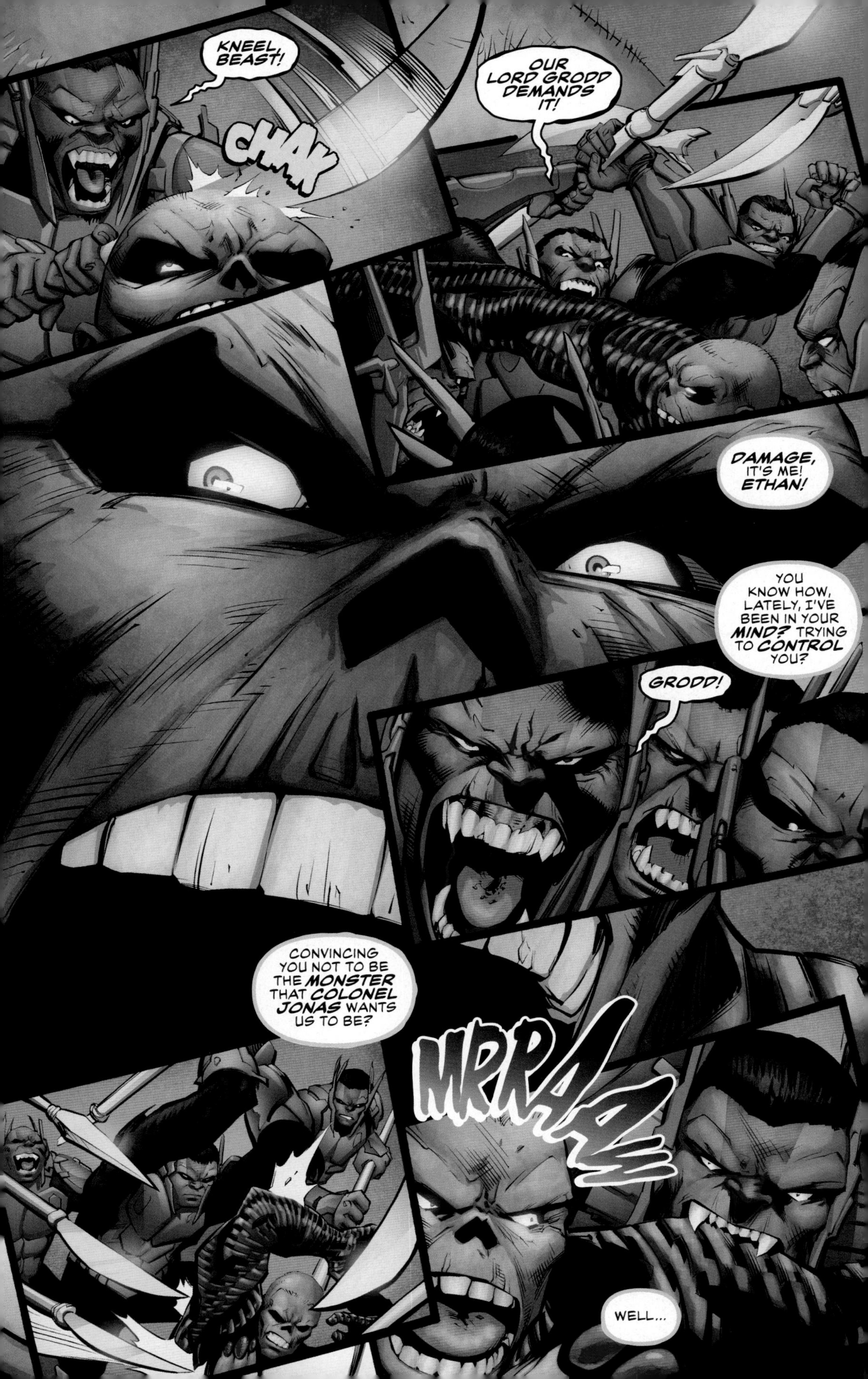
KNEEL, BEAST!
CHAK
OUR LORD GRODD DEMANDS IT!
DAMAGE, IT'S ME! ETHAN!
YOU KNOW HOW, LATELY, I'VE BEEN IN YOUR MIND? TRYING TO CONTROL YOU?
GRODD!
CONVINCING YOU NOT TO BE THE MONSTER THAT COLONEL JONAS WANTS US TO BE?
MRRAA
WELL...

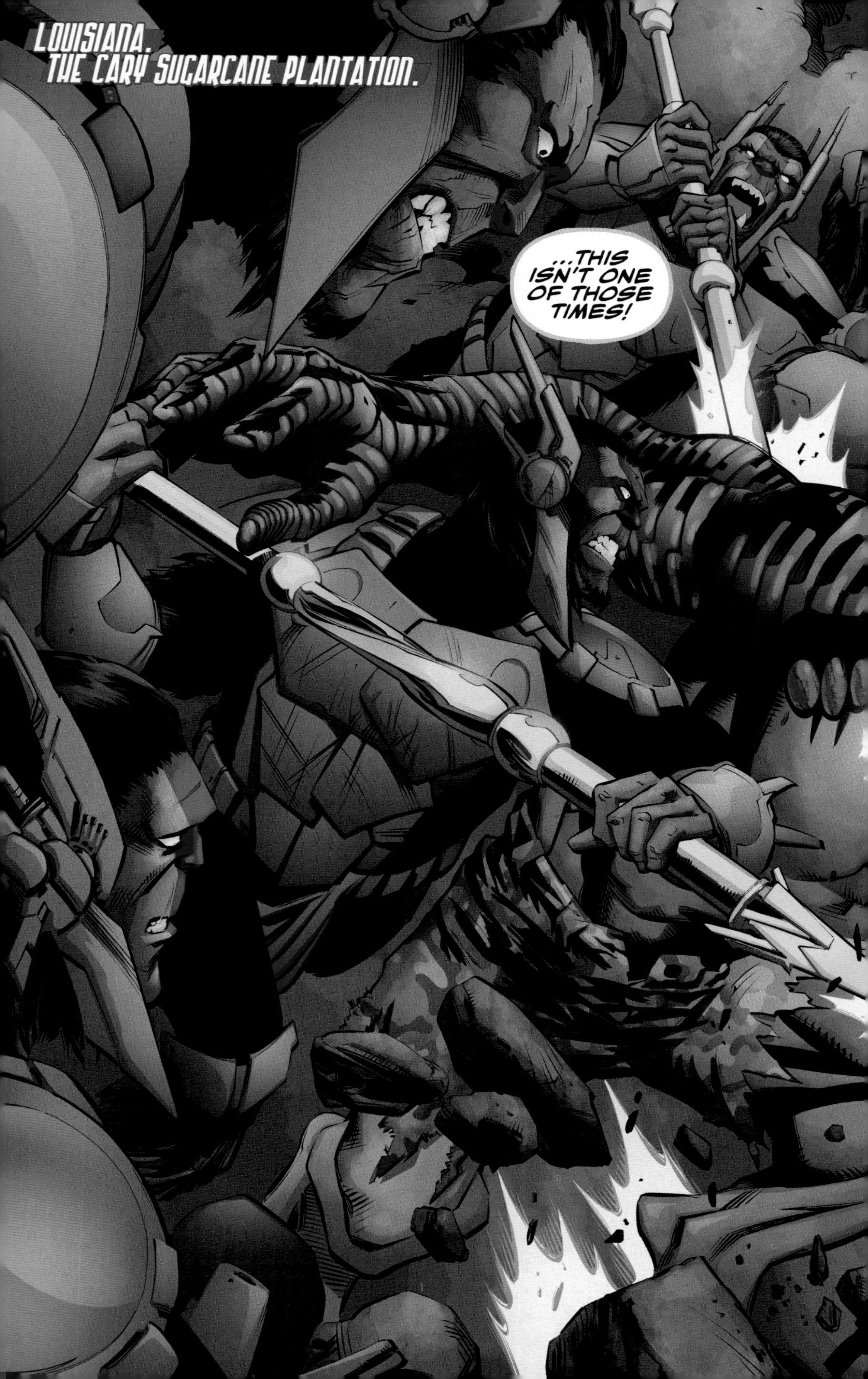
LOUISIANA.
THE CARY SUGARCANE PLANTATION.
...THIS ISN'T ONE OF THOSE TIMES!

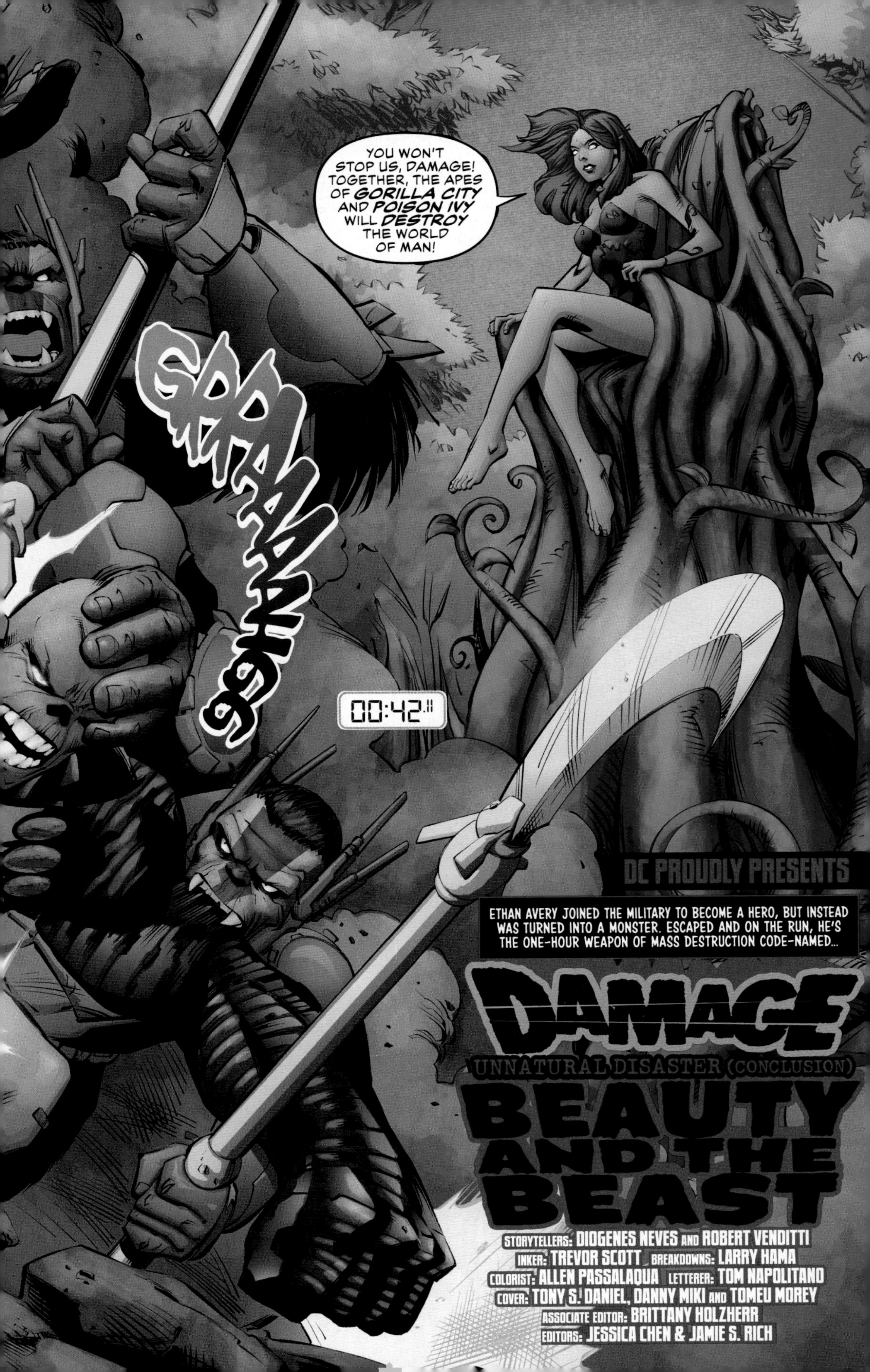
YOU WON'T STOP US, DAMAGE! TOGETHER, THE APES OF GORILLA CITY AND POISON IVY WILL DESTROY THE WORLD OF MAN!
GRRAAAAHGG
00:42.11
DC PROUDLY PRESENTS
ETHAN AVERY JOINED THE MILITARY TO BECOME A HERO, BUT INSTEAD WAS TURNED INTO A MONSTER. ESCAPED AND ON THE RUN, HE'S THE ONE-HOUR WEAPON OF MASS DESTRUCTION CODE-NAMED...
DAMAGE
UNNATURAL DISASTER (CONCLUSION)
BEAUTY AND THE BEAST
STORYTELLERS: DIOGENES NEVES AND ROBERT VENDITTI
INKER: TREVOR SCOTT BREAKDOWNS: LARRY HAMA
COLORIST: ALLEN PASSALAQUA LETTERER: TOM NAPOLITANO
COVER: TONY S. DANIEL, DANNY MIKI AND TOMEU MOREY
ASSOCIATE EDITOR: BRITTANY HOLZHERR
EDITORS: JESSICA CHEN & JAMIE S. RICH

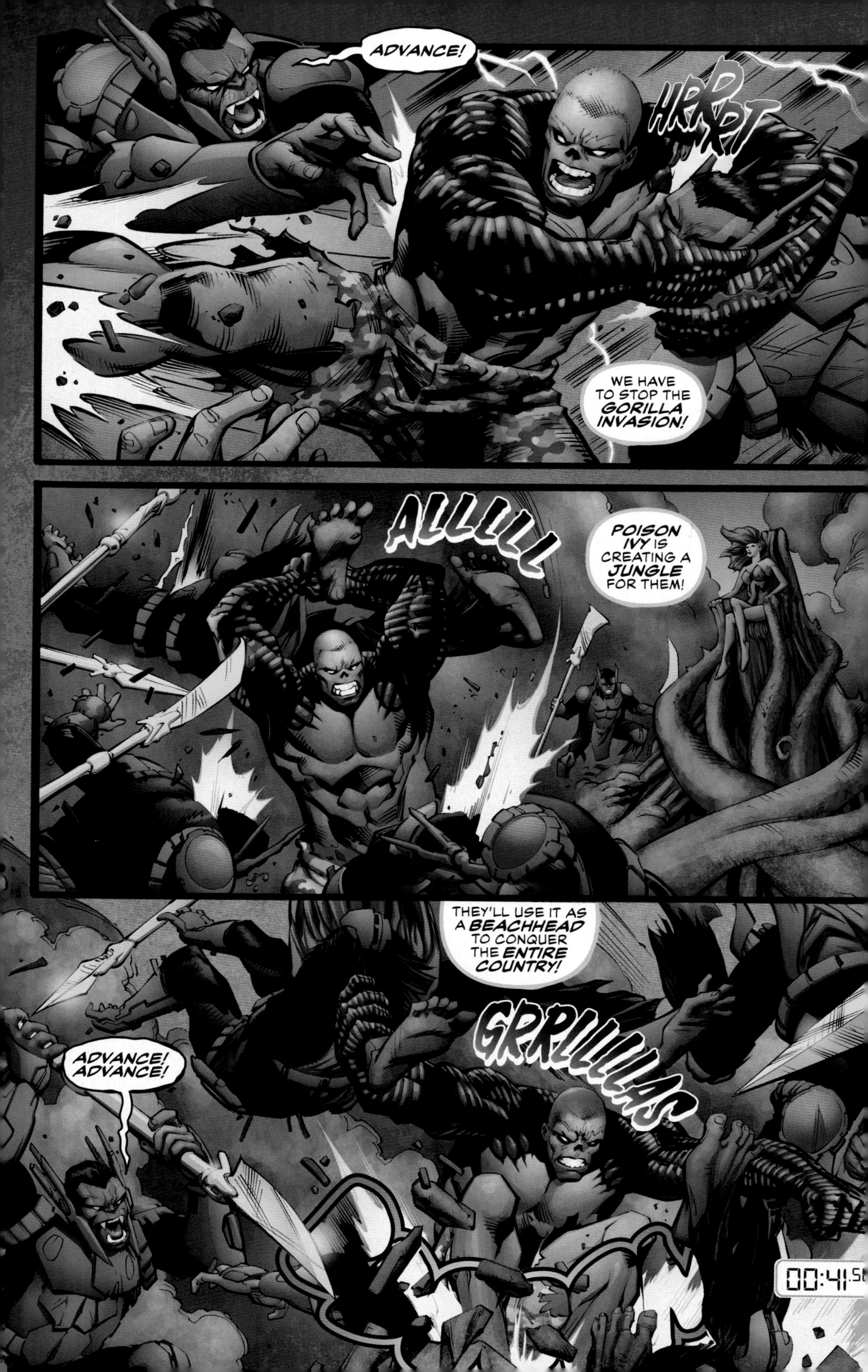
ADVANCE!
HRRRT
WE HAVE TO STOP THE GORILLA INVASION!
ALLLLL
POISON IVY IS CREATING A JUNGLE FOR THEM!
THEY'LL USE IT AS A BEACHHEAD TO CONQUER THE ENTIRE COUNTRY!
GRRLLLLAS
ADVANCE! ADVANCE!
00:41.5

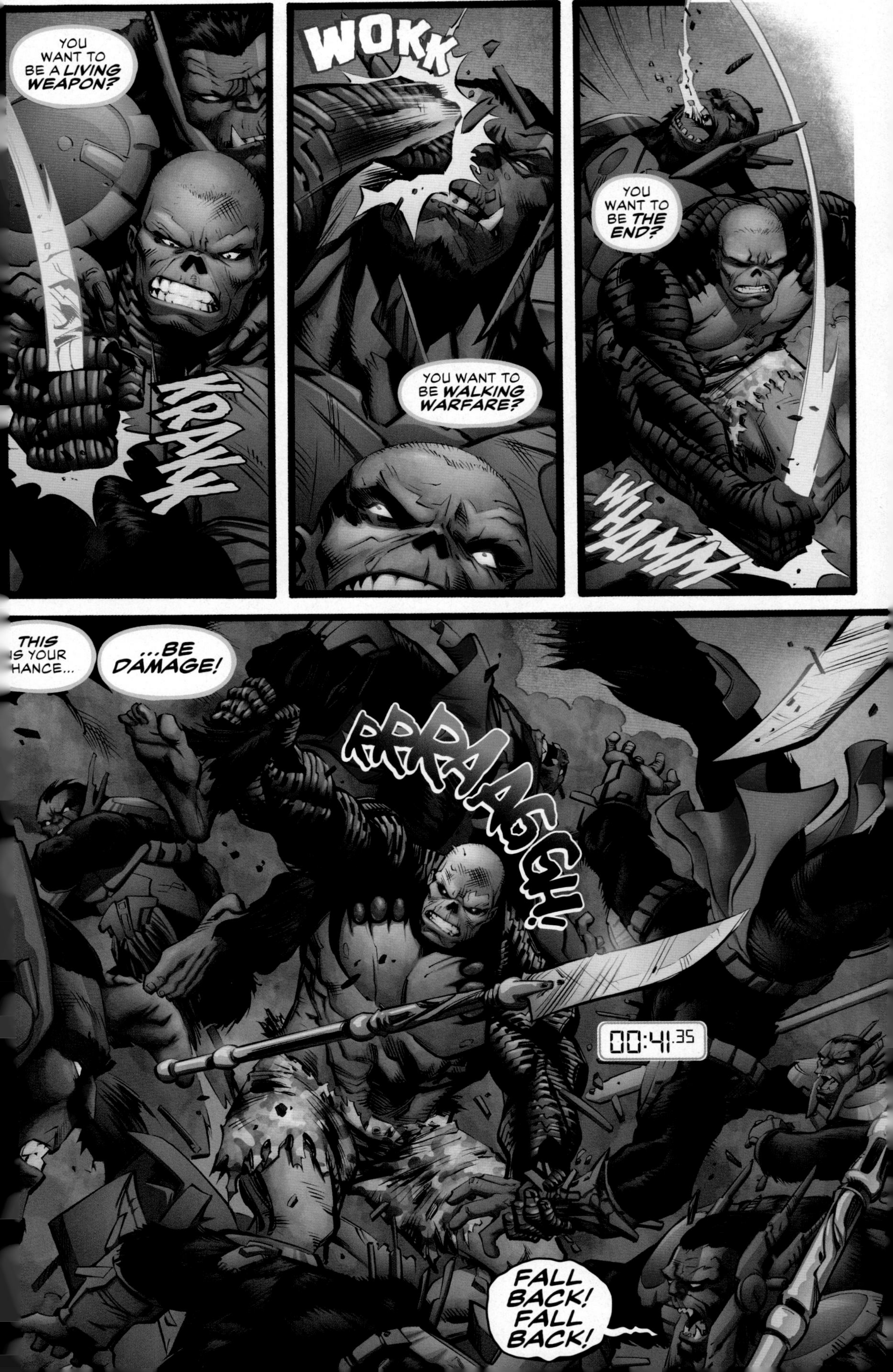
YOU WANT TO BE A LIVING WEAPON?
KRAKK
WOKK
YOU WANT TO BE WALKING WARFARE?
YOU WANT TO BE THE END?
WHAMM
THIS IS YOUR CHANCE...
...BE DAMAGE!
RRRAAGGH!
00:41.35
FALL BACK! FALL BACK!

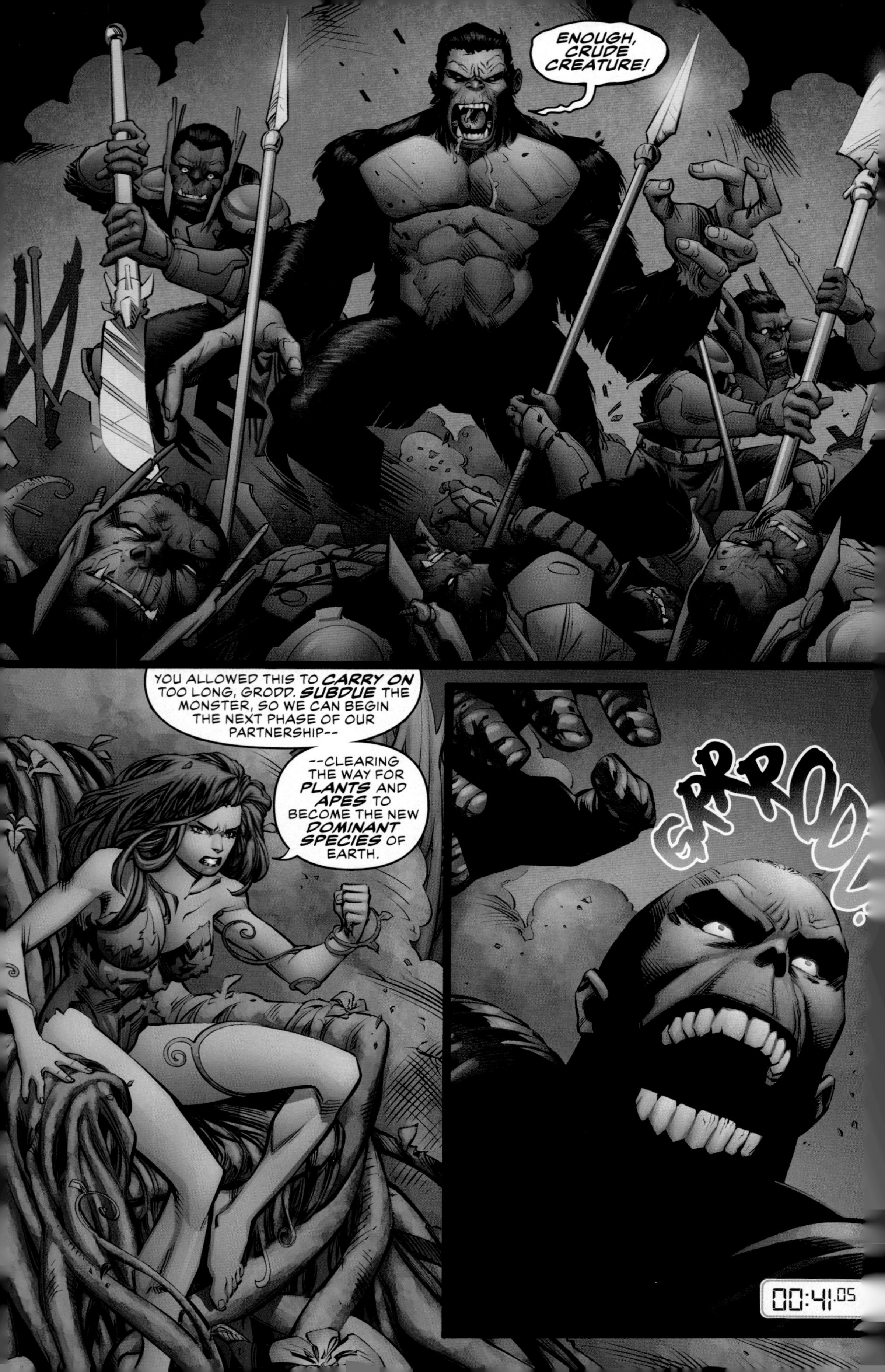
ENOUGH, CRUDE CREATURE!
YOU ALLOWED THIS TO CARRY ON TOO LONG, GRODD. SUBDUE THE MONSTER, SO WE CAN BEGIN THE NEXT PHASE OF OUR PARTNERSHIP--
--CLEARING THE WAY FOR PLANTS AND APES TO BECOME THE NEW DOMINANT SPECIES OF EARTH.
GRRROO!
00:41.05

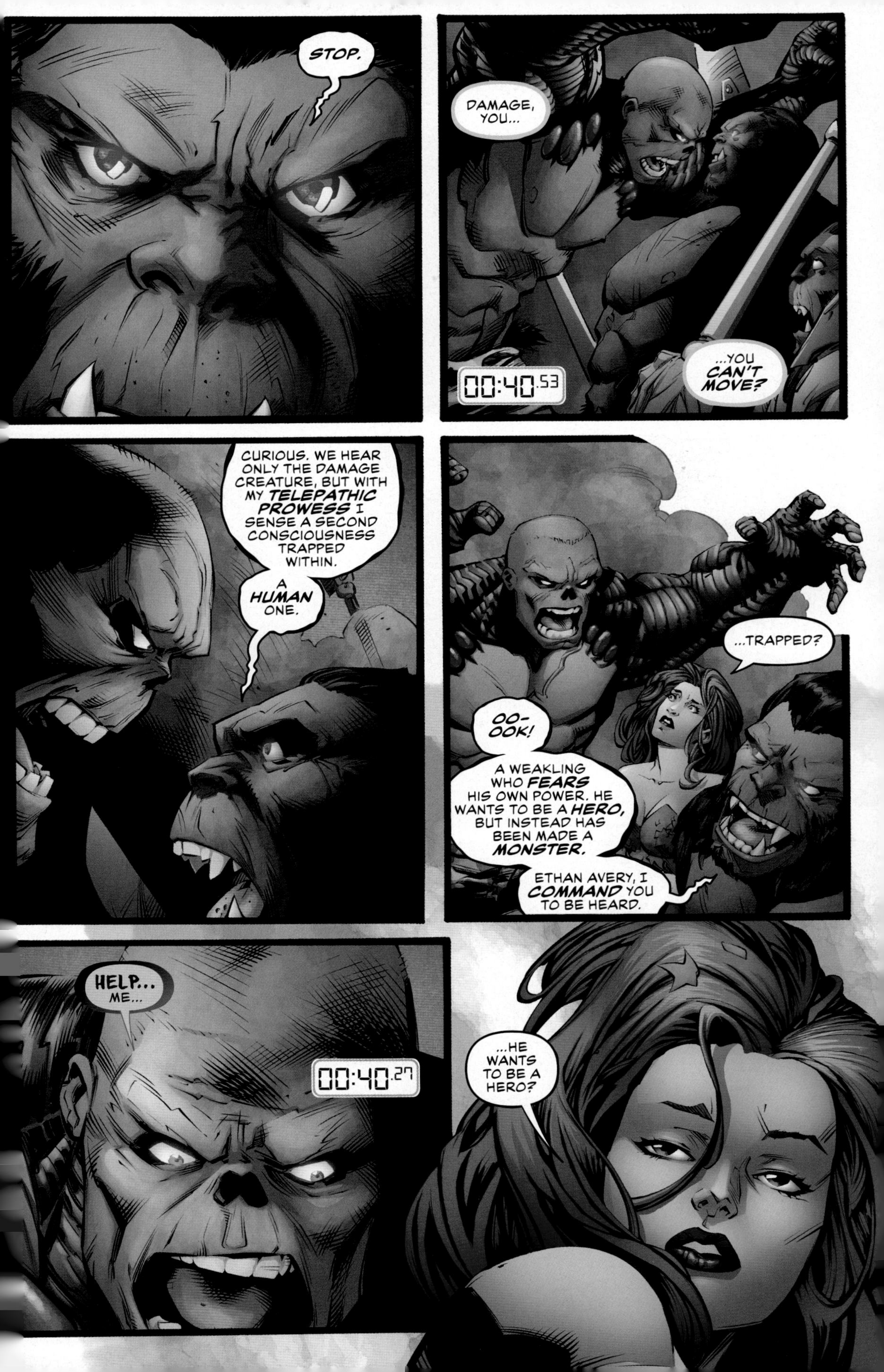
STOP.
DAMAGE, YOU...
00:40.53
...YOU CAN'T MOVE?
CURIOUS. WE HEAR ONLY THE DAMAGE CREATURE, BUT WITH MY TELEPATHIC PROWESS I SENSE A SECOND CONSCIOUSNESS TRAPPED WITHIN.
A HUMAN ONE.
...TRAPPED?
OO-OOK!
A WEAKLING WHO FEARS HIS OWN POWER. HE WANTS TO BE A HERO, BUT INSTEAD HAS BEEN MADE A MONSTER.
ETHAN AVERY, I COMMAND YOU TO BE HEARD.
HELP... ME...
00:40.27
...HE WANTS TO BE A HERO?

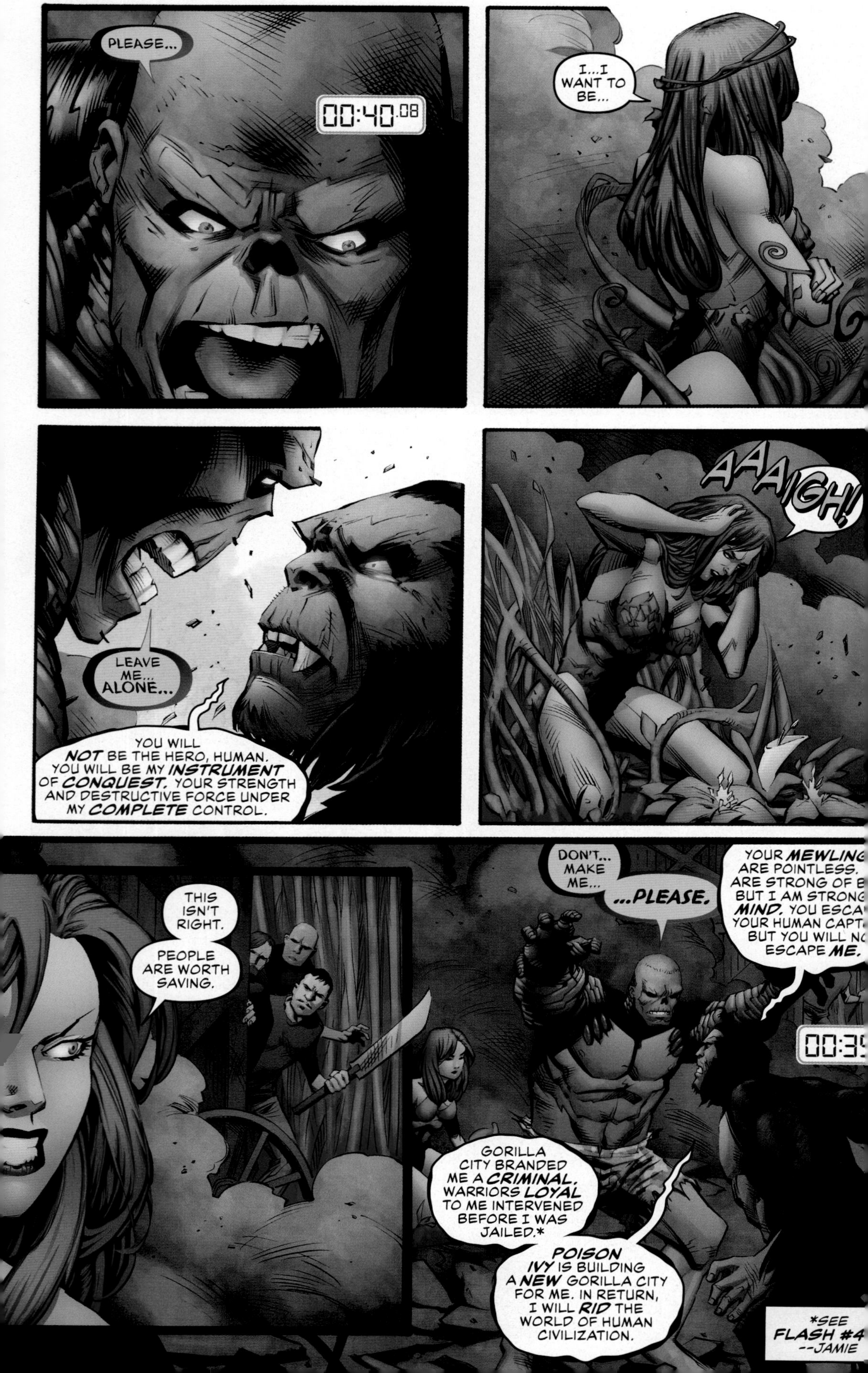
PLEASE...
00:40.08
I...I WANT TO BE...
LEAVE ME... ALONE...
YOU WILL NOT BE THE HERO, HUMAN. YOU WILL BE MY INSTRUMENT OF CONQUEST. YOUR STRENGTH AND DESTRUCTIVE FORCE UNDER MY COMPLETE CONTROL.
AAAIGH!
THIS ISN'T RIGHT.
PEOPLE ARE WORTH SAVING.
DON'T... MAKE ME...
...PLEASE.
YOUR MEWLING ARE POINTLESS. ARE STRONG OF B BUT I AM STRONG MIND. YOU ESCA YOUR HUMAN CAPT BUT YOU WILL NO ESCAPE ME.
GORILLA CITY BRANDED ME A CRIMINAL. WARRIORS LOYAL TO ME INTERVENED BEFORE I WAS JAILED.*
POISON IVY IS BUILDING A NEW GORILLA CITY FOR ME. IN RETURN, I WILL RID THE WORLD OF HUMAN CIVILIZATION.
*SEE FLASH #4 --JAMIE

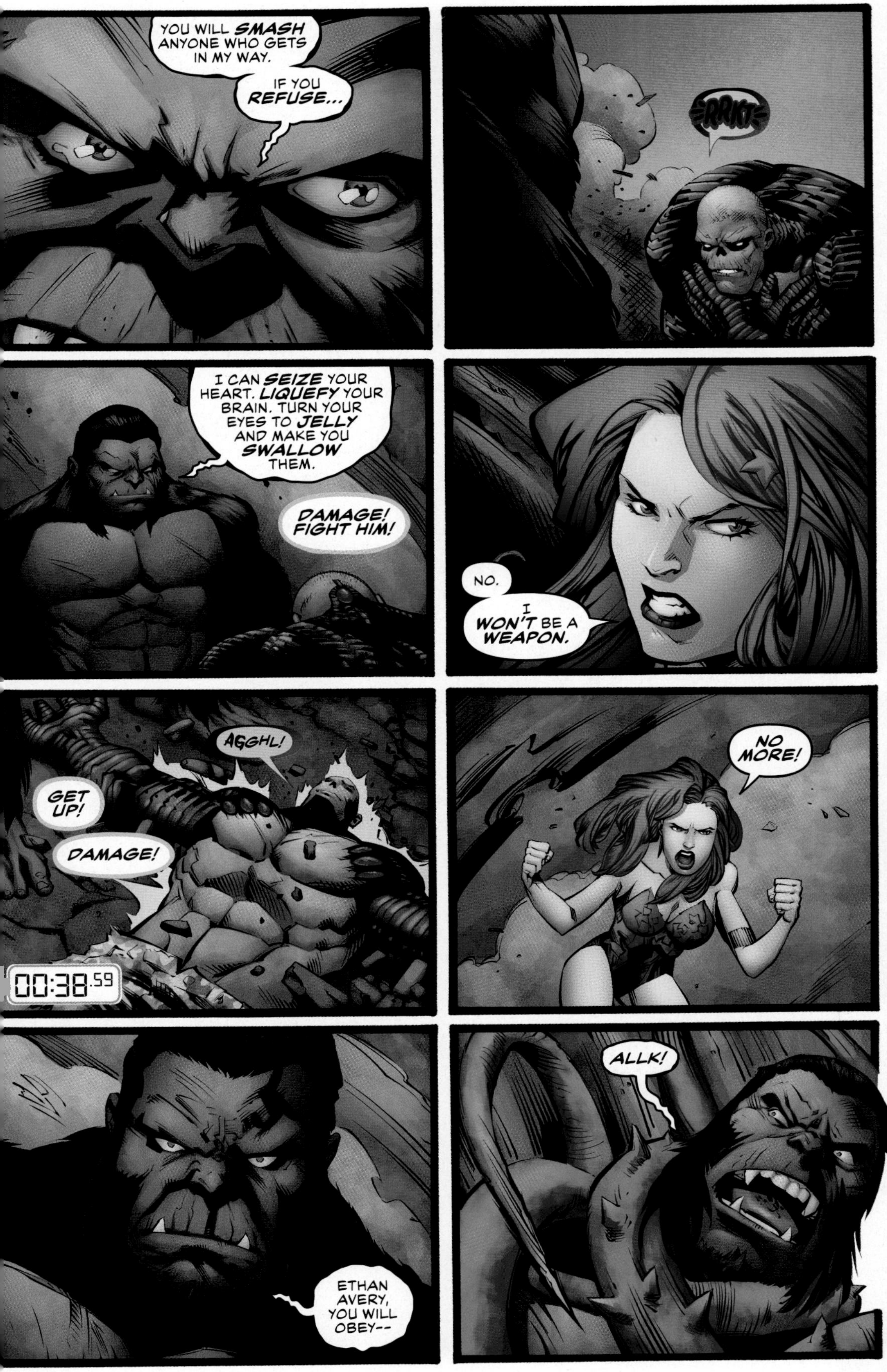
YOU WILL SMASH ANYONE WHO GETS IN MY WAY.
IF YOU REFUSE...
RRKT
I CAN SEIZE YOUR HEART. LIQUEFY YOUR BRAIN. TURN YOUR EYES TO JELLY AND MAKE YOU SWALLOW THEM.
DAMAGE! FIGHT HIM!
NO.
I WON'T BE A WEAPON.
AGGHL!
GET UP!
DAMAGE!
00:38.59
NO MORE!
ETHAN AVERY, YOU WILL OBEY--
ALLK!

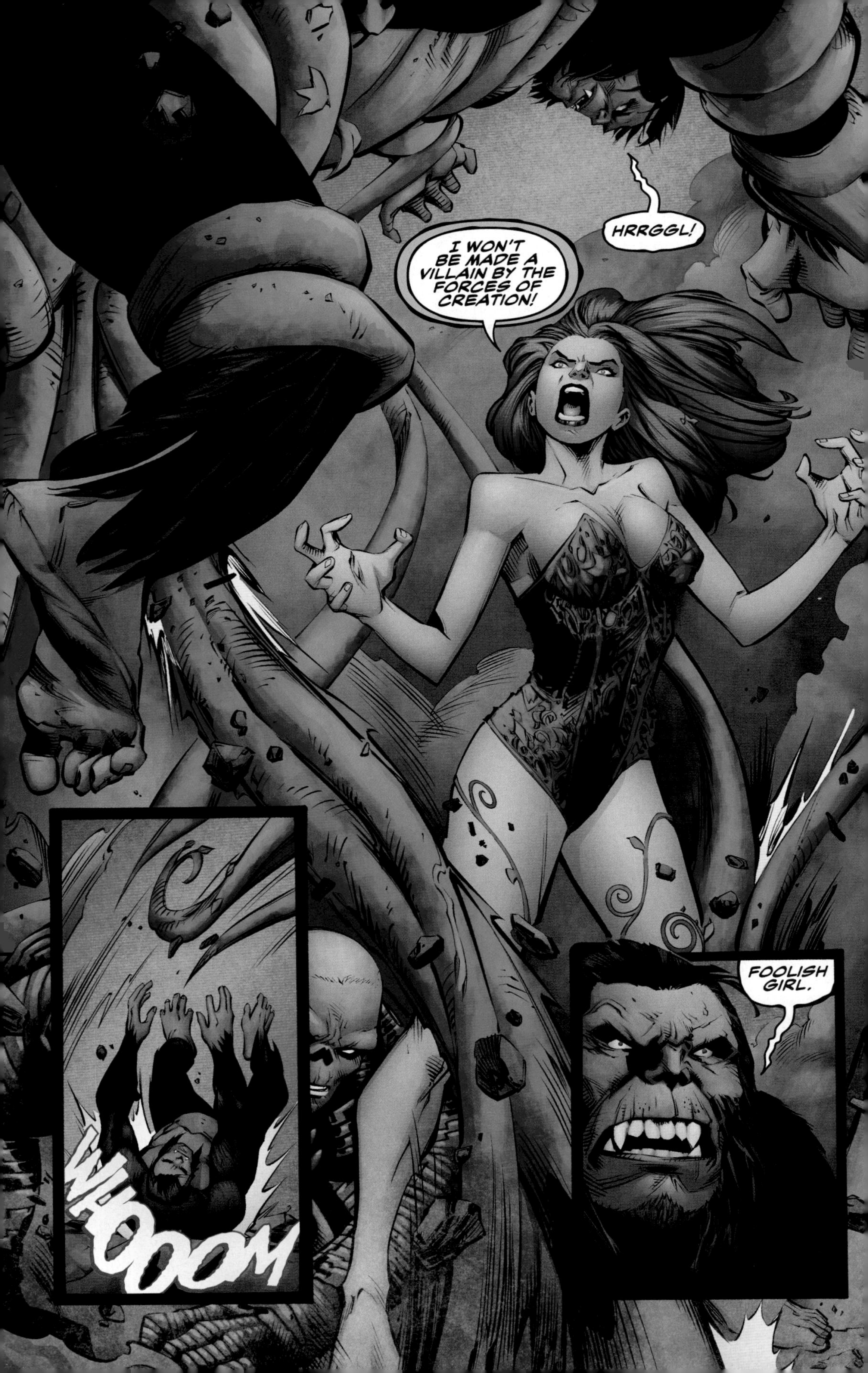
HRRGGL!
I WON'T BE MADE A VILLAIN BY THE FORCES OF CREATION!
WHOOOM
FOOLISH GIRL.

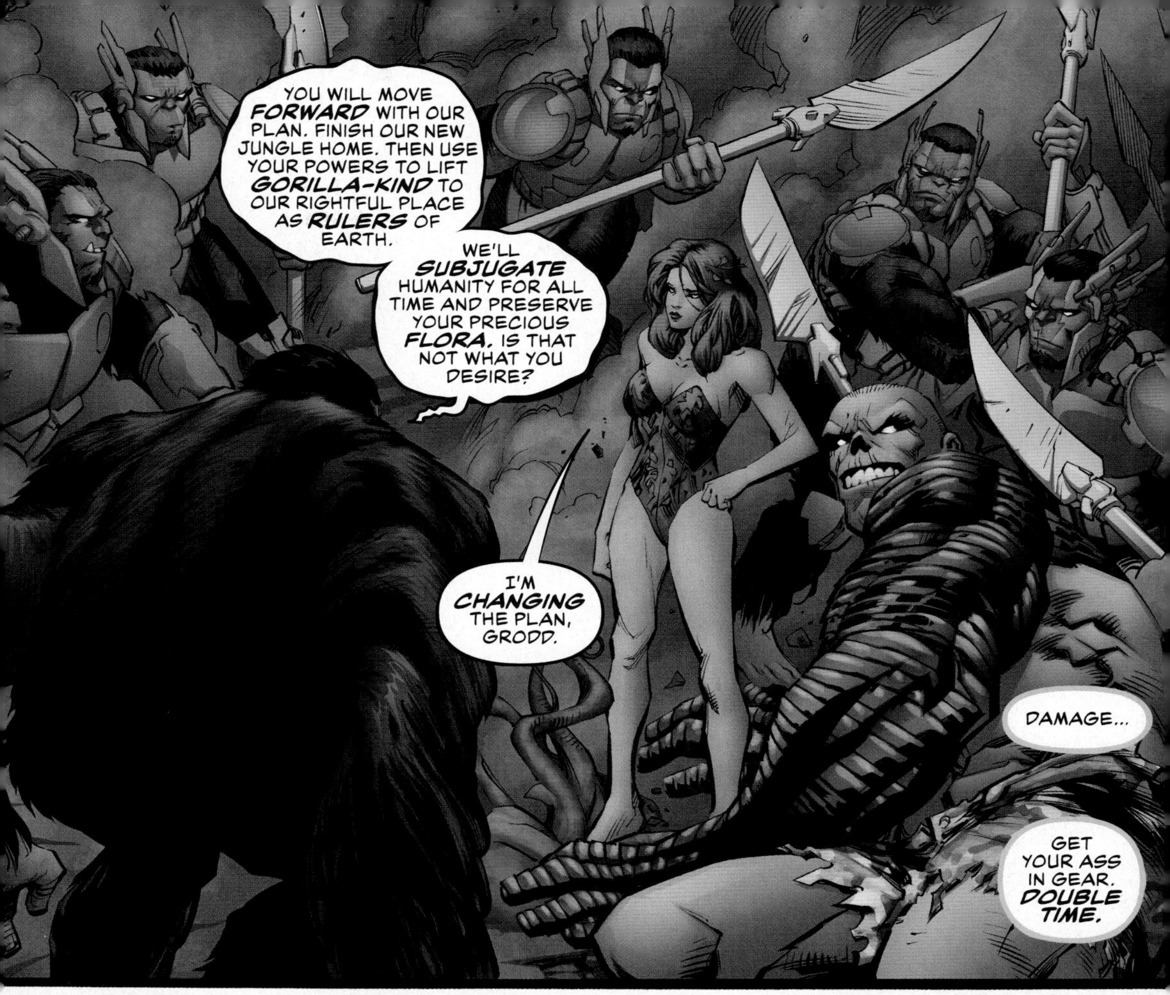
YOU WILL MOVE FORWARD WITH OUR PLAN. FINISH OUR NEW JUNGLE HOME. THEN USE YOUR POWERS TO LIFT GORILLA-KIND TO OUR RIGHTFUL PLACE AS RULERS OF EARTH.
WE'LL SUBJUGATE HUMANITY FOR ALL TIME AND PRESERVE YOUR PRECIOUS FLORA. IS THAT NOT WHAT YOU DESIRE?
I'M CHANGING THE PLAN, GRODD.
DAMAGE...
GET YOUR ASS IN GEAR. DOUBLE TIME.

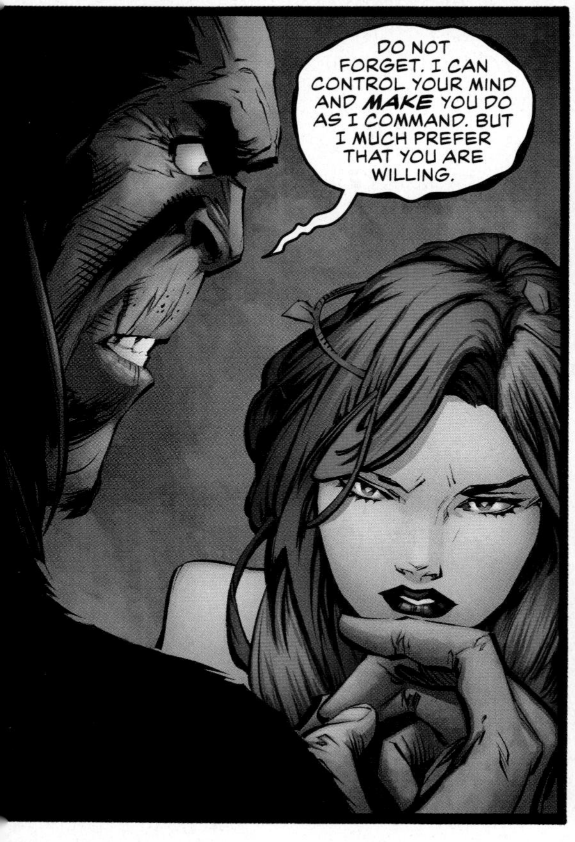
DO NOT FORGET. I CAN CONTROL YOUR MIND AND MAKE YOU DO AS I COMMAND. BUT I MUCH PREFER THAT YOU ARE WILLING.

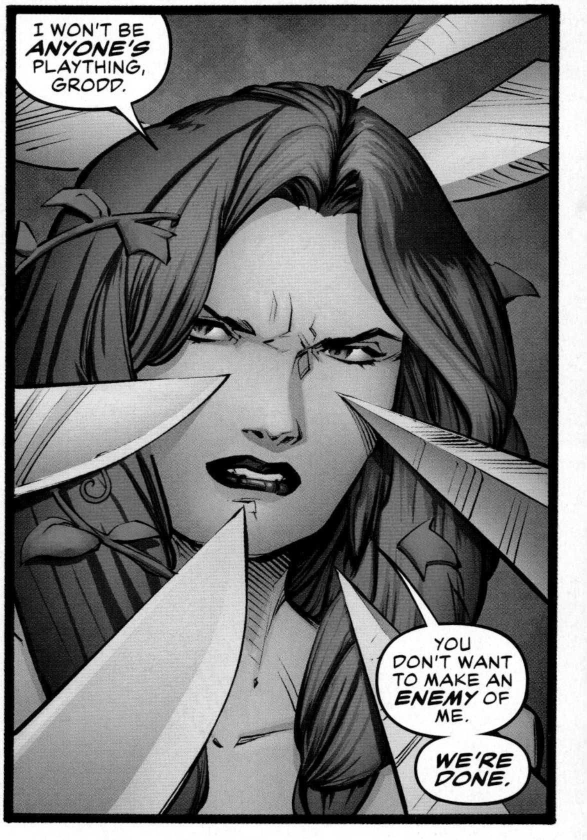
I WON'T BE ANYONE'S PLAYTHING, GRODD.
YOU DON'T WANT TO MAKE AN ENEMY OF ME.
WE'RE DONE.

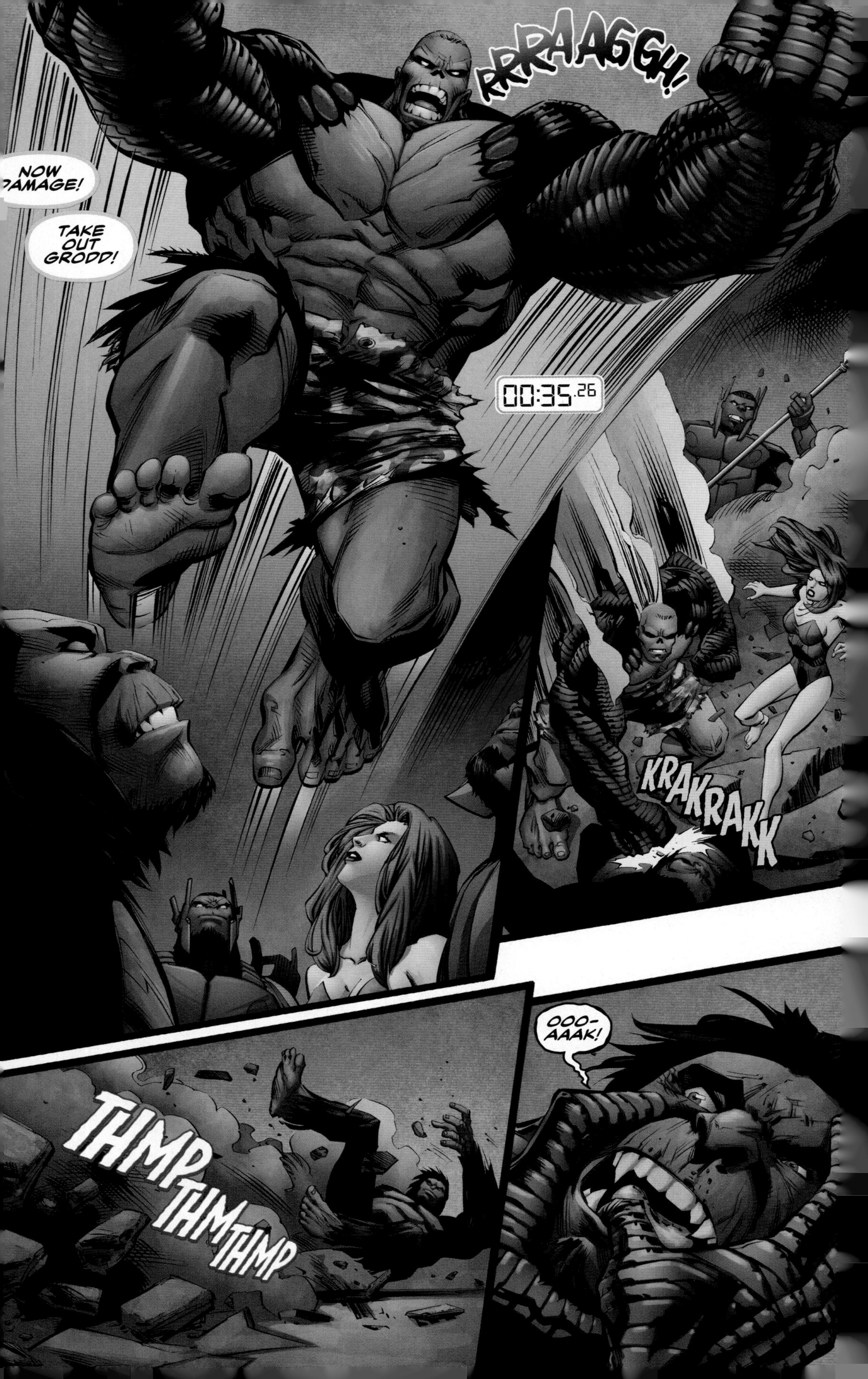
RRRAAGGH!
NOW DAMAGE!
TAKE OUT GRODD!
00:35.26
KRAKRAKK
THMP THMTHMP
OOO-AAAK!

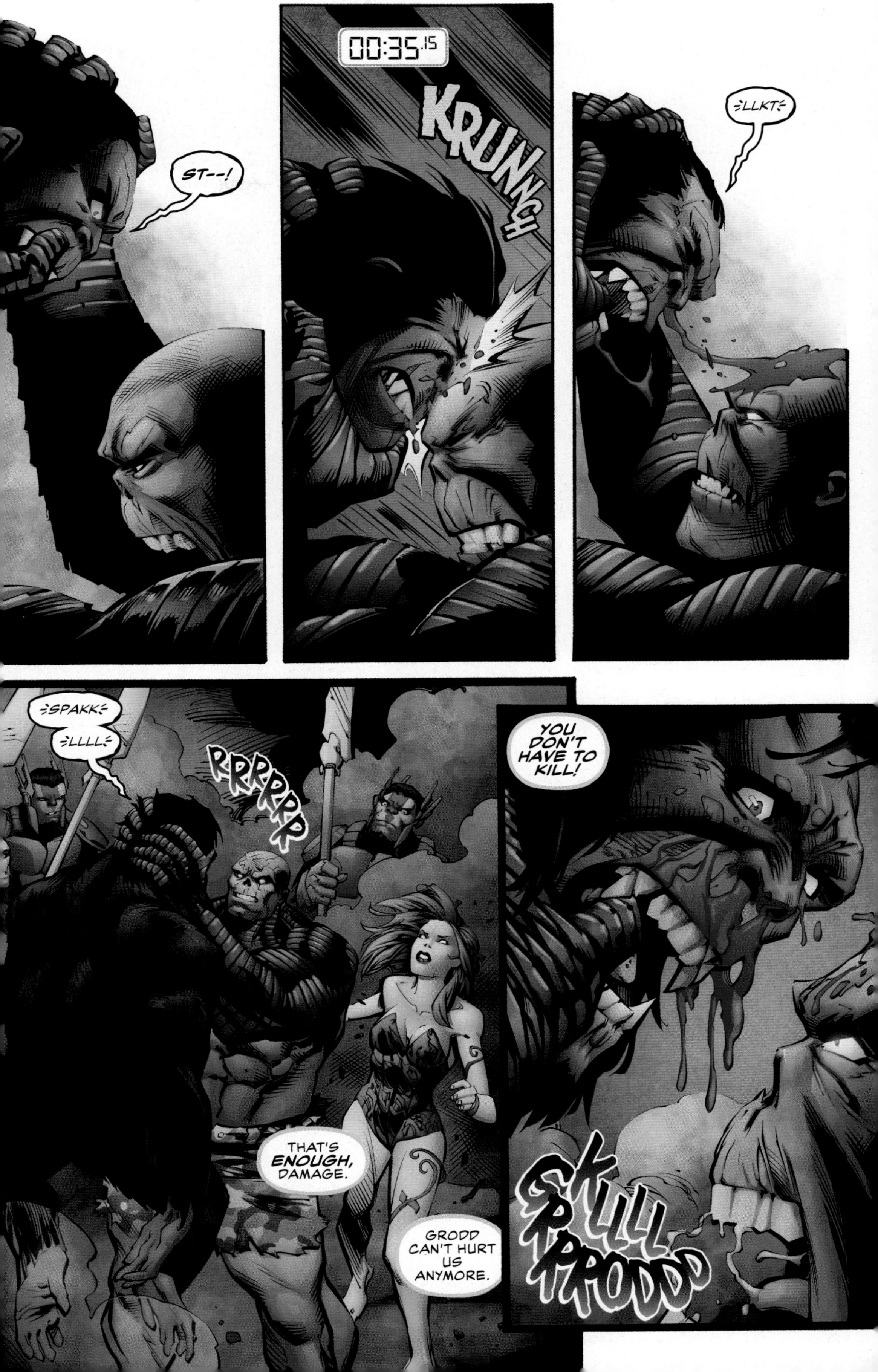

ST--!
00:35.15
KRUNNCH
LLKT
SPAKK
LLLL
RRRRRR
THAT'S ENOUGH, DAMAGE.
GRODD CAN'T HURT US ANYMORE.
YOU DON'T HAVE TO KILL!
SKLLL
PRODDD

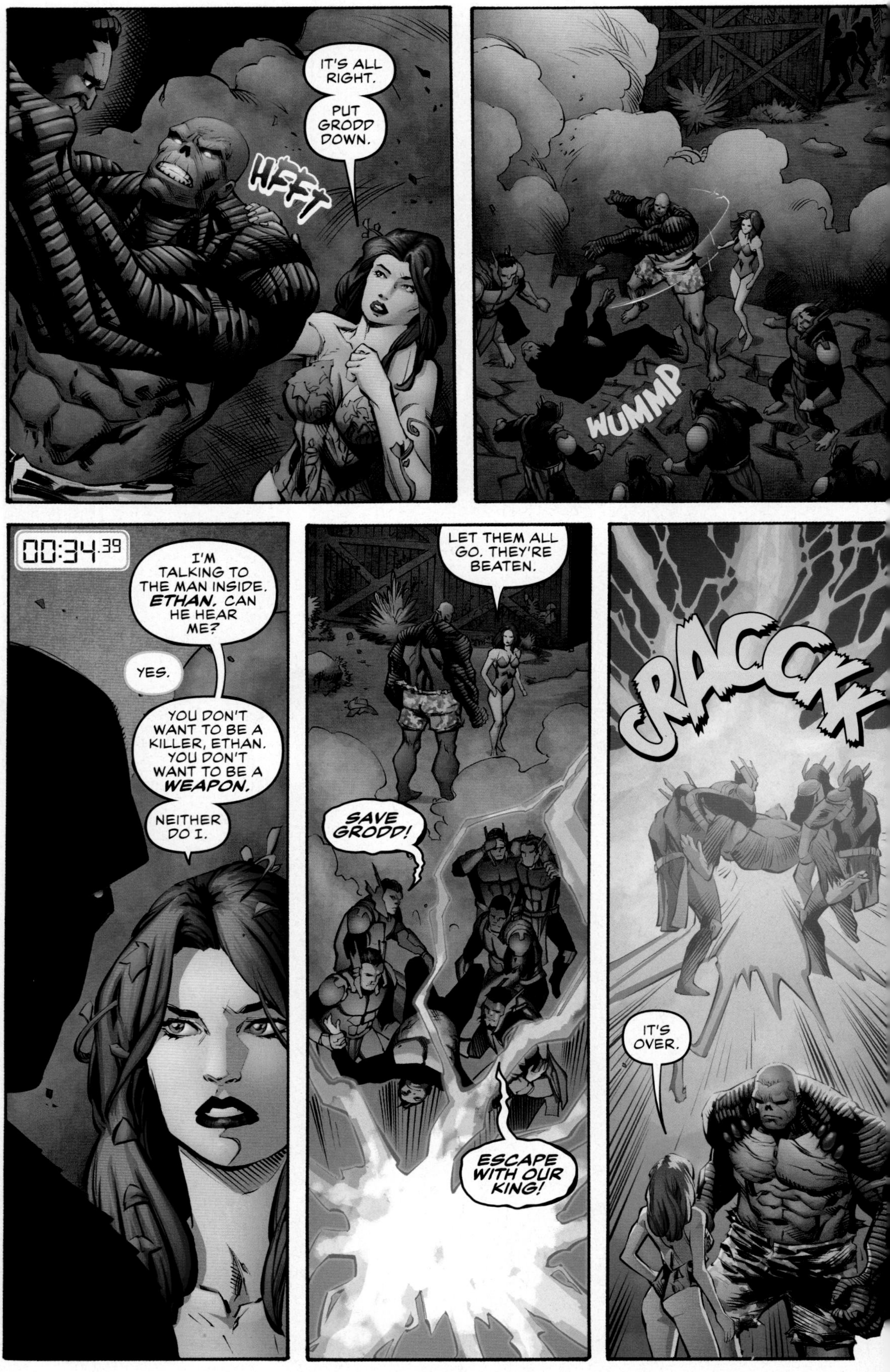
IT'S ALL RIGHT.
PUT GRODD DOWN.
HFFT
WUMMP
00:34.39
I'M TALKING TO THE MAN INSIDE. ETHAN. CAN HE HEAR ME?
YES.
YOU DON'T WANT TO BE A KILLER, ETHAN. YOU DON'T WANT TO BE A WEAPON.
NEITHER DO I.
LET THEM ALL GO. THEY'RE BEATEN.
SAVE GRODD!
ESCAPE WITH OUR KING!
CRACCKK
IT'S OVER.

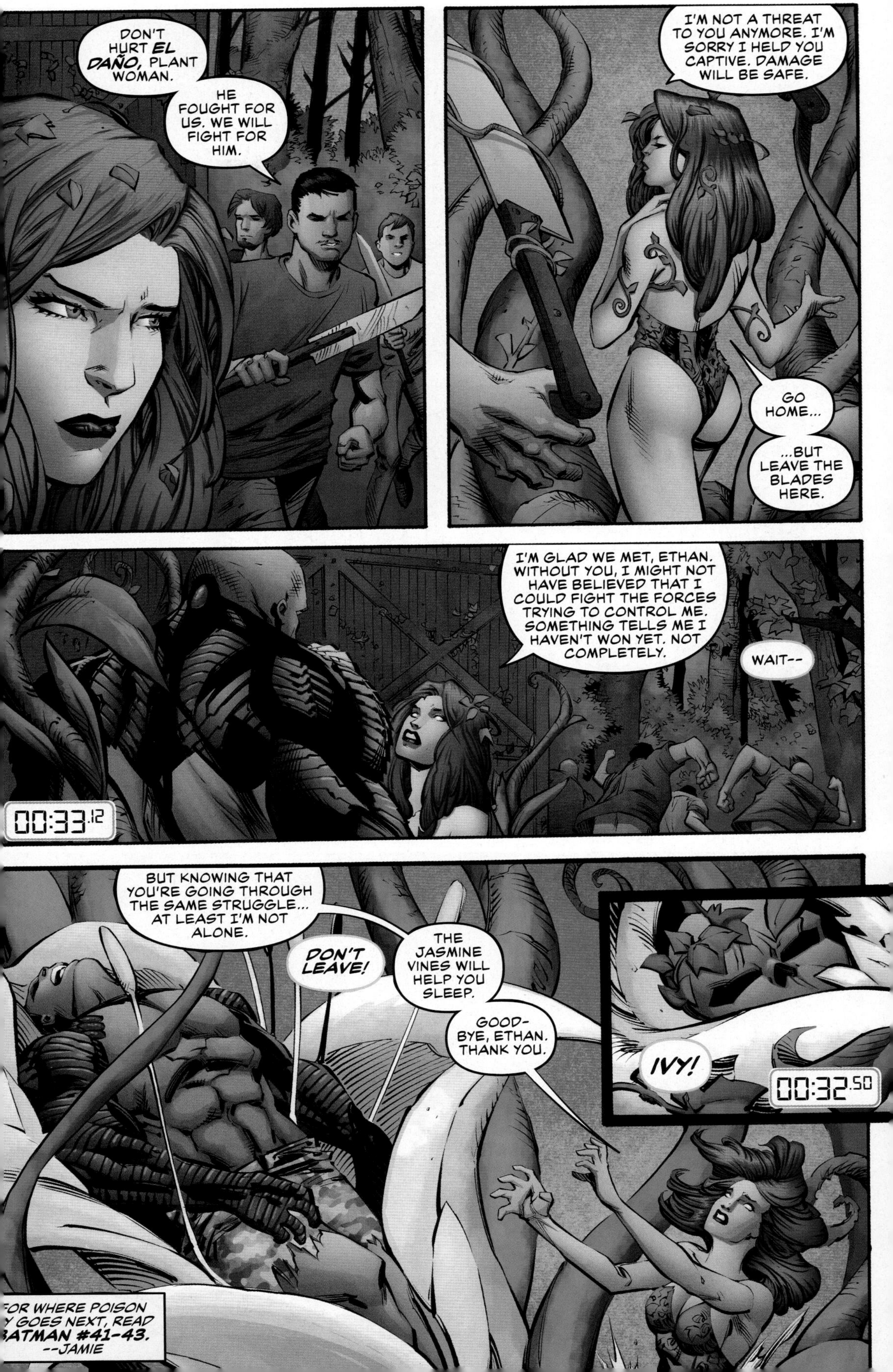
DON'T HURT EL DAÑO, PLANT WOMAN.
HE FOUGHT FOR US. WE WILL FIGHT FOR HIM.
I'M NOT A THREAT TO YOU ANYMORE. I'M SORRY I HELD YOU CAPTIVE. DAMAGE WILL BE SAFE.
GO HOME...
...BUT LEAVE THE BLADES HERE.
I'M GLAD WE MET, ETHAN. WITHOUT YOU, I MIGHT NOT HAVE BELIEVED THAT I COULD FIGHT THE FORCES TRYING TO CONTROL ME. SOMETHING TELLS ME I HAVEN'T WON YET. NOT COMPLETELY.
WAIT--
00:33.12
BUT KNOWING THAT YOU'RE GOING THROUGH THE SAME STRUGGLE... AT LEAST I'M NOT ALONE.
DON'T LEAVE!
THE JASMINE VINES WILL HELP YOU SLEEP.
GOOD-BYE, ETHAN. THANK YOU.
IVY!
00:32.50
FOR WHERE POISON Y GOES NEXT, READ BATMAN #41-43. --JAMIE

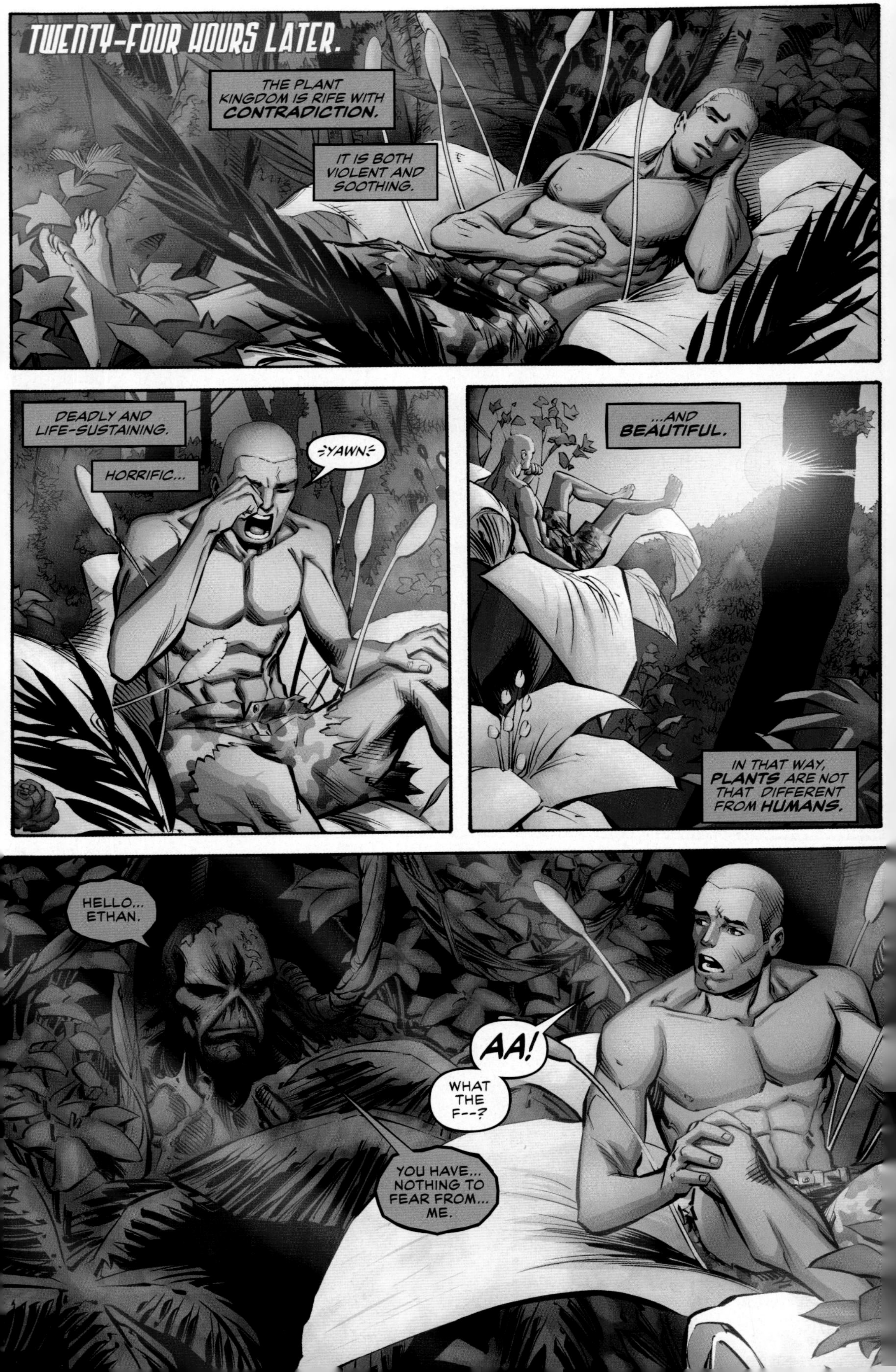
TWENTY-FOUR HOURS LATER.
THE PLANT KINGDOM IS RIFE WITH CONTRADICTION.
IT IS BOTH VIOLENT AND SOOTHING.
DEADLY AND LIFE-SUSTAINING.
HORRIFIC...
YAWN
...AND BEAUTIFUL.
IN THAT WAY, PLANTS ARE NOT THAT DIFFERENT FROM HUMANS.
HELLO... ETHAN.
AA!
WHAT THE F--?
YOU HAVE... NOTHING TO FEAR FROM... ME.

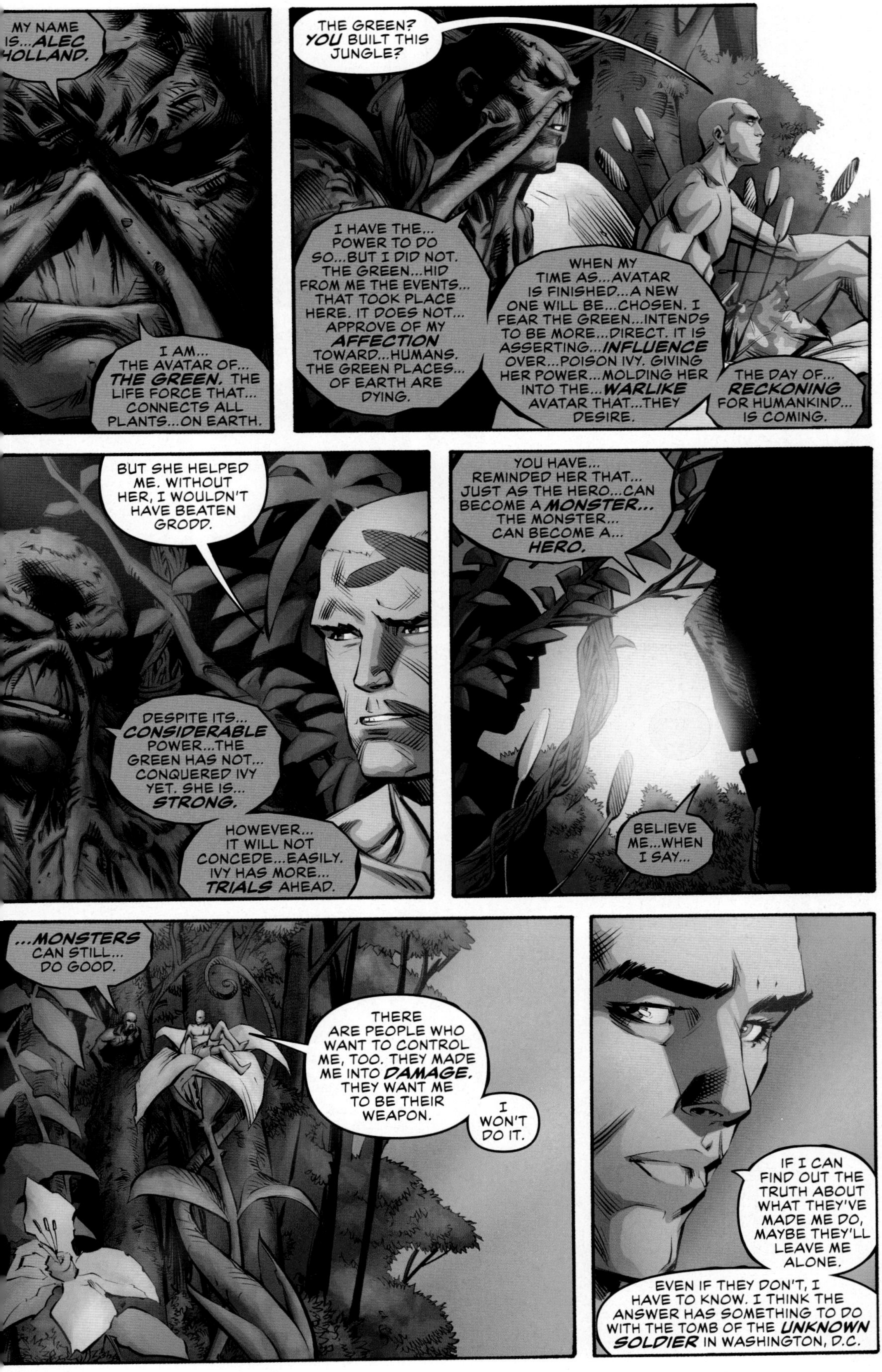
MY NAME IS...ALEC HOLLAND.
I AM... THE AVATAR OF... THE GREEN. THE LIFE FORCE THAT... CONNECTS ALL PLANTS...ON EARTH.
THE GREEN? YOU BUILT THIS JUNGLE?
I HAVE THE... POWER TO DO SO...BUT I DID NOT. THE GREEN...HID FROM ME THE EVENTS... THAT TOOK PLACE HERE. IT DOES NOT... APPROVE OF MY AFFECTION TOWARD...HUMANS. THE GREEN PLACES... OF EARTH ARE DYING.
WHEN MY TIME AS...AVATAR IS FINISHED...A NEW ONE WILL BE...CHOSEN. I FEAR THE GREEN...INTENDS TO BE MORE...DIRECT. IT IS ASSERTING...INFLUENCE OVER...POISON IVY. GIVING HER POWER...MOLDING HER INTO THE...WARLIKE AVATAR THAT...THEY DESIRE.
THE DAY OF... RECKONING FOR HUMANKIND... IS COMING.
BUT SHE HELPED ME. WITHOUT HER, I WOULDN'T HAVE BEATEN GRODD.
DESPITE ITS... CONSIDERABLE POWER...THE GREEN HAS NOT... CONQUERED IVY YET. SHE IS... STRONG.
HOWEVER... IT WILL NOT CONCEDE...EASILY. IVY HAS MORE... TRIALS AHEAD.
YOU HAVE... REMINDED HER THAT... JUST AS THE HERO...CAN BECOME A MONSTER... THE MONSTER... CAN BECOME A... HERO.
BELIEVE ME...WHEN I SAY...
...MONSTERS CAN STILL... DO GOOD.
THERE ARE PEOPLE WHO WANT TO CONTROL ME, TOO. THEY MADE ME INTO DAMAGE. THEY WANT ME TO BE THEIR WEAPON.
I WON'T DO IT.
IF I CAN FIND OUT THE TRUTH ABOUT WHAT THEY'VE MADE ME DO, MAYBE THEY'LL LEAVE ME ALONE.
EVEN IF THEY DON'T, I HAVE TO KNOW. I THINK THE ANSWER HAS SOMETHING TO DO WITH THE TOMB OF THE UNKNOWN SOLDIER IN WASHINGTON, D.C.

THERE ARE...PEOPLE WHO I HAVE...HELPED IN THE PAST. THEY WILL AID YOU...ON YOUR JOURNEY...BUT I ASK THAT...

...YOU HELP ME...WITH SOMETHING IN RETURN.

THE JUNGLE THAT... IVY CREATED...IS AN ABERRATION. INVASIVE SPECIES... THAT BELONG ON...ANOTHER CONTINENT.

BUT IT IS... PRISTINE...FULL OF GREEN LIFE... I CANNOT BRING MYSELF...TO DESTROY IT.

I UNDERSTAND.

...THANK YOU.

COME BACK FOR ME IN AN HOUR.

ADMIT IT, ETHAN.

SRFGG

EVERYONE WANTS DAMAGE.

GRRRAAAAAHHH

01:00.00

GRRAAAAUGG

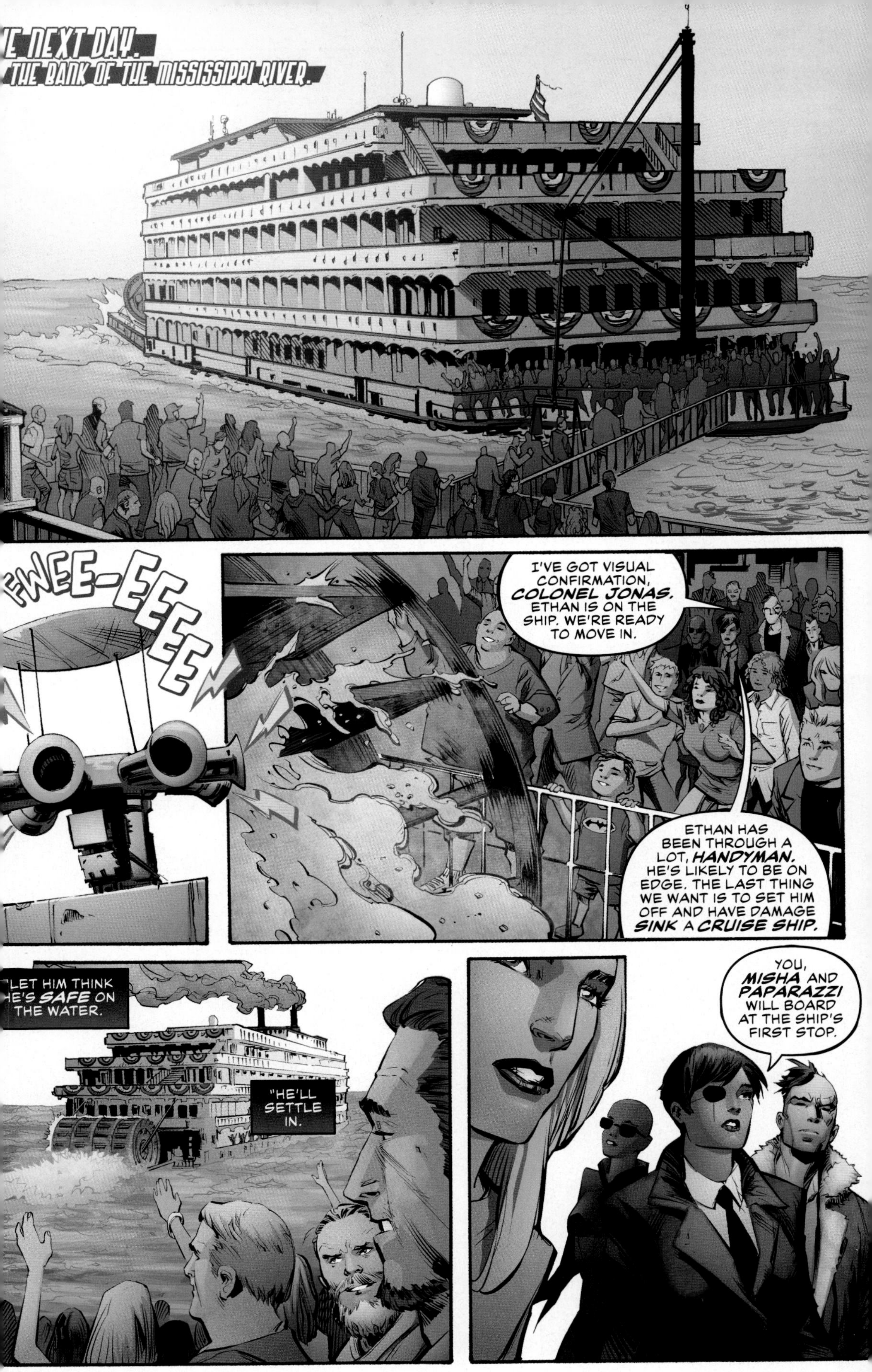
E NEXT DAY.
THE BANK OF THE MISSISSIPPI RIVER.
FWEE-EEEEE
I'VE GOT VISUAL CONFIRMATION, COLONEL JONAS. ETHAN IS ON THE SHIP. WE'RE READY TO MOVE IN.
ETHAN HAS BEEN THROUGH A LOT, HANDYMAN. HE'S LIKELY TO BE ON EDGE. THE LAST THING WE WANT IS TO SET HIM OFF AND HAVE DAMAGE SINK A CRUISE SHIP.
"LET HIM THINK HE'S SAFE ON THE WATER.
"HE'LL SETTLE IN.
YOU, MISHA AND PAPARAZZI WILL BOARD AT THE SHIP'S FIRST STOP.

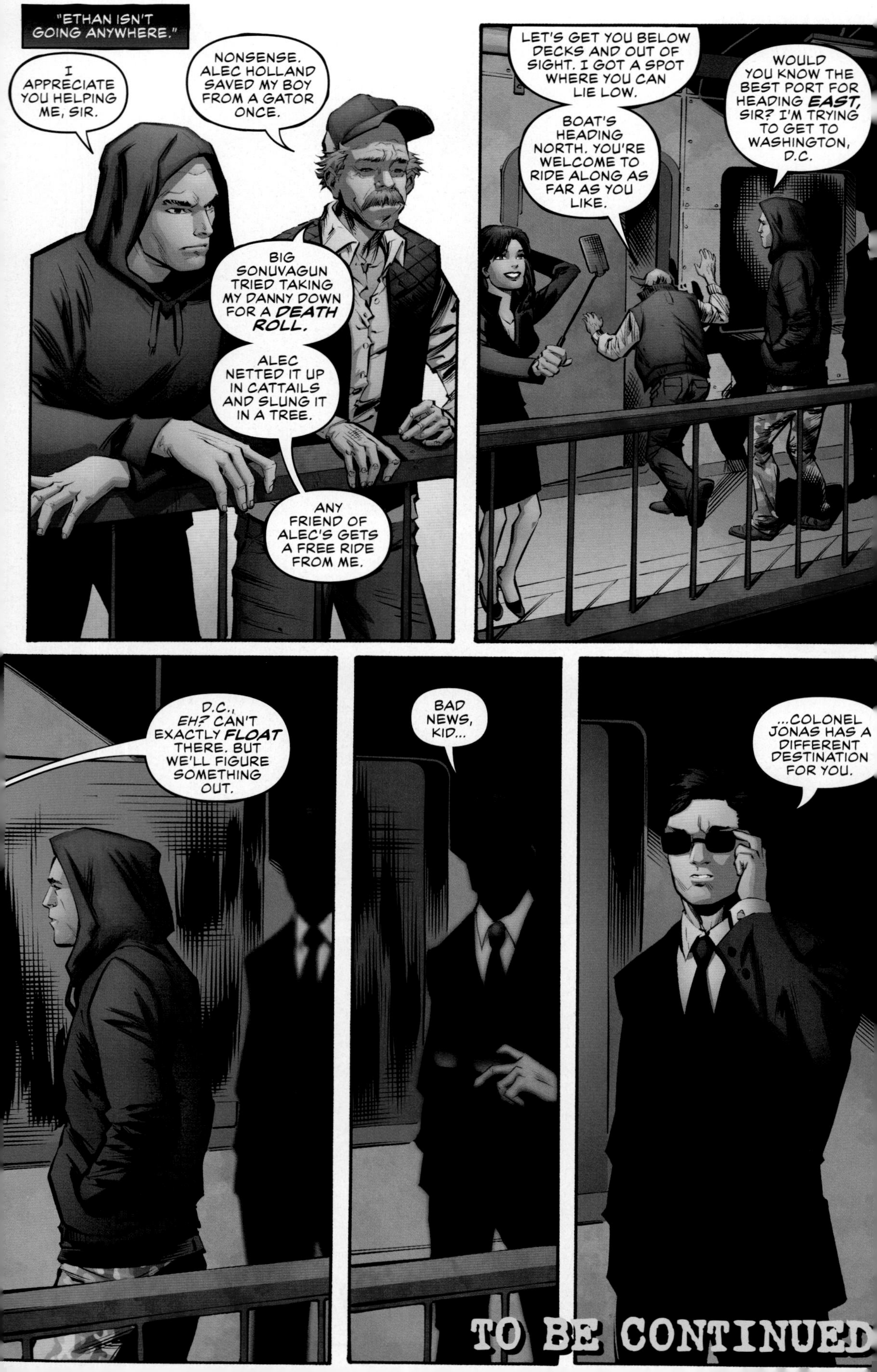
"ETHAN ISN'T GOING ANYWHERE."
I APPRECIATE YOU HELPING ME, SIR.
NONSENSE. ALEC HOLLAND SAVED MY BOY FROM A GATOR ONCE.
BIG SONUVAGUN TRIED TAKING MY DANNY DOWN FOR A DEATH ROLL.
ALEC NETTED IT UP IN CATTAILS AND SLUNG IT IN A TREE.
ANY FRIEND OF ALEC'S GETS A FREE RIDE FROM ME.
LET'S GET YOU BELOW DECKS AND OUT OF SIGHT. I GOT A SPOT WHERE YOU CAN LIE LOW.
BOAT'S HEADING NORTH. YOU'RE WELCOME TO RIDE ALONG AS FAR AS YOU LIKE.
WOULD YOU KNOW THE BEST PORT FOR HEADING EAST, SIR? I'M TRYING TO GET TO WASHINGTON, D.C.
D.C., EH? CAN'T EXACTLY FLOAT THERE. BUT WE'LL FIGURE SOMETHING OUT.
BAD NEWS, KID...
...COLONEL JONAS HAS A DIFFERENT DESTINATION FOR YOU.
TO BE CONTINUED

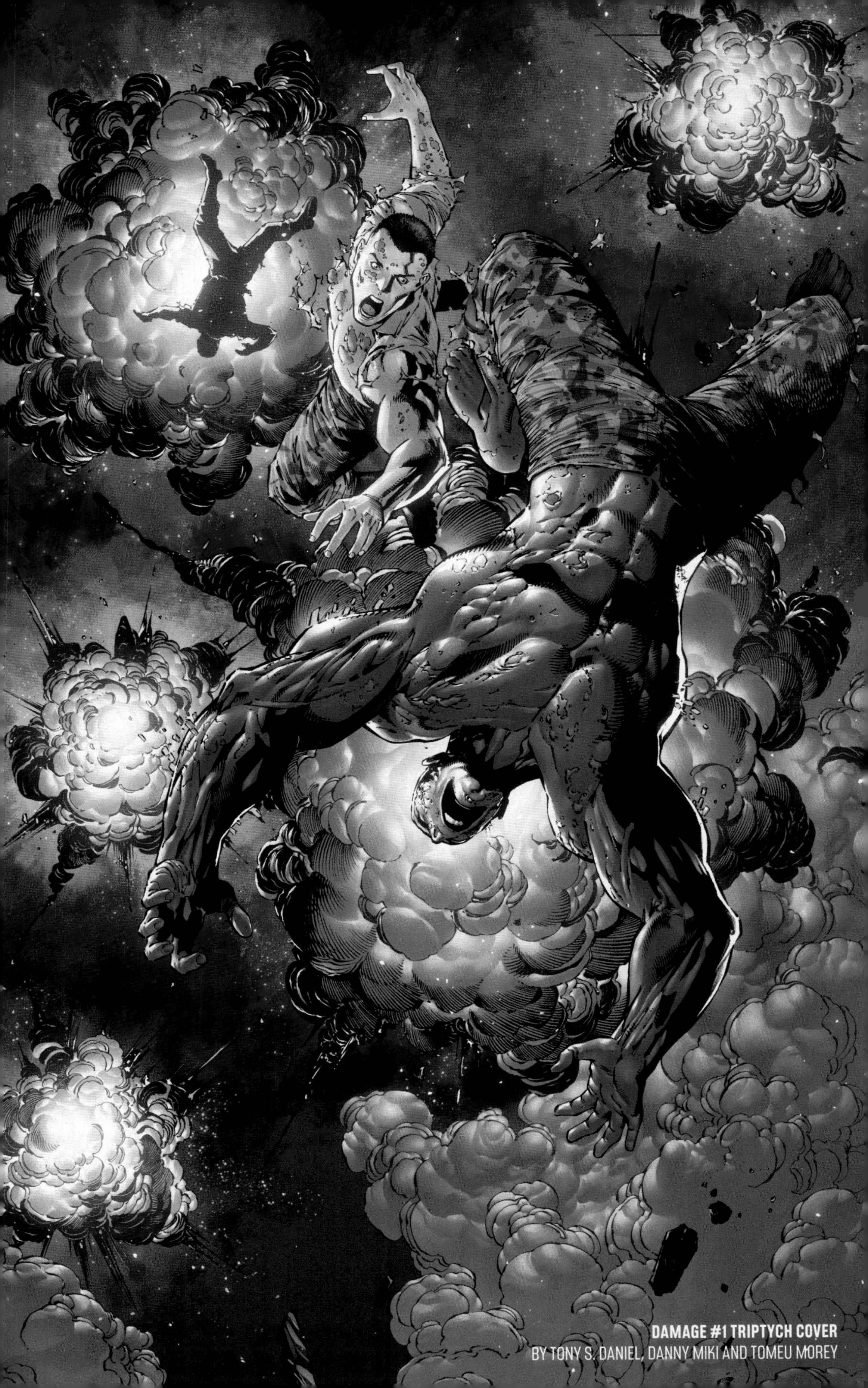

DAMAGE #1 TRIPTYCH COVER
BY TONY S. DANIEL, DANNY MIKI AND TOMEU MOREY

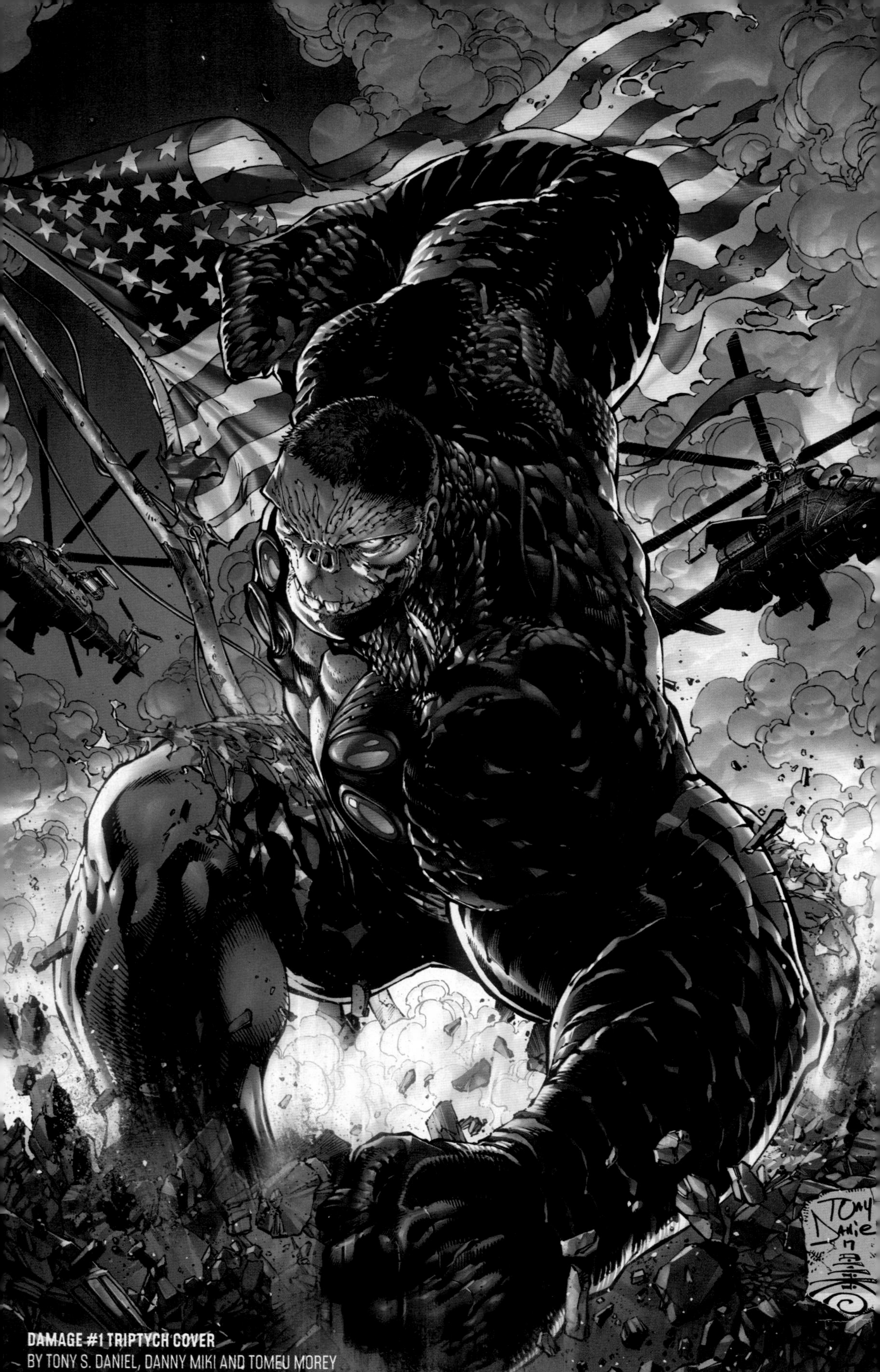

DAMAGE #1 TRIPTYCH COVER
BY TONY S. DANIEL, DANNY MIKI AND TOMEU MOREY

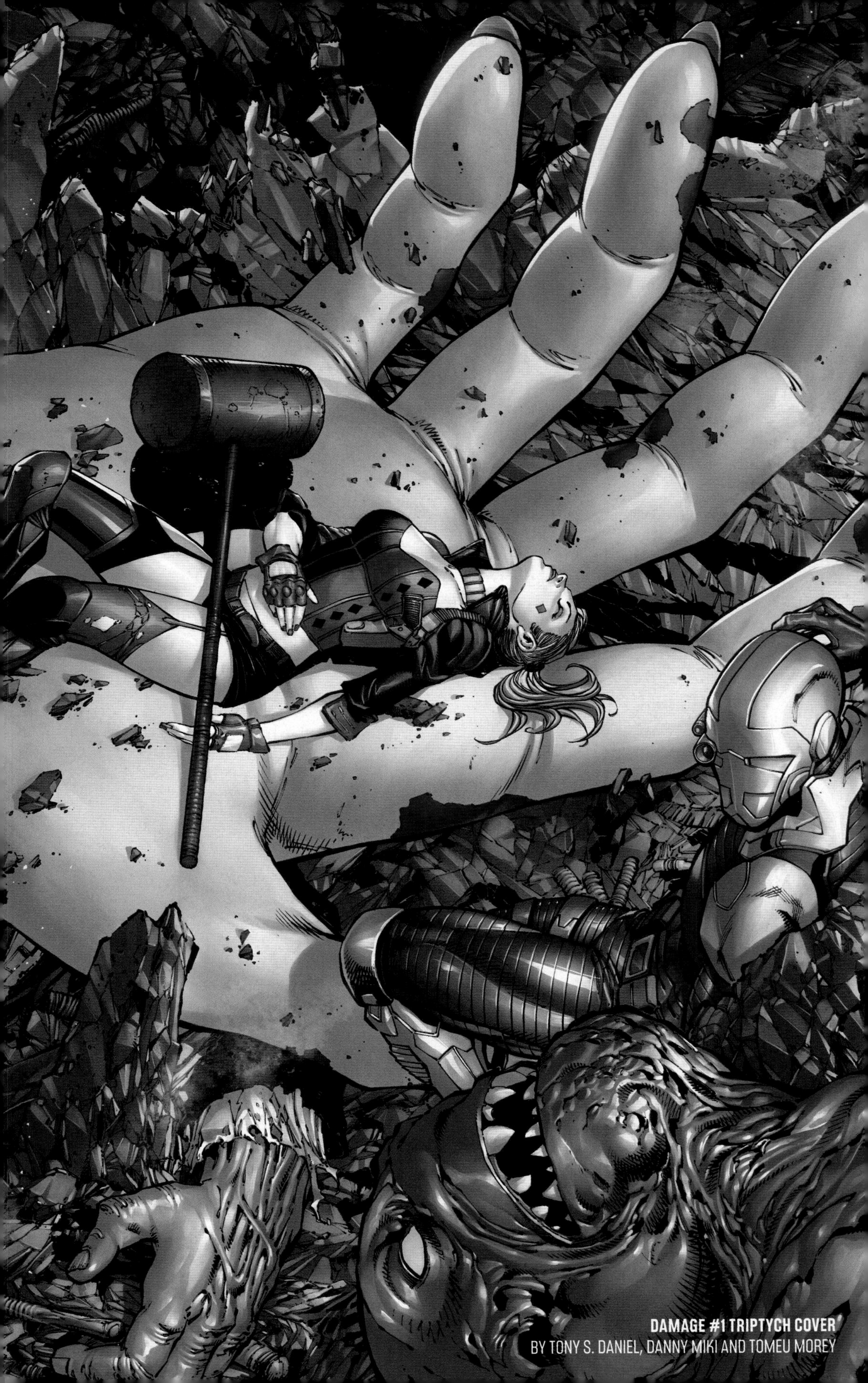

DAMAGE #1 TRIPTYCH COVER
BY TONY S. DANIEL, DANNY MIKI AND TOMEU MOREY

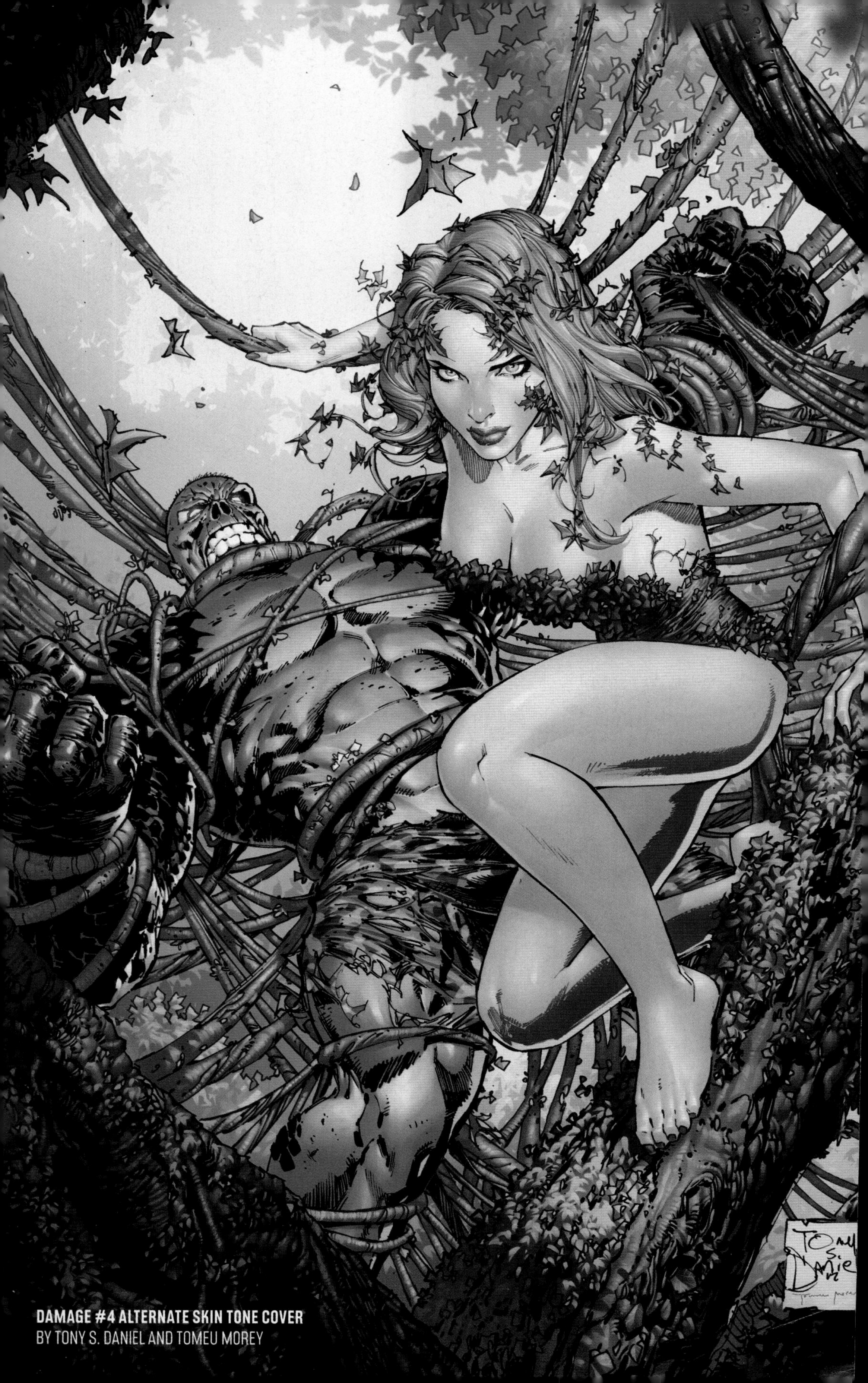

DAMAGE #4 ALTERNATE SKIN TONE COVER
BY TONY S. DANIEL AND TOMEU MOREY

"ead-spinning spectacular from
to bottom."
MTV GEEK

"is is your go-to book."
ENTERTAINMENT WEEKLY

ONY S.
DANIEL

ATMAN:
ETECTIVE COMICS
OL. 1: FACES OF DEATH

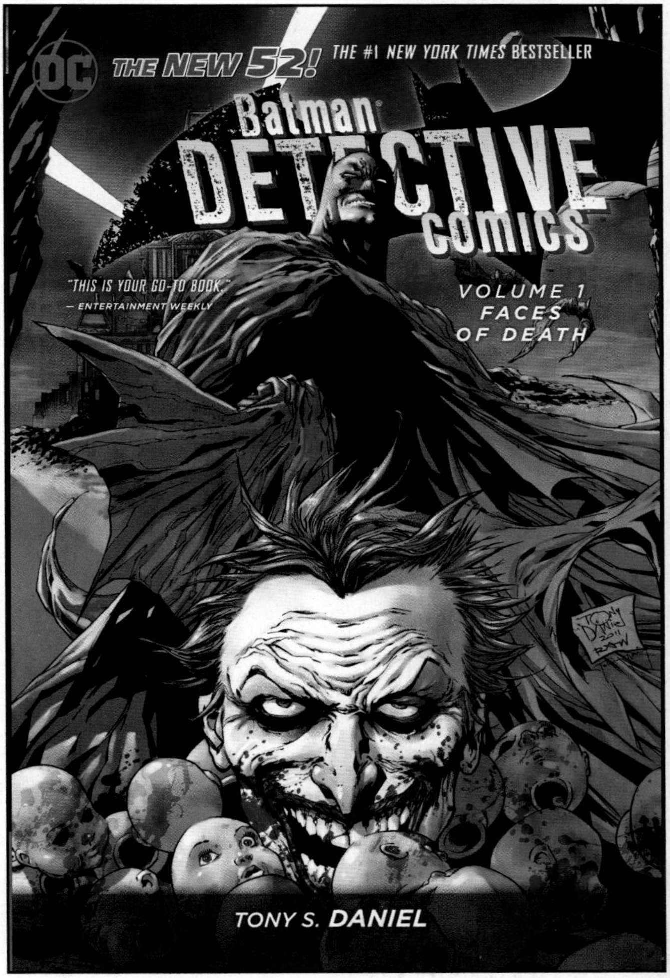
THE NEW 52!
THE #1 NEW YORK TIMES BESTSELLER
Batman
DETECTIVE
COMICS
"THIS IS YOUR GO-TO BOOK."
— ENTERTAINMENT WEEKLY
VOLUME 1
FACES
OF DEATH
TONY S. DANIEL

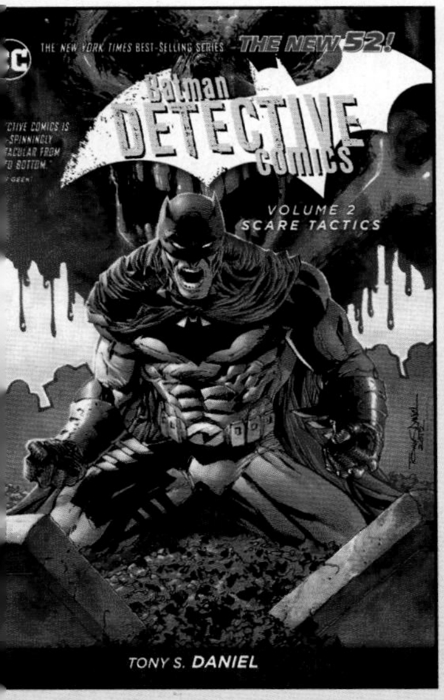
THE NEW YORK TIMES BEST-SELLING SERIES
THE NEW 52!
Batman
DETECTIVE
COMICS
VOLUME 2
SCARE TACTICS
TONY S. DANIEL

ATMAN: DETECTIVE COMICS VOL. 2: SCARE TACTICS

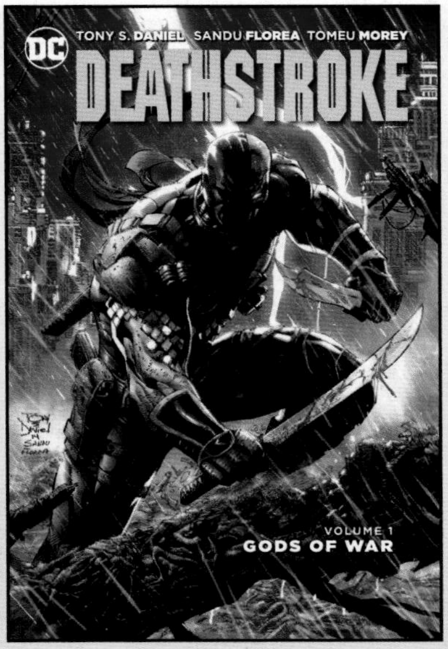
TONY S. DANIEL SANDU FLOREA TOMEU MOREY
DEATHSTROKE
VOLUME 1
GODS OF WAR

DEATHSTROKE VOL. 1: GODS OF WAR

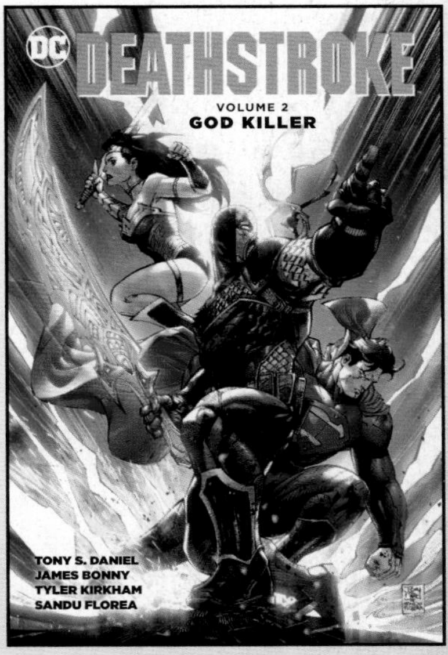
DEATHSTROKE
VOLUME 2
GOD KILLER
TONY S. DANIEL
JAMES BONNY
TYLER KIRKHAM
SANDU FLOREA

DEATHSTROKE VOL. 2: GOD KILLER

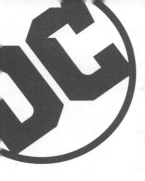

"Game-changing redefining of the Caped Crusader."
–ENTERTAINMENT WEEKLY SHELF LIFE

"One of the most exciting eras in Batman history."
–IGN

FROM *NEW YORK TIMES*
#1 BEST-SELLING WRITER

GRANT MORRISON

with ANDY KUBERT,
J.H. WILLIAMS III
and TONY S. DANIEL

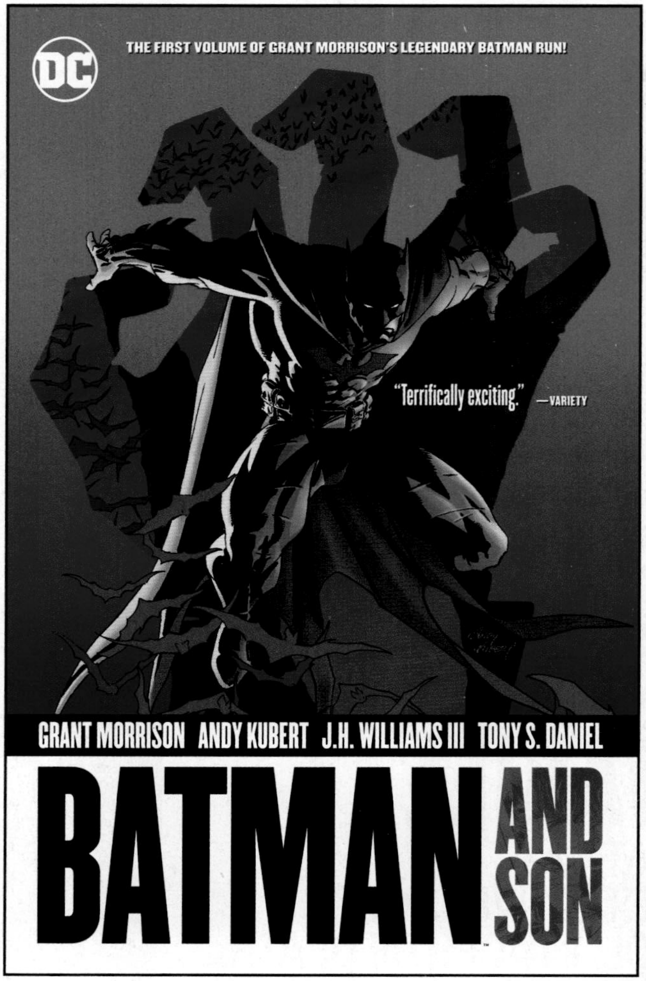
THE FIRST VOLUME OF GRANT MORRISON'S LEGENDARY BATMAN RUN!
"Terrifically exciting." —VARIETY
GRANT MORRISON ANDY KUBERT J.H. WILLIAMS III TONY S. DANIEL
BATMAN AND SON

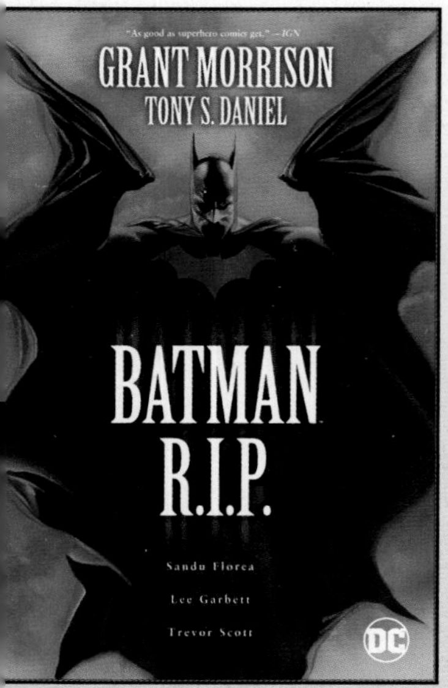
"As good as superhero comics get." – IGN
GRANT MORRISON
TONY S. DANIEL
BATMAN R.I.P.
Sandu Florea
Lee Garbett
Trevor Scott

BATMAN: R.I.P.
with TONY S. DANIEL

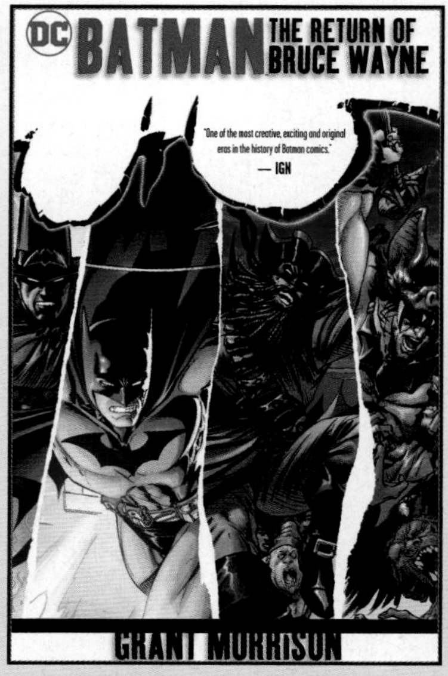
BATMAN THE RETURN OF BRUCE WAYNE
"One of the most creative, exciting and original eras in the history of Batman comics."
— IGN
GRANT MORRISON

BATMAN: THE RETURN OF BRUCE WAYNE
with FRAZER IRVING & RYAN SOOK

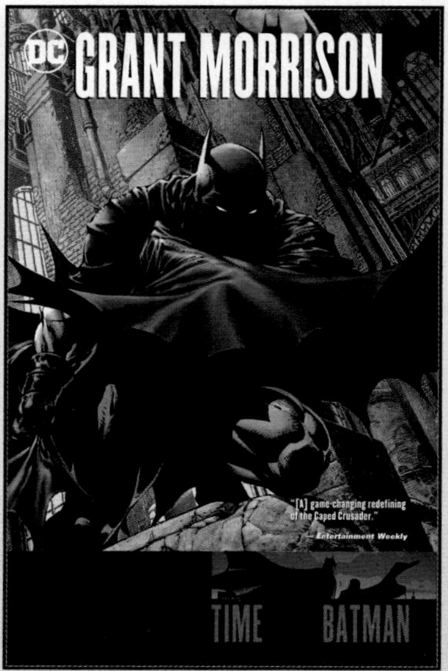
GRANT MORRISON
"[A] game-changing redefining of the Caped Crusader."
— Entertainment Weekly
TIME BATMAN

BATMAN: TIME AND THE BATMAN
with TONY S. DANIEL

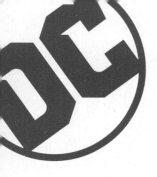